Tail Risk Hedging

Disclaimer

This publication contains information obtained from sources believed to be authentic and highly regarded. Reprinted material is used with permission, and sources are indicated. Reasonable effort has been made to publish reliable data and information, but the author and publisher cannot assume responsibility for the validity of all materials or for the consequences of their use. Certain information contained herein may be dated and no longer applicable; information was obtained from sources believed to be reliable at time of original publication, but not guaranteed.

This views contained herein are the authors' but not necessarily those of PIMCO. Such opinions are subject to change without notice. This publication has been distributed for educational purposes only and should not be considered as investment advice or a recommendation of any particular security, strategy, or investment product.

References to specific securities and their issuers are for illustrative purposes only and are not intended and should not be interpreted as recommendations to purchase or sell such securities. The author or PIMCO may or may not own or have owned the securities referenced and, if such securities are owned, no representation is being made that such securities will continue to be held.

This material contains hypothetical illustrations and no part of this material is representative of any PIMCO product or service. Nothing contained herein is intended to constitute accounting, legal, tax, securities, or investment advice, nor an opinion regarding the appropriateness of any investment, nor a solicitation of any type. This publication contains a general discussion of tail risk portfolio management; readers should be aware that all investments carry risk and may lose value. The information contained herein should not be acted upon without obtaining specific accounting, legal, tax, and investment advice from a licensed professional.

Tail Risk Hedging

CREATING ROBUST PORTFOLIOS FOR VOLATILE MARKETS

VINEER BHANSALI

New York   Chicago   San Francisco   Athens   London
Madrid   Mexico City   Milan   New Delhi
Singapore   Sydney   Toronto

Copyright © 2014 by Vineer Bhansali. All rights reserved. Printed in the United States of America. Except as permitted under the United States Copyright Act of 1976, no part of this publication may be reproduced or distributed in any form or by any means, or stored in a database or retrieval system, without the prior written permission of the publisher.

1 2 3 4 5 6 7 8 9 0   QVS/QVS   1 9 8 7 6 5 4 3

ISBN   978-0-07-179175-5
MHID   0-07-179175-2
e-ISBN   978-0-07-179176-2
e-MHID   0-07-179176-0

This publication is designed to provide accurate and authoritative information in regard to the subject matter covered. It is sold with the understanding that neither the author nor the publisher is engaged in rendering legal, accounting, securities trading, or other professional services. If legal advice or other expert assistance is required, the services of a competent professional person should be sought.

—From a Declaration of Principles Jointly Adopted by a Committee of the American Bar Association and a Committee of Publishers and Associations

Library of Congress Cataloging-in-Publication Data

Bhansali, Vineer.
  Tail risk hedging : creating robust portfolios for volatile markets / Vineer Bhansali.
      pages   cm
  ISBN 978-0-07-179175-5 (hardback : alk. paper)—ISBN 0-07-179175-2 (hardback : alk. paper) 1. Hedging (Finance) 2. Financial risk management. 3. Business cycles. 4. Risk management. I. Title.
   HG6024.A3B523   2014
   332.64'524—dc23   2013034580

McGraw-Hill Education books are available at special quantity discounts to use as premiums and sales promotions or for use in corporate training programs. To contact a representative, please visit the Contact Us pages at www.mhprofessional.com.

For my parents

Contents

Foreword by Mohamed El-Erian   xi

Introduction   xv

Acknowledgments   xix

Chapter 1   Introduction to Tail Risk and Tail Risk Management   1

Lessons Learned   1
Distressed Liquidation and Failure of Diversification   18

Chapter 2   Basics: Tail Risk Hedging for Defense   25

Formal Derivation of Portfolio Hedges Using Factor Hedges   30
Rolling Tail Hedges   32
Benchmarking Tail Risk Management   37
Cash Versus Explicit Tail Hedging   43

Chapter 3   Offensive Tail Risk Hedging   51

A Model to Compute the Value of Tail Hedging   56
Model Calibration   57

Chapter 4   Active Tail Risk Management   71

Creating a Long History   78
Active Monetization Rules   84

Chapter 5 Indirect Hedging and Basis Risk	**93**
Quantifying Basis Risk	95
Hedge Matching at the Attachment Point	98
"Soft" Indirects: Comparing Puts versus Put Spreads	104
Basis Risk from Correlated Asset Classes	107
Chapter 6 Other Tail Risk Management Strategies	**129**
Tail Risk Hedging versus Asset Allocation in a Multimodal World	129
The Hedging Value in Trends and Momentum	134
A Look at the Risks and Rewards of Costless Collars	138
Variance Swaps and Direct Volatility-Based Hedging	141
Dynamic Hedging	146
Chapter 7 A Behavioral Perspective on Tail Risk Hedging	**153**
Narrow Framing and Tail Risk Hedging	154
Pricing of Put Options on a Standalone Basis	161
Multiple Equilibria and Expected Returns on Tail Hedges	165
Precommitment and Procyclicality	169
Chapter 8 Tail Risk Hedging for Retirement Investments	**179**
Chapter 9 Inflation and Duration Tail Risk Hedging	**193**
Hedging at the Money Inflation versus Inflation Tails	195
Tail Hedging Realized Inflation versus Inflation Expectations	198
Inflation Dynamics and Inflation Spikes	202
Framework for Inflation Tail Hedging	210
Benchmarking Inflation Tail Hedges	211
Pricing of Inflation Options	212
Options on CPI	212
Options on the Breakeven Inflation Rate	215

Indirect Inflation Tail Risk Hedging and Basis Risk	217
Pricing of Tail Interest-Rate Swaptions	219
Indirect Hedges	221
Example of Gold Options as Proxy Tail Hedge	222

Notes — 225

Bibliography — 231

Index — 235

Foreword

Many astute and experienced professional investors will tell you that today's marketplace is, to use an old American expression, "not your father's Oldsmobile." Quite a few investors are seeking to evolve their approaches to keep up with changes on the ground, actual and prospective. Others have even decided to return funds to their clients rather than try to invest in a world that that they no longer sufficiently understand, let alone feel able to predict accurately.

Major global economic realignments and material regulatory changes are among the major reasons for today's more fluid investment landscape. But they are not the only ones.

Since the 2008 global financial crisis, most advanced countries have faced persistent difficulties in delivering high economic growth and sufficient jobs. With political polarization further limiting policy responses, the largest economies have embarked on a prolonged period of monetary policy experimentation that has seen central banks get more and more deeply involved in markets as both referees and players.

Undeniably, central banks have consequentially influenced how markets function, value securities, and allocate capital. And the deeper they have been pulled into this hyperactive involvement, the less obvious the route of exit. Indeed, it is far from clear how and when central banks will eventually be able to extricate themselves from what has become an intense influence on risk positioning, liquidity, and price-setting behaviors.

In such circumstances, investors are challenged to navigate several unprecedented and quite persistent disconnects. Whether it is the deviation of market prices from underlying economic and corporate fundamentals, or the more volatile and less predictable correlations among traditional asset classes, the trade-offs and hand offs between tactical and strategic positioning are no longer as straightforward as they once appeared.

The bottom line is a simple but consequential one. If investors wish to continue to generate superior long-term returns, they will have to work harder, smarter, and somewhat differently.

To succeed, investors will need to construct global portfolios with more agile alpha and beta engines, more forward-looking differentiation, and more resilient sizing of positions. Equally important, they will also need to limit their vulnerability to severe downturns that threaten to suddenly erase hard-gained returns and, judging from the insights of behavioral finance, also increase the probability of subsequent portfolio mistakes.

Portfolio diversification will remain a critical, *necessary* condition for all this, but it may no longer be *sufficient*. As investors seek to position themselves for durable success, they will be challenged to think more holistically about a distribution of potential outcomes with materially fatter tails.

For insights on these critical issues, including how to adapt risk management approaches to today's (and tomorrow's) realities, investors would be well advised to look to Vineer Bhansali's brilliant book. Drawing on his pioneering and highly regarded work on the subject, Vineer provides readers with valuable insights on the why, what, how, and when of portfolio tail hedging.

The book's added value is not limited to this already consequential and timely objective. Drawing on thought-provoking work that Vineer has delivered over the years, it also shows how a more holistic and modern approach to risk management enhances the ability to exploit temporary and reversible market dislocations.

As Vineer demonstrates well, smart tail hedging is about more than just better addressing the consequential two-sided extremes of distributions. Properly designed and executed, it has the potential to place portfolios in an improved position to exploit more consistently the opportunities that are provided in the belly of the distribution.

Whether your emphasis is on return generation, risk mitigation, or (hopefully) both, you will find Vineer's book informative and actionable. Simply put, it is a must-read for those investors seeking to excel consistently in what has become (and will remain) a highly fluid world.

Mohamed El-Erian
CEO and Co-CIO of PIMCO

Introduction

The conceptual origin of this book goes back to many years before my entry into finance. During one summer research project in physics at Caltech, it became obvious to the young undergraduate that was me that the "action," so to speak, was not in the middle part of the distribution but in the tails. Over the years, research papers (on power laws and fat tails) and popular books (on black swans) from all areas of inquiry made it obvious that the time was ripe for low-probability, high-severity events to assert their right to a proper analysis. And then, of course, the mother of all recent crises happened in 2008, and tail risk management entered the lexicon of investment management with a speed and intensity yet unmatched.

For me personally, the practice of tail risk management goes back to 2002, when an astute investor cherry-picked the tail risk management sleeve for a customized hedging portfolio. Despite the running cost of the explicit option premia, it became immediately obvious that by using a tail-hedging overlay at relatively low and finite cost, the investor had achieved three objectives: (1) he could hold his investments in other skilled managers while hedging out the common market tail exposure, (2) he could tune up or tune down the market exposure according to his needs and the opportunity sets with liquid instruments, and (3) he had more predictability about the distribution of returns; that is, he could plan his investment strategy ahead of the day-to-day implementation noise. These were clearly benefits, and in time, the success with these new portfolio design elements attracted others who embraced and implemented similar ideas.

This book is targeted to an audience familiar with the basics of option pricing and trading. I made no effort to provide an exhaustive exposition of option pricing models or theories, instead hoping that an interested reader would chase them down on the Internet or via the large number of books and papers now available. The target audience is a mix of traders and portfolio managers who have a solid analytical and quantitative tilt, though I have been told that some of the work in this book as originally published has been used in MBA and CFA classes. Most of the text is original or based on original work, so it is hard to attribute individually to all the written and oral inputs of so many that have gone into this book. But my thanks are due to all who have influenced and continue to subliminally influence my ongoing research and investments.

Chapter 1 lists a few major reasons for tail risk hedging and tail risk management. These are reasons that both ex post and ex ante strike me as valid for having tail risk hedging as an always-on (as opposed to just-in-time) risk-management tool in the investment tool kit.

Chapter 2 introduces a simple and transparent framework based on the core specifications of a tail risk management practice in terms of risk exposures, attachment points, and costs. While many investors approach tail risk management from many different angles, I believe that this trinity of inputs clarifies what the investor is intending tail risk hedging to achieve. Of course, this approach also highlights that the three inputs have to satisfy simultaneously; that is, exposures, attachment levels, and costs cannot be arbitrary and unbound.

Chapter 3 flips over the tail risk coin and provides a detailed exposition of how tail hedges allow portfolios to be positioned more offensively, thus offering a mechanism to subsidize the cost of running such a hedging program. In this way, tail hedging is not only risk-reducing but also can be return-enhancing.

Chapter 4 discusses the value and techniques for active tail risk management and monetization approaches. It is clear that tail hedging using options in particular can be expensive from the perspective of loss of value via time decay. I discuss how by managing the hedges as nonlinear, time-decaying assets, one can optimize the value of a tail-hedging portfolio.

Chapter 5 addresses indirect hedging using markets and instruments that are correlated with the direct hedging instruments. I define and quantify basis risk and how to create a good tradeoff between cost reduction of hedges and the probability of the hedge not delivering as planned because of correlations failing to realize.

Chapter 6 discusses other strategic tail-hedging approaches, such as dynamic asset allocation, "collars," variance swaps, and alternative betas. The ability to put all these approaches on a common platform (of cost versus tail convexity) allows an investor to maximize the potential hedging gains in a truly multifaceted way. None of the discussion is detailed enough for the reader who wants a deep dive, and I would point them to the rich literature for these approaches.

Chapter 7 looks at tail hedging from a behavioral perspective. Using models that rely heavily on Kahneman and Tversky's prospect theory, I approach the problem of tail hedging within the portfolio context, the variation in the skew, and time inconsistency in tail hedging that leads eventually to the opportunity to tail hedge cheaply over a market cycle.

Chapter 8 focuses on tail hedging for retirement accounts. The investment behavior of participants close to retirement says a lot about the implicit costs and benefits of tail hedging for their portfolios. With a complex interaction of varying time horizons, risk tolerance, and the underlying dynamics of the market, the retirement investment area is a natural place for practical application of the principles discussed so far.

Finally, Chapter 9 discusses hedging of inflation and interest-rate or duration tail risk. While most of the demand and supply of hedging so far has been in the domain of equity-like risks, I believe that in the years to come, the hedging of interest-rate and expected-inflation risk will be key to the construction of robust portfolios.

This book was written over a period of many years, and I happily concede that it is not complete in any form. Given a choice, I find it more fun to think in terms of the core concepts rather than an encyclopedic list of each and every alternative for tail hedging.

Realizing these limitations, to me this book is still a work in progress; it will have achieved its interim goal if investors recognize some value in the principles and are able to construct more robust investment portfolios for themselves.

Vineer Bhansali
Newport Beach, CA
Fall 2013

Acknowledgments

This book would not have emerged without the collaboration of numerous clients and colleagues. My understanding of portfolio management, investing, and risk management continues to be enhanced daily by the fruitful discussions and analyses with so many.

I would, however, like to specially thank four individuals who have been early collaborators on research on tail risk management as a part of portfolio construction: Mohamed El-Erian, Josh Davis, Mark Wise, and Bruce Brittain. A brief chat with Mohamed when he was the CIO of Harvard management revealed a few months before the financial crisis that we were independently thinking of financial tail risks and efficient ways of hedging them. This resulted in collaboration on asset allocation and tail risk hedging when he returned as CO-CIO of PIMCO. Josh has been a collaborator and indeed co-originator of many of the ideas in this book, particularly in Chapters 3–5. Mark and I go back decades—first when I was his SURF student at Caltech and then when we collaborated on papers relating to correlation matrices and swap spreads under stresses and to optimization of portfolios with higher moments. Finally, Bruce and his team have worked in connecting the dots that have helped tail risk hedging to become a unique new business for PIMCO. I would also like to thank numerous unnamed others who by their initial and in many cases continued skepticism have pushed me deeper into understanding the dynamics of options markets, rare events, and exploration of investors' sometimes unexplainable behavior when it comes to taking catastrophic risk of ruin.

There is a saying attributed to Gandhi: "First they ignore you, then they laugh at you, then they fight you, then you win." For the idea of tail risk hedging, one cannot yet declare victory and maybe never will, but at least skeptics are not laughing any more. The challenge of financial markets is to respond to changing dynamics in a timely manner, and it is this kind of intellectual and practical challenge that makes the application of research so fruitful.

From a personal perspective, first and foremost, I would like thank my wife Beka for her unwavering support and love in work and life. My parents, Rajendra and Vineeta, have always been the bedrock of support in whatever I do, and my children, Zane, Kieran, and Ara, have provided me with joy beyond words. My brother Roveen and my sister Vini have always been there for me cheering me on in my various projects. I should also thank the Western States Trail and the friends I have made there, which by accident provided me with another obsession that creates the space to have long periods of thinking without distraction.

Most of the analysis presented here is original work, done solo and with my collaborators, and I take full responsibility for any errors and omissions. This continues to be a "learn as you go" project, and that's what makes it so exciting.

1

Introduction to Tail Risk and Tail Risk Management

No risk-management term has entered the vernacular of investors as rapidly as *tail risk management* has in the last five years. Market participants have had to deal with not only a substantial loss to their wealth but also a loss of their confidence, most of all in the core principles of investing that they have held dear for almost forever. Even though the "crisis" is now over five years old, memories of risk-management mistakes are fresh in investors' minds. In fact, five years hence, we might be seeing a setup for the next crisis as much of the liquidity injected in financial markets in the aftermath of the crisis has begun to create other asset market valuations ripe for sharp and destructive corrections.

Lessons Learned

1. *Tail risk management is a necessity not a luxury.* Any automobile or home owner will attest that the benefit of having appropriate amounts of disaster insurance is financial survival. When applied to investing, there is a secondary benefit as well, that the

survivors are better able to take advantage of reduced liquidity and attractive prospective returns. Thus, tail "hedging" is an offensive strategy for the long term, even though it comes at a cost. When a home owner purchases insurance against a catastrophic event that might destroy the roof over her shoulders, she does not regret having paid the premium at the end of the year. If we think of investment portfolios in a similar vein, it seems almost dangerous to run portfolios without tail insurance.

2. *Diversification needs to be supplemented with explicit hedging:* The perceived benefits from diversification have been historically responsible for a large number of catastrophic financial crises. The reason has to do with the instability of correlations. For example, in a period of rapidly falling interest rates, almost all asset prices will likely rise because the effect of the increasing discount factor is the dominant influence on all assets, and this leads to the appearance that correlations have increased. Similarly, when rates rise by a large magnitude unexpectedly, all asset prices may fall together, which would appear to demonstrate increasing correlations as well, and the risk cannot be diversified away. When assets are levered, this dynamic can quickly result in large, correlated price swings. The only way to hedge against the failure of diversification in this case is to have explicit tail hedges against the rise in rates, that is, a static hedge on the variable that results in rising correlations. Another way to see this result is the following: Suppose that we estimate the beta of the government bond market to be negative to the stock market; that is, when the stock market falls by 1 percent, the bond market rises by x percent. If either the estimated correlation or the volatility ratio of the bond and equity markets were incorrect, then the implicit risk premium that we would have sacrificed by going from stocks to bonds for diversification would have been misspent.

3. *Tail risk at the portfolio level is almost always systemic risk.* Systemic risk brings under pressure the ability to carry levered holdings, so if leverage is a permanent risk in our economy, the likelihood of tail risk events increases as the risk of deleveraging increases. In such episodes, everyone desires liquidity, and no one is willing to provide it. Financing and liquidity are macroeconomic risks, and hence their proper valuation requires macro models, and proper hedges require macro tools and market instruments. This observation has far-reaching consequences. The main consequence is that tail risk becomes a macro risk, and to forecast and control against it, one needs to step away from and outside the world of historical estimates and calibration and forecast structural changes and imagine improbable, high-severity scenarios. The immense benefit of thinking of tail risk in these terms is that one only needs to extract the factor exposures to liquid market sectors (such as equity beta, duration, etc.). The net result is simplification and even cheapening of systemic hedges. Macro markets are the deepest markets, and typically there is some sort of hedge that remains attractively priced for long enough because of the sheer mass of capital reallocation needed to align all of them. When systemic crises happen, correlations rise in their absolute value. This provides an almost "free lunch" in that a completely disconnected macro market of normal times becomes a good hedge against the tails in distressed times. Often it is more efficient to sacrifice basis risk and close match of hedges by using correlation to our advantage to obtain cost-efficient hedges. For instance, credit-market tail risk events are frequently hedged better with equity options than with customized credit-hedge instruments. Indeed, this might blur the distinction between an active position and a hedge, but in the final analysis, the characterization of a position is less important than the economic benefits it confers.

4. *The cost of insuring against tail risk is an important factor and is highly variable.* Credit-market hedges were extremely cheap in 2007 because of the incessant selling of structured products and the demand driven by excess liquidity. We all know that catastrophe insurance can trade too cheaply in the natural insurance markets; it is possible for this to also happen in financial markets, especially in a world of innovative financial engineering that ports risks from one type of market to another type of market. Why can attractive tail hedges can be found in almost all market environments? There are many candidate reasons. For example, speculative demand of particular types and classes of assets may drive the price of those assets to very high valuation levels. In periods of low returns, as observed until the middle of 2007, the need for yield tempted options selling as a source of carry. The belief of mean-reversion participants is that out-of-the-money options will rarely be exercised. This is generally true, except that as the leverage in the marketplace increases because everyone is simultaneously doing levered option sales, the notional size has increased to generate the same carry. At some point this type of system becomes unstable to small noise and creates a domino effect of hedgers all trying to cover their hedge ratios (such as option deltas) at the same time. An example from the structured credit markets will show how explosive the gains and risks from some hedges can become. Prior to the crisis in June 2007, a 7-100 tranche on the IG8 10-year index cost 15.63 basis points (bp) per year. The running cost is the coupon divided by spread duration and equaled approximately 2 bp. Because the tranche rolls down to a shorter maturity, per year, the roll-down was 2.67 bp to give a total of 4.67 bp of cost. Then, to hedge $1 billion notional, total lifetime cost is about $12 million (cost times PV01 of 7.45). The same tranche in February 2008 was trading at 91 bp/year. Then, running cost (coupon) per year of

spread duration increased to 10.1 bp, and roll-down equaled 2.2 bp, resulting in a total of 12.3 bp/year. The new total lifetime price was then about $67 million. The delta of the tranche before the crisis was approximately 0.53, which when multiplied by the spread duration of the 10-year index of 7.45 gives an approximate sensitivity of 3.95 percent per 100 bp of index widening. In February 2008, the delta rose to 0.77 (because the index widened and was closer to at-the-money), giving almost 5.66 percent of spread risk. With increased value and risk, one can immediately see why supersenior levered notes went into severe distress. First, the mark-to-market loss for the seller of protection is huge (five times) because it equals the net present value (NPV) of premium change. Second, the mark-to-market is more variable (because the delta has increased), and third, the collateral that has to be posted to make up for the mark-to-market fluctuations is much more expensive (lower Treasury bond yields). The fact that all these things happened simultaneously is typical of systemic tail events. In most cases, the gains from tail hedging arise from the mark-to-market of hedges rather than the underlying going "into the money."

5. *There is more than one method to implement tail hedges that can be unified in an option cost versus benefit framework.* The simplest way to hedge is to buy linear securities that are negatively correlated with what's being hedged. For instance, credit-market crises almost always occur with deleveraging and a grab for liquidity, which usually results in Treasuries rallying in price terms, especially those at the shortest maturities. Thus, short-term cash and Treasuries are a natural asset-based hedge for tail risk. But these securities can become overpriced for other technical reasons. The second option is to buy contingent claims or "option-like" securities. Prior to the crisis, as discussed in the preceding example, tranches on CDX and ITRAXX indices were literally being given

away because of the demand for default remote structured transactions such as constant-proportion debt obligations (CPDOs), levered superseniors, and so on. These option-like payoffs were priced below their theoretical expected value under a systemic risk outcome. The third alternative is to invest in strategies that are negatively correlated with tail risks. Essentially this approach balances risks in portfolios with risk-factor exposures that are likely to negate some of the adverse returns embedded inside the portfolio. Among the traditional established strategies, systematic, trend-following, managed futures strategy provides positive correlation with tail risk indicators such as the Volatility Index (VIX) while also being largely uncorrelated with the stock market. A copious amount of research has been done to demonstrate that trend-following strategies behave like a long position in lookback straddles and hence are naturally long tail risk (Fung and Hsieh 2001), and I will discuss this later in the book. The fourth approach is to move the portfolio off the optimal frontier, that is, accept less return for the same amount of risk. This approach explicitly recognizes that the simplest mean-variance optimal frontier falsely assumes that risk can be measured by volatility alone and that the investor has perfect forecasting ability. One example of this approach to risk management is to reduce the exposure to spread products such as corporate bonds or low-quality mortgages, which have higher yield because of embedded default and illiquidity options. Risk management of investment portfolios, thus, can be visualized in terms of a continuum of four distinct regimes (Exhibit 1.1). These regimes correspond to the potential of losses; because larger losses naturally happen with lower probability, a natural and practical approach to loss mitigation seamlessly transitions between them.

For the smallest fluctuations in the markets (say, from 0 to −5 percent), the best way to manage risk is by dynamic rebalancing.

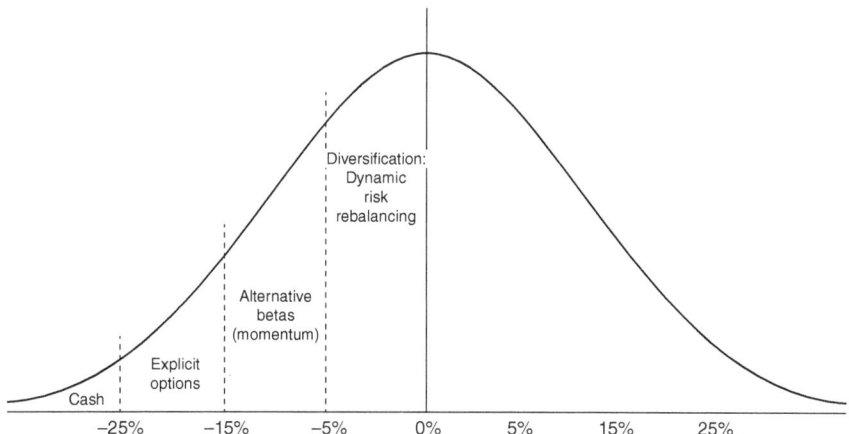

Exhibit 1.1 The four modes of practical portfolio construction and risk management.

The algorithms that investors have found useful here are some sort of targeting of volatility. This is implemented by allocating with relatively high frequency between stocklike or bondlike instruments and cash.

To protect against losses larger than, say, 5 percent but less than perhaps 15 percent, a realignment of the underlying betas, or key exposures, is found to be more useful. Predominant among these are alternative, diversifying betas such as momentum. The expanded palette of diversifying betas makes this exercise increasingly powerful and potent.

For even deeper losses (say, −15 to −35 percent), we find explicit tail risk hedging, via option-like strategies, to be more effective. Options are indeed the easiest way to outsource the jump-risk component of dynamic risk balancing, and for highly improbable events, this method of portfolio risk management is indispensable.

Finally, cash is indeed the ultimate king as long as one is not worried about the return on capital. For catastrophic loss events, there is no substitute for having a pristine source of liquidity. However, in a world where nominal yields are low and inflation is likely to rise, the "real" (nominal minus inflation) return on cash should be considered against the other alternatives.

Because losses can follow a continuum, breaching these ad hoc boundaries, the mixture of how much of each type of risk-management strategy one uses depends on one's perception of the probability of particular losses of a particular magnitude and the market's pricing of those same expected losses. However, it would be too narrow minded to focus on only one regime and eliminate the gains to be had from adding elements from the others.

The unifying framework that ties all four alternatives together is the application of an option theoretic approach to the relative pricing of each mode. Diversification has an option cost because it requires one to give up yield in order to obtain correlation benefits (think of the costs of holding low-yielding Treasury bonds in a portfolio). Investing in macro or commodity trading advisors (CTA) strategies has an implicit cost from reading trends incorrectly (the "whipsaw effect"). Explicit options purchase, of course, has an explicit option cost. Finally, cash has a real option cost as well as an option benefit. It provides the investor with the choice to deploy capital later, but in the meantime, it loses nominal opportunity and real purchasing power.

Putting the four regimes in a common framework allows us to think in terms of the proper balance of risk versus cost. It also allows us to think of what we can and should do to mitigate the short-term costs of prudence and risk management with long-term gains from more favorable portfolio repositioning. In a world where policy risk is one of the predominant drivers of asset returns, having an open-minded and dynamic approach to managing portfolio risk for all magnitudes of positive and negative surprises is no longer a luxury but a necessity. This book takes such an option-based approach to risk management broadly and tail risk management specifically.

6. *Tail risk management is much more than dynamic replication.* The problem with many types of zero-cost tail solutions is that they assume that liquidity will be present in crises, and usually liquidity evaporates during systemic shocks. When everyone else is trying to put on the same hedges, there is no assurance that an investor will be able to do so before others with low transactions costs. In the explicit hedging approach I am describing, the portfolio is subjected to reasonable but rare supershocks, and hedging is achieved using one of the four preceding techniques. Thus there is an explicit cost of the hedge. The role of the portfolio manager is to reduce the cost of these hedges over the hedge horizon. Frequently, especially with a long enough horizon, hedges can be bought very cheaply. For instance, right after the crisis, long-dated options on foreign exchange such as the dollar-yen exchange rate had negligible economic cost over a one-year horizon (due to the roll-up of forward rates from the interest-rate differential between dollar rates and yen rates). In periods of stress, one common outcome is deleveraging and flight to low-yielding currencies such as the yen. This directionality of particular exchange rates with risky assets and the associated increase in volatility makes the real-world expected value of the hedging package much higher than the theoretical, risk-neutral value one would obtain from dynamic hedging of the underlying risk using equity-market instruments. Thus, it is the possibility of asymmetric payoffs in particular states of the world that make the hedges worth more to the investor

than their standalone theoretical value. In his most recent book, *Antifragile*, the author of *The Black Swan* and *Fooled by Randomness*, Nicholas Taleb (2012) takes another step forward in expanding our basic understanding of complex systems and financial markets and portfolio construction in particular. Taleb points out that it is not enough to classify systems as fragile and robust but rather to expand the duality to a more symmetric triad where the opposite of the fragile is *antifragile*, not simply *robust*. His definition of antifragile is something that actually benefits under stress or increasing volatility, that is more than the robust, and that is largely indifferent to such variability. Under this lens, the valuation of most asset markets is fragile and exposed to significant asymmetric outcomes. In traditional portfolios, increasing cash holdings makes the portfolio more robust but does not make it antifragile because the value of the cash does not increase in value under a shock. Hedging with explicit tail hedges using options where volatility is cheap is a manifestly antifragile approach. But it costs premium, low as it may be today in the face of historic asymmetries. Therefore, accumulating these convex positions cheaply is key.

7. *Risk-neutral models should not be exclusively relied on to value tail hedges, especially in a period of policy activism.* To ascertain the value of a particular tail hedge, it is critical that the scenario analysis be performed with many variations of the inputs for the parameters. The inputs are actually more important than the level of refinement of the models. In the simple language of Black-Scholes options, this boils down to running the performance of option positions under various maturity, rate, volatility, and spot-rate environments. The option model is simply a crude nonlinear transformation machine between inputs and outputs. Special attention has to be paid to consistently taking the volatilities and correlations to extreme values because

the underlying assumption of joint lognormality undervalues the tails of the distribution (see Bhansali and Wise 2001). It is also possible to approach the problem by specifying other distributions with naturally fat tails, and today's computational power makes it easy to substitute for theoretical, closed-form solvable models empirical distributions that can be evaluated numerically, especially on the tails. Correlation sensitivity plays a key role in both quantification of the risks and constructing powerful hedge portfolios against the risks. Macroeconomically, this makes sense because correlations tend to rise during crises. As an example, consider the effect of rising correlations on the value of a credit tranche. As correlations rise, the senior tranches in credit will start to perform more and more like deeply out-of-the-money puts in equities because the probability of reaching the attachment point or "strike" of the option becomes larger. Also, risk-neutral models do not capture the influence of external participants on pricing, which has become a part of the current financial fabric. Thus, understanding the role of the government in creating or mitigating outlier events is critical. For example, in some of my own work (Bhansali, Gingrich, and Longstaff 2008), my collaborators and I break down the credit-index spreads for various indices using a three-jump approach. The third component of the spread that corresponds to systemic risks became elevated in the recent financial crisis and reverted to normal levels with a long lag and after substantial liquidity was provided to alleviate solvency fears. Statistical regression of other markets, such as municipals, asset-backed securities, and so on, on the systemic component of the spread shows significant dependence of prospective returns on how the systemic risk factor changes. In other words, many asset classes carry large amounts of systemic illiquidity risk, which have a tendency to become correlated at the worst time. Prior to the Bear Stearns event in spring of 2008, the systemic component had already started to rise and became the same order of magnitude as the idiosyncratic spread component. When the government provided unprecedented liquidity, this component of spreads started to narrow. With the mid-September failure of Lehman, the authorities had to make a choice in which they sacrificed the interest of common equity holders relative to senior debt holders. Credit derivatives markets immediately responded to this choice with the idiosyncratic component widening out. This coincided with the meltdown of the equity market that saw a decline of almost half its capitalization. If we think of modeling asset prices as a product of payoffs, probability distributions, and discounting, then a government with unlimited legal and monetary powers can quickly change any or all of these elements of pricing, altering asset values and risk in a fundamental way, which is not captured in traditional risk-neutral models.

8. *The relationships between assets through risk factors drive tail risks.* Proper tail risk hedging requires an understanding of the risk factors that drive asset returns and then building hedges for the risk factors in the most efficient manner. For example, bond investors like to think of bonds as a separate asset class from equities. The performance of fixed-income markets in 2008 showed us that most types of bonds (with the exclusion of government bonds) have a lot of equity risk in them. Until the Lehman bankruptcy, the equity market was living in its own world; but the default brought home the truth that equity holders ultimately take the bulk of the enterprise risk. Since then, every bond class other than Treasuries has tracked the gyrations of the equity markets. Conceptually, this makes sense because equity markets are where the collective animal spirits live, and increasing risk-aversion is experienced first-hand when

equity markets free fall. The well-known Merton model that links credit spreads to equities is indeed based on the relationship of both equities and bonds issued by a corporation to the underlying assets, and so the observation that a fall in the asset value of companies affects both corporate stocks and bonds is hardly surprising. What is shocking is that so many asset classes that have nothing to do with corporations and their assets also have become correlated with equities. Over the last few years, a watchful investor generally could guess the daily direction of bond levels and yield-curve shape, currencies, commodities, and credit just by observing the changes in the equity market. This "risk-on, risk-off" correlation of assets at the macro level has brought home the fact that much of the real risk of investments resides in a few risk factors, and among those factors, the equity market becomes the final risk shock absorber. In a levered economy in which assets are being supported by a diminishing equity base, each unit of falling equity prices will very drastically magnify the economy-wide leverage. If we are on a path of deleveraging that is not at its final resting place, then this "denominator effect" (where equity is the denominator and the net assets are the numerator) can require a further downward adjustment of the numerator, that is, of asset valuation broadly. To see the impact of this simple approach at the portfolio level, let's go back to the basics of asset pricing. By definition, the beta of the stock market to itself is 1. The beta of any other security is the correlation of its returns times the ratio of the volatility of the asset to the volatility of the stock market. Thus, if a security such as a Treasury bond shows a beta of -0.10, this means first that its returns are negatively correlated with the stock market. On the other hand, high-yield bonds show an equity beta of almost 1; that is, not only are they positively correlated with the stock market, but they also have volatility of the same order of magnitude as the equity market. One would only want to buy such a security if the compensation for holding the default risk exceeded the risk from the market volatility of the equity market by a good margin. Higher-equity beta should, in efficient markets, compensate with higher return, but higher beta also means higher drawdown and tail risk. Thus, evaluating core factor exposures at the portfolio level, in aggregate, is a precursor to thinking of how to hedge the risk.

9. *The probability of tail events is less important than the severity.* The probability question for tail events cannot be addressed accurately by looking at traded option prices. The models used to explain the prices are based on assumptions that typically fail for very rare events. The reason is that the pricing of tail options in particular carries a significant amount of risk-premium compensation to the seller ("lottery-ticket risk") that alters the probability distribution of the underlying asset. Simulation (e.g., "bootstrapping" by sampling from history) is good but also not a totally satisfactory approach because each crisis is different in severity and magnitude. The practical approach to coming up with probabilities can take a number of parallel approaches that blend history and forecasts. One approach is to sample from historical events with replacement and to magnify the rare-event likelihood by a dynamic scale factor based on user forecasts of risks in the system (this effectively reshapes the tails). Simultaneously, changes in a tail risk indicator such as the VIX, even with its inherent limitations, can be measured to indicate the likelihood of being in a crisis versus a normal environment in which correlations and volatilities from a distressed regime are used. Regardless of how these probabilities are estimated, it should be emphasized that because tail hedges are essential to managing

portfolio risk, the probability calculation is less important than knowing that hedges exist that can make the difference between survival and almost certain ruin.

10. *Tail hedges have to be monitored and adjusted actively.* This might seem to be a contradiction because we are used to hedges being relatively static. But a static approach simply does not work in stress environments. For example, as I discuss later, once a tail hedge changes in value, its prospective future potential performance can change in complex, nonlinear ways. Also, the interdependence of market tail risks and counterparty risk becomes important. The risks to such contracts are many, and not controlling portfolios against failure to pay is a recipe for disaster. For instance, many participants found that insurance written by insurers was not as solid as they had thought. In addition, once we allow for indirect hedges, there are frequent opportunities to add value that reduces the cost of the hedge; markets don't all react together and create short-term dislocations between them. Monetization, when and how to take gains on hedges that have performed, is also crucial for adding value. I will discuss the tools for active management in this book.

11. *Tail hedges create "nonlinear, explosive" liquidity when liquidity is hard to obtain.* Tail hedging allows the portfolio to be more efficiently positioned both ex post and ex ante. In my experience, the fact that tail events are accompanied by deleveraging transfer, the transaction benefits the party who is long the hedges; that is, when there is a demand surge for hedging, the seller of existing hedges is the price setter for liquidity. Whereas it is obvious that explicit tail hedges allow one to have defense in the portfolio, that is, protect the portfolio from permanent losses, it is also important to note that having tail hedges in the portfolio allows carrying of positions through volatile periods

that subsequently may result in longer-term gains. Changing the objective function for portfolio construction to one that targets permanent capital losses indeed even allows portfolios to take more of the preferred risks. I call this *offensive risk management* and will discuss how it can lead to better portfolio construction.

12. *Proper accounting of tail-hedging costs and benefits in the portfolio context is critical.* As I will discuss in Chapter 7, it is important to ensure that the accounting for tail hedges is done in the context of the overall portfolio. Just as one does not regret buying automobile insurance despite the fact that the insurance premium is lost at the end of the year, one should think of tail risk hedging as an essential part of managed portfolios against systemic risk. Overcoming many of the behavioral biases makes the value of tail hedging clearer. In Chapter 7, I discuss these issues, which underline the need for tail hedging as an asset-allocation decision, a design feature of modern portfolio construction. Such precommitment to looking at portfolio and hedge performance in unison simply creates a better distribution of prospective returns.

13. *When hedging, it pays to be countercyclical.* Tail risk hedging is most beneficial as an anticyclical asset-allocation design element. Investors have a tendency to buy tail hedges during and after a crisis and run their portfolios "naked" when markets are relatively quiet and tail hedges become cheap. In my view, the best way to construct robust portfolios is to increase tail hedges when they are cheap, but at the same time to maintain essential portfolio risks. It is a well-known phenomenon that quiet markets, low volatility, and the lack of visible risks on the horizon breed complacence and increasingly dangerous levered positions. In doing so, these market conditions are a setup for the

next set of deleveraging and losses. What has also been apparent by experience is the predictable behavioral response to this cycle. When the markets suffer large losses, tail risk hedging comes back into fashion, and there is a "demand surge" that drives up volatilities across markets. This reduces the overall potency of naive hedges, and one has to be smart about when and where to spend the premium. On the other hand, when markets are quiet, we quickly forget the pains we suffered during prior crises and choose to take off the guard-rails of tail hedging or, even more dangerously, become sellers of the tails.

14. *Tail hedging is an asset-allocation decision.* I believe that tail hedging is not just a "trade" but also an asset-allocation decision for robust portfolio construction. In this light, variations in valuation levels make it easy to be countercyclical and add to tail hedges when they are cheap. If one integrates tail hedging into the overall asset-allocation approach that mitigates long-term risks of sharp losses and potential improved risk-adjusted returns, the benefits of following tail hedging as part of investment policy become obvious.

In summary, the essential insight from my experience is that tail risks for typical diversified portfolios occur from systemic risks and rising correlations. Thus, a proper tail risk hedging program takes into account the relative pricing of broad macro markets and strategies and evaluates the best alternatives from combinations of these alternatives to immunize the portfolio against improbable but not impossible shocks. Rather than using one approach for risk mitigation (which has been dominated by diversification or dynamic risk reduction), I believe that a multipronged approach that uses active explicit tail risk hedging as an alternative is not only more powerful but also more cost-efficient in the long run.

In the following chapters I will explain the framework and the details that I think other investors will find useful.

Distressed Liquidation and Failure of Diversification

As discussed earlier in this chapter, one reason tail risk hedging is necessary as a supplement to diversification is that under stress, market liquidity falls drastically, volatilities of both assets and portfolios can rise, and correlations between assets can change, sometimes significantly. This may result in the failure of diversification under stress. As a matter of fact, the impact of large-scale liquidations anecdotally almost always results in rising correlations between risk assets in tail events. Clearly this happened during the 2008 crisis when many large and small investors, who appeared to be cosmetically diversified, realized that their portfolios were exposed to hidden tail risk. Thus, it is important to understand how large-scale liquidations may endogenously result in the covariance structure between asset returns to change, and contagion may occur.

As discussed in Cont and Wagalath (2011)[1], in a simple model where asset returns are driven by a combination of normal uncertainty and the market impact of liquidation under stress, the realized covariance of assets is the sum of the fundamental covariance (that is, the long-term covariance expected as a consequence of economic relationships between asset returns) and an excess covariance. This excess covariance turns out to be path dependent and varies inversely with market liquidity. In particular, *even assets that are fundamentally uncorrelated may become correlated on the tails if they are affected by a common liquidity factor.* Although this observation clearly confirms the limited benefits obtained from diversification, it also gives us a powerful insight into the use of multiasset hedges for tail risk hedging. In other words, if the market cheaply prices a hedge instrument that is normally uncorrelated to the equity market and becomes correlated under stress events, then this hedge instrument can be used to create more efficient hedging strategies. We think of this as "using tail correlations to your advantage." For example, if we believe that there are concentrated carry positions in some currency pairs that will come under liquidation pressure if the equity or credit markets come under pressure, then a carry currency put option bought in advance of the stress would prove to be a cheap way of hedging.

Using such a model, the excess covariance generated under stress is driven by the ratio of a large liquidating fund's holdings to the market depth of the liquidated holdings. When such a security has infinite depth, then the resulting asset correlation is simply equal to the fundamental correlation. Under stress, and with less than infinite depth, the fund holdings endogenously become correlated. Such liquidation also results in an increase in the volatility of the assets that the fund holds, and indeed in the volatility of the fund itself, since the fall in the value of the total portfolio below a threshold triggers the fire sale of other assets. In addition, such large-scale liquidation by one fund may result in contagion and tail risk exposure (and rising volatility) to other smaller funds, proportional to the commonality of holdings as well as the overall market liquidity for the common holdings.

This is an important lesson that tail risk hedging is necessary—not only for a large fund with leverage that might be forced to liquidate under an adverse shock, but also for smaller, less leveraged funds that have similar strategies but might seem safer from not being large enough to affect market liquidity directly. As discussed later in this book, estimating the crowdedness of particular investments through high-frequency signatures such as intraday correlations may help in preparing for potential contagion events.

Can Tail Events Be Predicted?

One of the repeated themes of this book is that unprecedented central bank activism is creating the potential for extreme volatility in the markets. Another theme is that the markets can implode without warning and precursory phenomena, not unlike "phase transitions" that occur in physical systems.

When Japan's Nikkei Index dropped 15 percent over eight trading days in early June 2013, many global investors were caught off-guard. Despite the nearly 80 percent run-up in share prices since November 2012, market sentiment remained bullish thanks to Japan's new hyperactive monetary policy aimed at reflating the economy. As a result, it seems that many investors had not hedged their portfolios in advance against the impact of a market correction. In short, the subsequent Nikkei "minicrash" was an excellent example of a real tail event—a seemingly unlikely occurrence with an extreme outcome.

Looking back, I believe that the Nikkei crash can yield important lessons. With careful observation and analysis, investors *can* potentially anticipate a tail event, hedge their portfolios inexpensively, and potentially improve their investment returns. In the case of the run-up in the Nikkei, many hedges that would have proved profitable had become very inexpensive.

Tail events are easy to identify in hindsight. The difficulty, of course, is predicting them with any degree of accuracy in terms of both time and magnitude. Based on commonly available economic data evaluated through sufficiently pessimistic lenses, one might even predict tail events that don't happen. However, just observing the speed and performance of markets also can be sufficient reason to be careful. In the case of the Nikkei, a 72 percent cumulative return over six months was reason enough for caution. While I am no technician, some interesting research that has its origin in the physics of earthquakes leads to an interesting explanation of the imminence of the bursting of bubbles. I was tracking the daily closing prices of the Nikkei against a model based on research into economic bubbles by Sornette (2003). A cursory observation of the closing prices shows that each new high happened at a rapidly decreasing time interval (roughly halving each time), which is "amplification and oscillation" that precedes a correction in Sornette's theory (this is also observed in a variety of natural and social phenomena). In my model fit for the Nikkei, the duration of the peak to peak, according to the model, should be reduced by a factor of 1.62. The theory is that once the oscillation becomes "log-periodic" (see Exhibit 1.2 with a

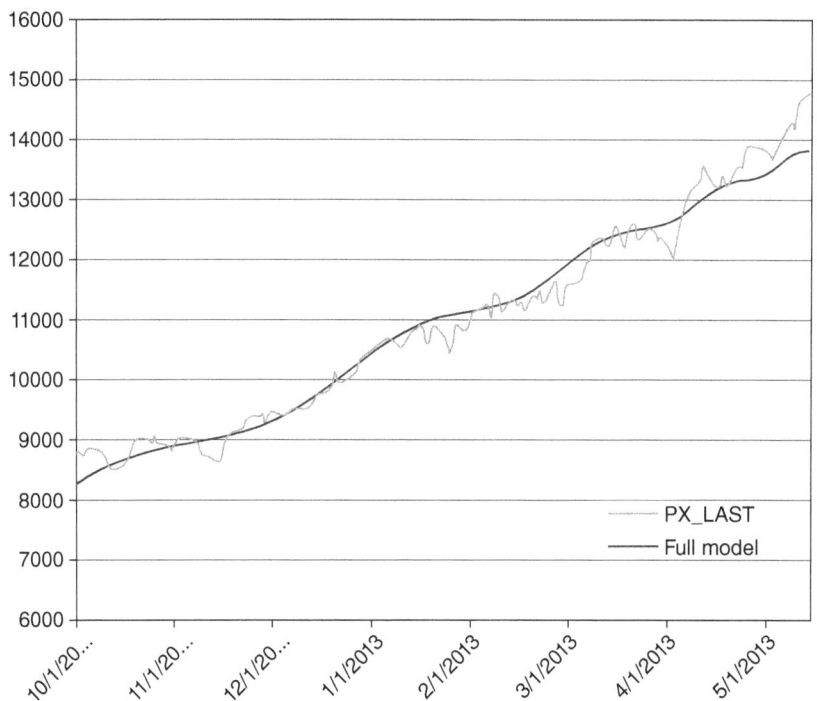

Exhibit 1.2 Tracking the daily close of the Nikkei Index: October 2012–May 13, 2013. Model results are hypothetical and are intended for illustrative purposes only. Nikkei 225 Index versus fit of log-periodic oscillation model to the index from May 13, 2013. (*Source: PIMCO*)

log-periodic fit to the market and Exhibit 1.3 for the predicted deviations from the model), one can forecast a distribution of the critical time and magnitude of a correction/collapse. (The magnitudes have varied from 15 to 35 percent in the case of the Nasdaq bubble, the gold bubble, and so on). Within two weeks, the Nikkei had made a quick 5.7 percent gain and then corrected 15 percent over eight trading sessions to land approximately 10 percent below its starting level. This example demonstrated that

1. *Tail risk can be hidden and unanticipated both in timing and in magnitude.* In the case of the Nikkei, almost no one anticipated the correction, and even after the fact, pundits are searching for proximal causes; the lesson is that sometimes

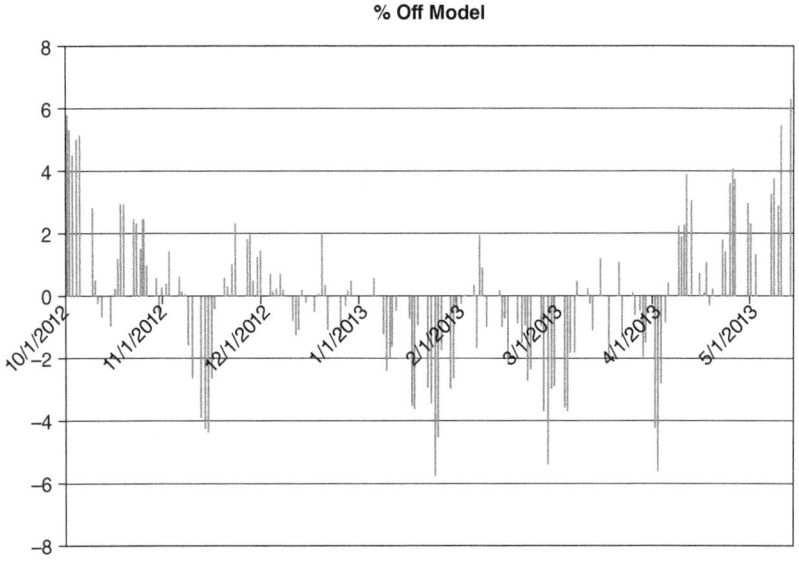

Exhibit 1.3 Mapping the Sornette model to the Nikkei: potential for a correction as of May 13, 2013. Model results are hypothetical and are intended for illustrative purposes only. (*Source: PIMCO.*)

markets do collapse under their own weight, especially if they are "pumped" up for artificial reasons.
2. *The markets allow, even encourage, the hedging of many of these tail risks in advance at attractively priced levels.* Before the Nikkei collapse, both puts and put spreads on the Nikkei Index were extremely cheap, after the Nikkei collapse, the VNKY volatility index (the equivalent of the VIX for the Japanese equity index) doubled, raising the price of out-of-the-money puts multifold.
3. *Hedging may offer not only a degree of protection from possible losses but also the potential for improved investment returns.* I don't advocate going out and buying lots of tail hedges simply to increase exposure without thought, but where necessary, tail hedges may allow investors to hold onto positions despite volatility and potentially reap gains from markets later if they do rally.

Monetary policies around the world have created extraordinary levels of liquidity, which, in turn, have driven substantial rallies in many markets. Not all of these can be justified by fundamentals (although some can). As talk of liquidity withdrawal hits investors' radar screens, the financial markets are likely to find even more severe and frequent air pockets without warning or fundamental explanations. Thus, even though prediction may be hard, anticipation of sharp corrections and adjusting portfolio exposures and tail hedges make sense.

2

Basics: Tail Risk Hedging for Defense

In this chapter I outline the basic elements for building a framework for tail risk hedging. I start with definitions of the key terms that I have found to be useful in designing a hedge program. Next, I discuss the costs and benefits of changing the hedge horizon based on market conditions. This "rolling" aspect of hedges is important if you think of tail hedging as an asset-allocation decision rather than as a "trade." Finally, I discuss benchmarking of tail hedges, which, though obvious, sets the stage for the discussion of active tail risk hedging later. Note that for the purpose of this chapter, I discuss hedging of the primary risk factor in most investment portfolios, that is, equity market–driven risk. The extension to other risk factors is straightforward.

Let us start with a very simple example. Suppose that we have a portfolio with a current value of $1 billion. Further, assume that it is 100 percent indexed to the Standard and Poor's 500 Index (S&P500); that is, it has a beta of 1 to the equity market. Finally, let us assume that the investor wants protection if the terminal value falls below $850 million in one years' time. We also assume that the investor wants to make sure that there is no basis risk; that is, the hedge should perform with complete certainty. The simplest solution is to purchase a European put option. The two basic questions are (1) which strike to buy and (2) how much of the option to buy. To answer these questions, we first note that the portfolio falls one for one with the S&P500 at the terminal horizon. Thus, if the current level of the S&P500 is, say, 1,294, then we want a payoff such that beyond 0.85 of 1,294, that is, below 1100 (0.85 × 1,294), every dollar of portfolio loss is covered. Therefore, the "direct" strike is 1,100. If we execute this in the listed S&P500 options market, then, by contract definition, each option contract pays off 100 times the S&P points. Thus, on one contract, the S&P500 falling from 1,100 to 1,000 will make 100 points, which equals $10,000. For the whole portfolio, the fall from 1,100 to 1,000 will be a 9.09 percent loss. At 1,100, the value of the current portfolio will be $850 million. A 9.09 percent loss of this amount is $77,265 million. To make this up with the option, we need to have 7,726 options contracts. Now the price per contract is 57.34 (using a simple Black-Scholes model), so the total premium spent will be 57.34 × 7726 × 100 = $44,300,884. Of the $1 billion current notional, this is approximately 4.43 percent.

We could have short-circuited this long computation by just going to a simple Black-Scholes calculator and pricing the 1,100 strike option. We would have found the cost to be 4.43 percent of the current S&P500 Index value. The reason I went through the long-winded computation was to show in detail the steps that will be relevant for hedging more complex portfolios with broader hedging needs.

Let us change the parameters to see the impact. Now let us suppose that the $1 billion portfolio we are hedging is only 50 percent equities (indexed to the S&P500), and the rest is cash. Suppose that the investor wants the same protection on this portfolio as before, that is, if the value of the portfolio falls below 85 percent of its current value at a one-year horizon. Now, for the portfolio to fall 15 percent, the equity market has to fall 30 percent. When the equity market falls 30 percent,

Basics: Tail Risk Hedging for Defense

the 50 percent portion that is in equities (i.e., $500 million) falls to $350 million, and the 50 percent cash portion remains unchanged at $500 million. Thus the total portfolio falls to $850 million. In this case, therefore, the appropriate equity-market strike is 30 percent out of the money or approximately at 900 strike. If the equity market falls from 900 to 800 (an 11.11 percent decline), the equity portion of $350 million falls by $38.89 million. To make this up, we need 3,889 contracts (3,889 × 100 × 100 points = $38.89 million). The current price of this contract is 26.45 points, so the total cost is 26.45 × 100 × 3,889 = $10,286,405. As a fraction of the current notional, this is 1.0286 percent.

Now note that if we had directly priced this option, we would have found that the 30 percent out-of-the-money strike (900 strike) would have cost 2.0447 percent. But this is on the full portfolio, so to adjust for the 50 percent equity exposure, we only need half as much, that is, 0.50 × 2.0447% = 1.023 percent, or $10.3 million.

There are three key inputs and one output that I have used here that I should now define. These are the terms we have been using for over a decade around which our framework is built and executed. First, the billion-dollar *notional* is the reference notional on which the hedge is written. Second, the 85 percent of current portfolio value is used to compute the *attachment* point of 15 percent (100 percent − 85 percent) where the protection is designed to produce a one-for-one benefit. The response of the portfolio of 0.50 is the factor *beta*. In the preceding example we only used one factor, equities, for the beta. Finally, we solve for the *cost* (1.02 percent in the second example). Typically, the investor specifies all four, and they have to solve simultaneously; otherwise we have to use indirect hedges (or take basis risk), which I will discuss later.

Let's explore why focusing on the factor exposure is so important. Exhibit 2.1, shows that both a traditional portfolio of equity and bonds and a broadly diversified portfolio of alternative and conventional assets are (1) dominated by equity-factor risk and (2) have similar tail profiles.

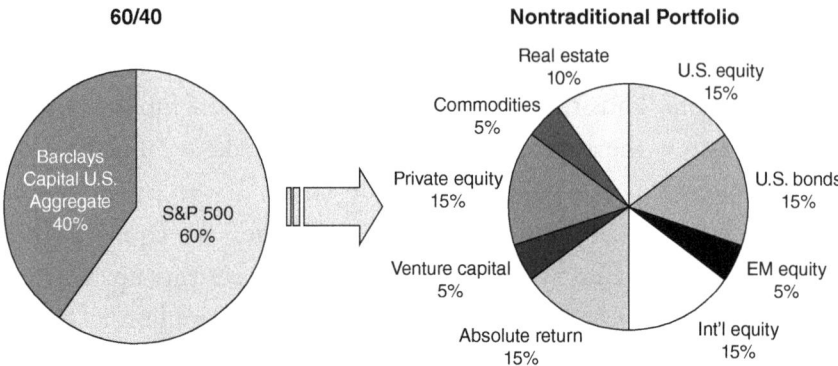

Exhibit 2.1a A 60/40 portfolio and an endowment style "diversified" portfolio.

Common risk factors end up driving the asset allocation and indeed the behavior of quite distinct asset classes, especially on the tails. In particular, the liquidity characteristics of the cosmetically more "diversified" alternative portfolio during market shocks makes the need for tail hedging even more important for that portfolio. This illustrates two important points in my approach—first, asset diversification and risk

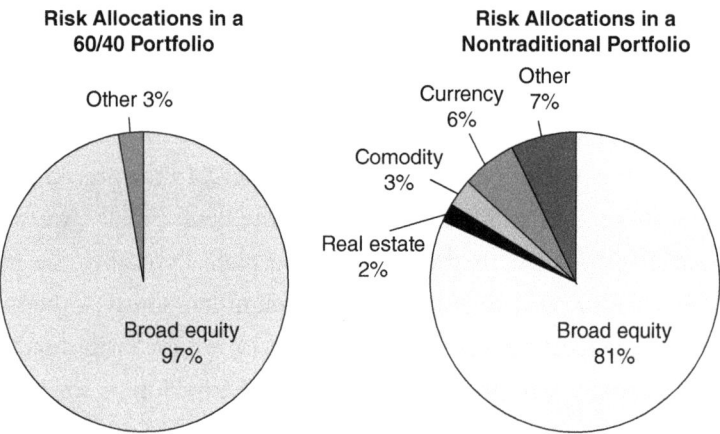

Exhibit 2.1b Risk decomposition of a 60/40 portfolio versus a nontraditional portfolio.

Basics: Tail Risk Hedging for Defense

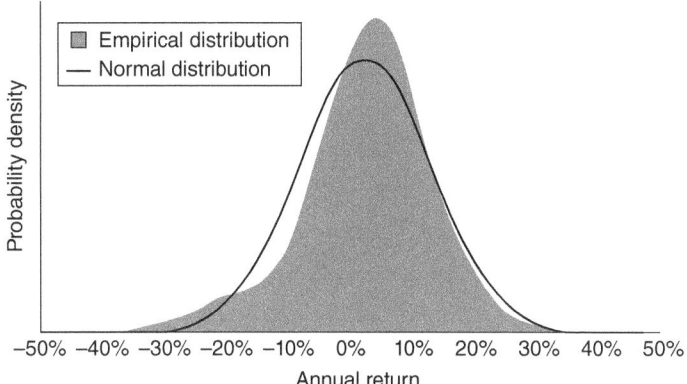

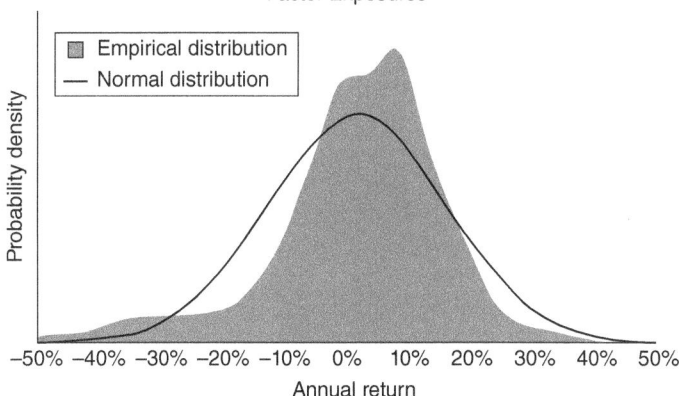

Exhibit 2.1c Tail risk profile of a 60/40 portfolio versus a nontraditional portfolio based on statistical bootstrap.

diversification are different, and second, as long as the indirect hedge has a high degree of probability of replicating the payoff of a direct hedge, we consider the indirect hedge to be superior to the direct hedge because it reduces the cost of carrying the tail hedge.

Formal Derivation of Portfolio Hedges Using Factor Hedges

In this section I show how the factor-based approach may be used to derive the right scaling for factor hedges that track portfolio hedges for the same strike.

If the attachment is denoted by A (say 15 percent = 0.15), the current level of the portfolio by P_0, and the future level at time T by P_t, then the European option tail payoff is simply $\max[(P_0-P_t)/P_0 - A, 0]$, which equals [we replace A by $(P_0 - K_P/P_0)$]

$$\max\left[\frac{P_0 - P_t}{P_0} - \frac{P_0 - K_P}{P_0} -, 0\right] = \max\left[\frac{K_P - P_t}{P_0}, 0\right]$$

We can expand this as follows:

$$\max\left[\frac{K_P}{P_0} - \frac{P_t}{P_0}, 0\right] = \max\left[\frac{K_P - P_0}{P_0} - \frac{P_t - P_0}{P_0}, 0\right]$$

which, in terms of returns (lowercase), is

$$\max\left[k_p - r_p, 0\right]$$

Now we can use the beta to replace portfolio returns and strikes with stock-market returns and strikes $r_p = \beta r_S, k_p = \beta k_S$:

$$\max\left[\beta k_S - \beta r_S, 0\right]$$

And finally manipulating

$$\beta \max\left[k_S - r_S, 0\right] = \beta \max\left[\frac{S_0 - S_t}{S_0} + \frac{K_S - S_0}{S_0}, 0\right]$$

$$\beta \max\left[\frac{K_S - S_t}{S_0}, 0\right] = \frac{\beta}{S_0} \max[K_S - S_t, 0]$$

Basics: Tail Risk Hedging for Defense

Ultimately, therefore, we have the result that the payoff of the option is simply beta over the initial stock value times the price of the stock price put option priced at the beta-adjusted strike K_S. Thus, as a shortcut, remember that the beta comes into play twice when computing the hedge cost. First, we have to adjust the attachment of the portfolio by dividing by the beta ($k_S = k_p/\beta$). For a 15 percent attachment point on the portfolio, the attachment point on the stock market is 15 percent divided by the beta (if beta is 0.6, the equity attachment is 15 percent/0.6 = 25 percent). Second, the amount of the payoff required is β-scaled. The price of this option is in the last formula. It is simply the price of a put option on the stock in percent times the beta of the portfolio (remembering that the strike is adjusted down by the beta first).

In the discussion so far we have assumed that the only risk in the portfolio arises from the equity beta. However, a true portfolio has many different types of assets and has other factors that create tail risks as well. For generic 60/40 portfolios, duration, or interest-rate sensitivity of the portfolio, is second only to the equity risk factor (there are also other fixed-income risk factors that matter; see my book *Bond Portfolio Investing and Risk Management*). For a typical 60/40 portfolio, 40 percent of the allocation is to fixed income. If this 40 percent allocation is indexed to a broad market index, then assuming that the 60 percent in equities has no duration, we need a hedge if rates or credit spreads rise substantially. Some of the credit-spread risk is generally already captured in the equity beta (because credit and equity risk are correlated). To hedge the interest-rate duration, we can go through a similar exercise as before; for example, if the portfolio duration is 10 years and the attachment point is 5 percent away, then rates have to rise 50 basis points (bp) for the attachment point to be breached. Note that when both the equity and bond parts are risky, the 15 percent attachment level refers to the whole portfolio, and for different levels of correlations between stocks and bonds (equity beta and duration risks), the 15 percent attachment level can be achieved through an infinite combination of equity- and bond-market movements. This option price can be easily computed through a basket option put pricing formula.[1] Similarly, other factors can be included, and the portfolio hedging problem is basically a problem of hedging the basket. The critical element to note is that diversification between factors is likely to reduce the overall cost of portfolio hedging. In other words, tail hedging is cheaper when diversification is working. When diversification fails, each component of the hedge becomes more expensive, and the absence of any factor hedge can create losses that are not hedged. Knowing how diversification can fail, by running correlation sensitivities, we can see how much explicit hedging is needed to supplement the internal hedging from portfolio diversification.

Rolling Tail Hedges

When we implement tail hedges, to standardize the discussion, we usually begin with one year as the default hedge horizon. For a given premium, we thus price the "direct" one-year hedge and then propose indirect ways of reducing its premium. In addition, on an ongoing basis, we usually actively manage the hedges to reduce the realized cost of hedging over this investment horizon.

The instruments themselves, of course, can be shorter or longer than the horizon, but by starting with a one-year hedge horizon, we can standardize the discussion. Of course, in practice, there is no reason to use the one-year hedge as the reference. In this section we will briefly discuss the costs versus benefits of rolling hedges at a shorter or longer horizon.

Frequently there is a desire to move toward more frequent rebalancing of hedges. One popular frequency is quarterly. There are numerous reasons for this. First, having more frequent hedges "averages" out the premium spend and the attachment point. Second, it avoids a "cliff" effect on the hedge becoming more distant as we near expiration.

Finally more frequent rebalancing might allow a recalibration of the portfolio exposures within the one-year period.

Of course, we cannot make a blanket statement as to the efficacy or superiority of one hedge algorithm. Even without a lot of work, one can anticipate that tradeoffs will arise from the variation in the volatility term structure or the shape of the volatility curve. Because the price of an option scales as volatility times the square root of time left to expiration, we can expect a more frequent hedge to do better if the volatility curve is steep and upward-sloping (shorter-term volatility lower than longer-term volatility) or when the term structure is flat and is expected to remain that way. If the volatility curve is inverted (as usually happens after a market shock), then the more frequent hedging costs more than when the curve is steep or flat. This also argues for flexibility in varying the rebalance frequency in the aftermath of market events as part of active management.

To provide a flavor of the key considerations on how rolling hedges work relative to holding longer-term hedges, I will anchor the discussion around a one-year hedge on the S&P500, with a strike that is 25 percent out of the money. This is an often-used "benchmark" direct hedge. To see why, recall that when we are hedging a 60/40 portfolio with a 15 percent attachment point, the effective strike for the direct S&P option is 15 percent/0.6 = 25 percent. Let us assume that the one-year volatility for this 25 percent out-of-the-money strike is 30 percent. The Black-Scholes price of this option is 250 bp (2.5 percent) by plugging into a Black-Scholes option calculator. Our objective will be to quantify the tradeoffs of more frequent hedges (cost, sensitivities, etc.) relative to this one-year hedge. For theoretical clarity, we ignore the transactions costs of unwinding existing hedges to replace with new hedges, although these considerations are critical in running an actual hedge program.

Suppose first that the volatility of the S&P options market is flat at 30 percent for the whole year. Then we can think of replacing the annual option with a string of daily options expiring in one day, two days, three days, and so on all the way to 365 days, each one of which would have 1/365 of the notional associated with it. Clearly, no one would want to have 365 daily options for practical reasons, but as with many problems, taking the limit sheds important light on the nature of the problem. Because the time value of shorter-expiry options is lower than those of longer-dated ones, the total cost of the daily options is only 94 bp (see Exhibit 2.2*d*) which is obtained by pricing each option and dividing by 365. Also, the shorter options will expire with the passage of time and will need replacement, whereas the longer-dated options remain alive. If we go to the more sensible quarterly rebalancing (where 250/4 of the premium is used each quarter), the total cost is only 127 bp or half the "bullet" one-year hedge. Also observe from Exhibit 2.2*a* that the pricing depends on the shape of the volatility curve. We created

Total Cost	Flat Vol	Steep Vol	Inverted Vol
Daily	94	60	170
Monthly	105	71	181
Quarterly	127	95	202
Bi-Annually	166	137	229
Annually	250	250	250

Exhibit 2.2*a* Prices of tail hedges for different volatility curve shapes.

Cost Ratio	Flat Vol	Steep Vol	Inverted Vol
Daily	0.38	0.24	0.68
Monthly	0.42	0.28	0.72
Quarterly	0.51	0.38	0.81
Bi-Annually	0.66	0.55	0.92
Annually	1	1	1

Exhibit 2.2*b* Ratio of prices to one year options.

Total Delta	Flat Vol	Steep Vol	Inverted Vol
Daily	−0.071	−0.048	−0.1
Monthly	−0.077	−0.054	−0.11
Quarterly	−0.089	−0.066	−0.12
Bi-Annually	−0.1	−0.087	−0.13
Annually	−0.14	−0.14	−0.14

Exhibit 2.2c Deltas of tail hedges for different volatility curves.

Delta Ratio	Flat Vol	Steep Vol	Inverted Vol
Daily	0.51	0.34	0.71
Monthly	0.55	0.39	0.79
Quarterly	0.64	0.47	0.86
Bi-Annually	0.71	0.62	0.93
Annually	1.00	1.00	1.00

Exhibit 2.2d Ratio of deltas to one year puts.

Delta Adjusted Cost	Flat Vol	Steep Vol	Inverted Vol
Daily	185	175	238
Monthly	191	184	230
Quarterly	200	202	236
Bi-Annually	232	220	247
Annually	250	250	250

Exhibit 2.2e Delta adjusted cost of tail hedges for different volatility curves.

three idealized curves: The "steep" curve starts at 15 percent volatility and goes to 30 percent volatility linearly, which is usually associated with a calm equity market (note all volatilities here refer to the out-of-the-money put options). A flat volatility curve stays at 30 percent all the way, and an inverted curve starts at 50 percent volatility for the shortest option (a one day option) and ends up at the 30 percent volatility for the one-year option with linear interpolation. The exhibit shows that the inverted volatility curve requires twice as much premium for daily rebalancing relative to the flat volatility curve and three times as much as for the steep volatility curve. For quarterly rebalancing, the inverted volatility curve creates a 60 percent higher cost relative to the flat volatility curve, and the steep volatility curve creates a discount of 25 percent. In terms of higher-frequency rebalancing, a flat volatility curve makes the total cost of quarterly hedging 127 bp versus 95 bp for the steep volatility curve and 202 bp for the inverted volatility curve. In all three cases, more frequent hedging is cheaper than locking in the one-year hedge. But this is not a free lunch! As Exhibit 2.2c shows, more frequent hedging has a lower delta than longer-term hedging. Because the delta is the sensitivity of the hedge to the movements in the underlying, what this analysis shows is that the sensitivity of a hedge portfolio goes down as compensation for the lower cost. One can see why this happens intuitively. First, more frequent hedging means that the hedges expire more frequently; that is, the daily hedge will have 1/365 of the notional expire each day. Second, the shorter hedges have lower deltas because the probability of a large market move is much lower, so the hedge is theoretically less likely to go in the money. Of course, one can argue that if event risk is higher in the short term, having more short-term hedges cheaper can be a better hedge. This would be an active view on the level of the volatility term structure that one might want to take, for instance, right around a big policy decision, elections, or any similar event with potential unpriced jump risk.

Exhibit 2.2d summarizes the ratio of the potency, or deltas, of the various frequencies of hedges relative to the benchmark one-year hedge. As is obvious, the quarterly delta ratio (0.84) for the inverted volatility curve is higher than the quarterly delta ratio (0.47) when the volatility curve is steep and upward-sloping.

To put all the discussion and tradeoffs together, Exhibit 2.2*e* shows the cost for the same unit of delta. In other words, if we impose the condition that we want the same delta regardless of the frequency of hedging, what should be the total equivalent cost? The conclusion from the exhibit is that more frequent rebalancing does add some benefit in all cases relative to the once-a-year hedge (ignoring transactions costs), but the benefits are larger when the volatility curve is flat or steep. Also, once each period's hedge expires, new extension hedges have to be added on to replace them. Because the normal volatility term structure is expected to appear more than 75 percent of the time (inversions are associated with large downside market events), we expect, on average, to improve some hedging efficiency by moving to a reasonable (quarterly) hedging program. This also highlights two other major issues: (1) hedging has to be a systematic, repeated asset-allocation decision to obtain best long-term benefits, and (2) the hedge program has to be active and consider pricing levels so that efficient rebalancing can be implemented. I will discuss the active management of hedges more thoroughly in Chapter 4.

Benchmarking Tail Risk Management[2]

The term *tail risk hedging* and its practice have been open to much interpretation; this phenomenon of initial confusion is not particularly different from the growing pains experienced by many other new markets. Mutual funds, hedge funds, and even exchange-traded funds (ETFs) at the very beginning of their life cycle operated without much uniformity or proper reference indexes. As the market for tail-hedging solutions evolves, it will become critical that end users at least have a framework within which to evaluate the potential and realized costs and benefits of particular ways of implementing solutions. I believe that to add value over time, tail risk management has to be active rather than purely passive; thus a proper benchmarking framework is important to measure value added. The purpose of this section is to start to lay out exactly such a framework, which I have evolved over almost a decade of implementation.

As discussed earlier, a small set of inputs or guidelines is the natural starting point for defining a tail-hedge program. In my view, the minimal set consists of the following:

1. Exposures
2. Attachment
3. Cost
4. Basis risk

Any benchmark we use should have these four elements available for continuous and accurate measurement.

The first step is quantifying exposures. My analysis of the long-term history of many different types of assets shows that a small set of risk factors drives the returns of these assets. The two major secular exposures are the equity beta and interest-rate or duration exposure. In addition, over cyclical periods, factors such as liquidity, currency exposure, momentum, and monetary policy also play important and significant roles. In my practice, I first try to quantify the exposures of each underlying portfolio to these key factors, both for normal and stressed periods. Interestingly, both my research and the work of others show that even very diversified portfolios exhibit similar exposures to the key risk factors, with equity beta as the dominant risk exposure. This was illustrated earlier in this chapter, and hence the benchmark should have the breadth to capture the exposures that will be hedged.

The second step is to select the *attachment* level (taking a term from the reinsurance industry). The closer the attachment level is to the current value of the portfolio, the higher one should expect the cost of the tail risk program. Generally, I believe that broadly diversified portfolios should have an attachment level anywhere from 10 percent to 15 percent below the current portfolio value. The reasons for this are partly based on the psychological tolerance for risk and partly on the empirical observation that a diversified portfolio over long history has delivered a volatility of 8 to 12 percent annualized, and this roughly corresponds to a drawdown of 10 to 15 percent. But this is variable, and the benchmark should have enough flexibility to allow for variability of the attachment level.

This brings me to the important question of cost. I generally do not believe that tail hedging can be done efficiently in a perfectly costless manner over short-term horizons. Yes, there are structures (especially exotics) that purport to reduce the cost or in many cases even eliminate the cost, but usually they consist of embedded sales of options that one would frequently rather not sell or at the cost of illiquidity when it is time to unwind the hedges. Instead of this hidden discount, I believe that an explicit cost target is essential to thinking of tail risk management as both an asset-allocation decision and a commitment that one can continue to support in periods where fat tail events do not occur. Because of the natural difficulty in forecasting the time and form of the next tail event, I believe that tail hedging is an "always on" part of any risky investment portfolio rather than a "just in time" approach. My empirical and theoretical research, discussed in the next few chapters, validates the belief that over longer periods (three to five years), tail hedging is generally self-financing when one accounts for both the ability to tilt portfolios more aggressively and following a systematic approach to rebalancing in the presence of such hedges.

Finally, one has some freedom to replace what might be expensive direct hedges with relatively cheaper indirect hedges, taking advantage of the tendency for correlations to increase, especially when extreme events happen. This cheapening comes with a tradeoff that indirect hedges will not perform as well as direct hedges conditional on the extreme event happening. To quantify this basis risk, I specify a level of confidence within which the outcomes of the actual portfolio are likely to fall relative to the direct hedge. The performance of a particular hedge program should be quantified in terms of the trade off between basis risk and cost savings relative to a low- or no-basis-risk benchmark.

Once the framework for proper tail hedge construction is defined, the task of creating a proper index becomes relatively straightforward. If the benchmark is equity beta, we can use the most liquid traded market sectors that carry the key risk-factor exposures to start with a shortlist of potential benchmark constituents. For instance, it would make sense to use S&P500 Index options close to the maturity of the hedge mandate as a reference instrument because, by definition, this index has an equity beta of 1 to itself (one can choose another equity index for this reference, e.g., the MSCI World, if that is the index of reference for the underlying portfolio). If the reference portfolio is a blend of equity beta and fixed income—for instance, something like the MSCI World Index combined with the Barclays U.S. Aggregate Bond Index—then the tail hedge will be a blend of the best equity beta and duration hedges for this combination. The best reference market instruments therefore will be options on the equity and bond indexes. But because options on bond indexes are generally not very liquid, it makes sense to select options on tradable markets such as Treasury futures for index construction. Also, note that tail options on a portfolio are not the same as the sum of options on the individual constituents, so adjustments for the correlations of the underlying constituents need to be made.

Once the proper sectors are identified, the next step is to set a *strike* for the portfolio of reference market options. As an example, if the attachment level for an overall 60 percent equity, 40 percent bond portfolio is set at 85 percent (i.e., 15 percent out of the money for the whole portfolio), then assuming that the bond part remains static, the reference equity option strike is 15 percent/0.60 = 25 percent. Thus the natural strike of the reference equity option is 25 percent out of the money.

One can proceed in a similar manner for the other underlying risks as a crude starting point.

The advantage of constructing the basket of reference securities in such a way is that they can be monitored in real time. Options-based tail hedges have various *Greeks*, such as time decay, gamma, vega, theta, and so on that are very dynamic and have to be actively monitored and traded. The value added by an investment is proportional to how the actual portfolio of hedges behaves over time relative to the theoretical benchmark. It also solves the problem of behavioral aversion to the cost of hedging. Once the actual hedge cost and time decay are put relative to the cost of a theoretical hedge, it is much easier to commit to the cost as a long-term asset-allocation decision and to compare this cost versus the implied cost of derisking or buying government bonds. The important point is that all types of tail hedging cost something, either implicitly or explicitly, and this includes derisking and moving to cash. The process of going through the relative-value comparison of different types of hedges allows the investor to anchor the tail-hedging analysis to something realistic and measurable.

I should emphasize that the use of market-traded options is a simplification that works only if the underlying hedge objective is rather plain vanilla. If the objective is more complex, for example, "hedge so that at no point in time does the portfolio suffer a loss of more than x percent," the reference index security would have to be more of an exotic option such as a knock-in option. Although these options are traded heavily in the over-the-counter (OTC) markets, their prices are not as easily available as those of vanilla index options. More complex replicating option portfolios can be constructed to index these payoffs; they just require more complex replicating portfolios that have to be dynamically managed, and this means more cost and possibly counterparty risk. Complexity versus transparency is an important tradeoff when it comes to tail hedging. I generally recommend erring in the favor of simple portfolios and, hence, simple benchmarks to measure them against.

Quantifying Performance

For portfolios indexed to traditional portfolios, the task of performance measurement is relatively straightforward. One can look at the returns of the actual portfolio versus the index and discern whether the decisions of the manager are adding or subtracting value. For tail risk hedging, the problem is only simple if all the hedges are relatively plain vanilla and the underlying instruments are liquid and replicate the portfolio without any basis risk. The moment the hedges become complicated, performance measurement takes a new twist. The reason simply is that the current price of the hedge does not reflect the potential it has for a large tail payoff, and because tail events are rare events, observation of a few nontail periods is not sufficient to identify the prospects of the tail hedge. Naively, a tail hedge could look like it is performing better than a reference index of securities by losing time value more slowly than the reference hedges, but this is most likely to offer less potential for payoff if there is a jump event in the market (if the option hedges have less time decay, they probably, though not necessarily, have less gamma as well). To compensate for this shortcoming of real-time performance measurement, I believe that tail hedges need to be evaluated on the basis of scenario analysis. By identifying scenarios of concern and shocking the underlying market factors at different horizons, one can evaluate the potential of these hedges to pay off in the situations that matter. Robust technology and sensible stress-testing systems are thus of paramount importance for this exercise.

While tail risk hedging is a new and critically important area of modern portfolio management practice, the relative newness of the area means that standard frameworks for benchmarking such portfolios have not yet developed. Although much work remains to be done,

I believe that standardization and benchmarking in this area will result in the same value added to investors as they have done in the areas of traditional equity and bond portfolio management. Most important, they will give end users a means by which to quantify the "distance" of a bespoke tail hedge portfolio versus an easily measurable index to evaluate the cost-versus-benefit tradeoffs.

Cash Versus Explicit Tail Hedging

As discussed in Chapter 1, proper tail hedging does not have to be unidimensional. We should use cash, diversification, alternatives, and explicit hedging within a consistent cost-benefit tradeoff to construct the most efficient and practical solutions. This list includes two choices at opposite extremes—hold cash or buy options-based hedges—with lots of alternatives in the middle. Note that cash provides liquidity, and the option to purchase assets later rather than now is a very valuable option. However, how much cash to keep should be evaluated against the cost of holding the cash.

In this respect, it seems, cash may not always be king. The main difference between cash as a hedge against systemic risk and, say, put options is that a dollar of cash remains a dollar of cash regardless of the market, but option values change as either the underlying asset moves down or as the perception of risk changes. As observed during the brunt of the credit crisis in 2007–2009, during the stock market "flash" crash of 2010, and during many other similar episodes, the value of not just equity put options but options in many other risk assets exploded up as the markets felt more insecure.

This *explosive liquidity* of explicit options can be a potential benefit because it can far exceed the value of old-fashioned simple cash in a period of crisis. (See Exhibits 2.3 and 2.4 for the performance of an S&P500 Index put option and one-month Treasury-bill yields, essentially the rate you are paid to hold cash.) This happens in two ways.

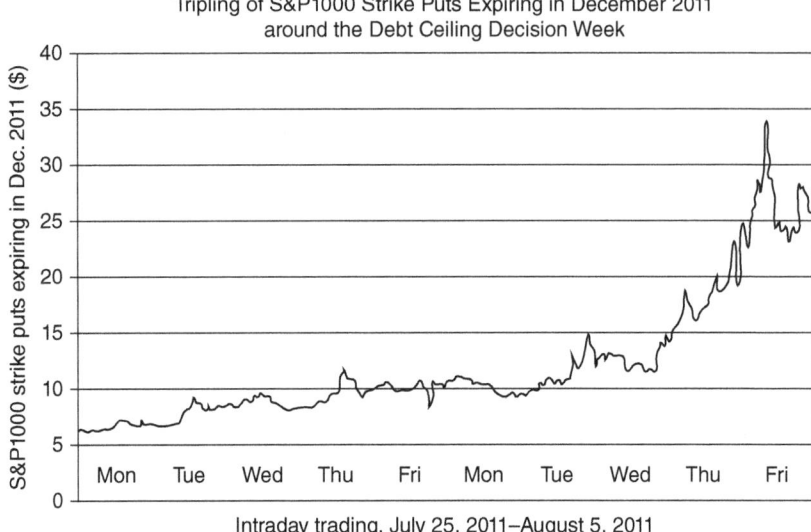

Exhibit 2.3 Increase in the value of an S&P500 put option.

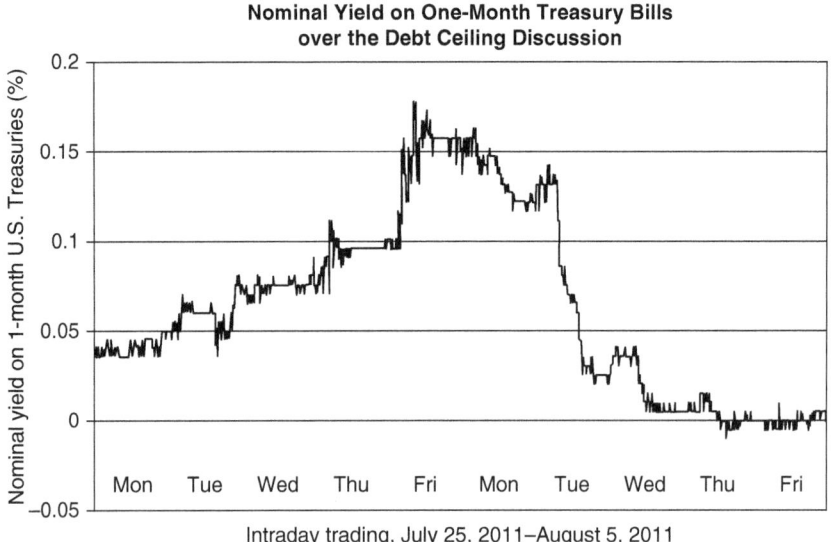

Exhibit 2.4 Nominal yield on Treasury bills.

First, portfolio holdings often show increased correlation (tendency of holdings to move in lock step) when markets move downward while tracking equity markets less closely on the upside. Thus, having cash might not match this downside convexity properly. To match it, one needs convex instruments, for which options are one of the simplest tools. Second, and beyond this defensive aspect, excess cash can be used to enter the markets at an attractive level. Put another way, if you believe that risk premia increase when the equity markets are doing badly, then each extra dollar is worth a lot more in bad states. The more of these dollars you have, the less likely it is that the cost of the hedge is a cost over the long run and the more likely it is a benefit.

To be sure, this potential benefit comes at a cost. Options are decaying assets; that is, if time passes and nothing happens, the options lose their value, whereas cash does not. If uncertainty falls, the mark-to-market value of options also falls. The magnitude of the time decay also changes depending on what initial price was paid (the larger the price, the more time decay there is in absolute terms) and the distance to the options' exercise price.

When choosing to set aside cash, therefore, one has to make a similar judgment. What is the drag on the cash? Currently, short-term rates are close to zero, so saving a large amount of cash creates a significant opportunity cost for the investor. The saved cash cannot be deployed into attractive investments, and if inflation is high, the cash loses real purchasing power and buys much less in the future. Indeed, the "costs" of holding cash as a vehicle of safety will become more and more expensive in both nominal and real terms.

Another aspect of cash as a safety vehicle is that cash is indifferent to the risks and asset mix in the portfolio. Most portfolios are much more complex. To evaluate the risks to these portfolios, I apply a risk-factor-based approach—indeed, looking through the portfolio in an effort to identify the risks that drive the assets and hence the portfolio. Knowing the details of the exposures, I believe, allows us to design custom strategies that use a proper combination of cash-and-options-based tail hedges from different asset classes dynamically.

The use of cash solely as a safety vehicle also depends on the ability of investors to time the markets well. As widely noted in the body of investment literature and discussed in Chapter 7, investors have overconfidence in their ability to time the markets and also tend not to follow through on plans.

I believe the solution to these biases is to follow a strategy of delegation and precommitment—in other words, combine cash-based hedging with "renting" a process and hardwire it so that the plans are implemented when optimal to do so. The options markets achieve this precommitment and delegation strategy.

As an analogy, let's compare two drivers. One keeps cash in his pocket in case of a flat tire or other more serious mishap but carries no insurance. Our second driver carries some insurance. In order to cover himself for all possible contingencies, our first driver would need to hold a great deal of cash. He should also make sure that the cash he is counting on is of the highest quality and will be sound and liquid in the event of the worst catastrophe. Of course, our second driver would want some cash because her insurance cannot cover all bad scenarios, but the amount of cash she needs to hold is relatively small compared with that of the other driver. Given that she wants the insurance to pay off in the worst of circumstances, she must take care to purchase her insurance from a provider or counterparty that is reputable and of more than sound financial status. Whereas it may make sense for some people to self-insure or drive more slowly, in the aggregate it would be highly inefficient for all people to hold sufficiently large sums of cash to adequately insure against all catastrophic outcomes.

I believe that guarding against the tails is best achieved by a mix of approaches rather than blind adherence to one. And fortunately, we can get a good sense of what the mix should look like by putting the choices on the same conceptual footing. First, we create a large set of scenarios on which to evaluate potential outcomes for both alternatives. Second, we evaluate the opportunity cost of using either the cash or the option-based alternative. Third, we evaluate the ability and the cost of switching into risk at each future point. None of this can be done without reference to the underlying portfolio and the objective function of the specific client—the client's own utility function, tolerance for risk and return, and investment horizon, as well as, critically, the price that the client is willing to pay now for the opportunity to truncate the "left tails."

Granted, this requires modeling and much computation, but technical details aside, the concept of using all the tools at your disposal is obvious.

Estimating Tail Probabilities

As mentioned in Chapter 1, I think that investors should focus more on the severity of tail events rather than on the probability of such events. However, understanding of the probabilities of severe events is a useful exercise. Over a long history of the equity markets, we can first compute an empirical probability density of returns and then estimate the probability of one-year returns falling below a particular threshold. Here I show *Mathematica* code on how to achieve this.

First, obtain history (here I am using annual returns):

```
returns=Table[(spxhistory[[i+12]]-spxhistory[[i]])/
spxhistory[[i]],{i,1,l-13,1}];
```

Next, compute the empirical smoothed distribution using a smoothed *kernel* estimator (Exhibit 2.5):

```
empdist=SmoothKernelDistribution[returns]
```

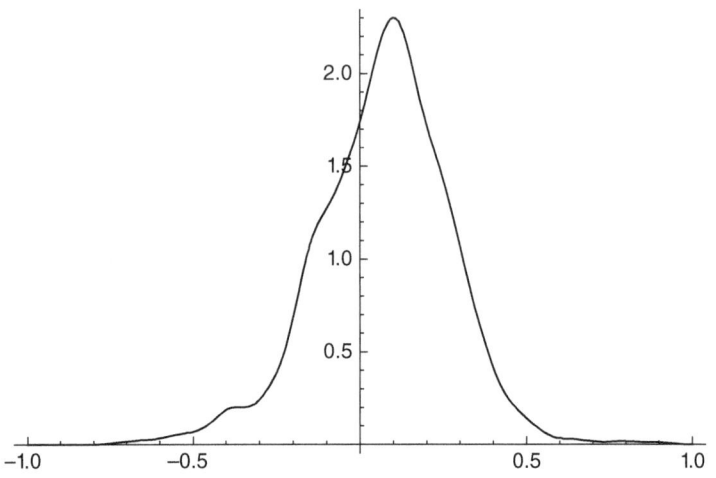

Exhibit 2.5 Empirical kernel distribution of annual S&P500 returns from January 1930 to 2013 sampled monthly. *Source: Author calculations.*

Now we can compute the statistics, for example, the empirical mean:

```
empmean=Mean[empdist]
```

which is 7.36 percent over the period 1930–2013.

Next, we can plot the smoothed empirical distribution of returns, which exhibits fat left tails:

```
Plot[PDF[empdist,x],{x,-1,1}]
```

We can compute tail probabilities using the built-in symbol `Probability`:

```
Probability[x<0,x≈empdist]
```

which yields 33 percent (i.e., the probability that we return a negative annualized return is a one in three).

What about the probability that the annual return is less than the rolling one-year average return by more than 15 percent?

`Probability[x<empmean-0.15,x≈empdist]`

This turns out to be only 20 percent. Similarly, the probability of a 20 percent loss below the mean return is 15 percent, the probability of a 25 percent loss below the mean return is 10 percent, and the probability of a 50 percent return below the mean return is empirically only 1.5 percent, that is, a very rare event. If we compute the same numbers relative to zero, that is, the probability of negative annualized returns based on history, we find that the probability of a negative return is only 33 percent, the probability of a 5 or greater loss is 25 percent, the probability of, 10 percent or greater loss is 18.5 percent, of a 15 percent or greater loss is 12.5 percent, of a 25 percent or greater loss is 5.5 percent, and the probability of a 50 percent or greater loss is only 0.8 percent.

3

Offensive Tail Risk Hedging[1]

Long-horizon investors traditionally have assumed that they need not purchase tail risk hedges against rare and severe events that can adversely affect their portfolios. Even when tail risk hedges are justified, they are interpreted as a cost that reduces the expected returns of the portfolio. Our experience over many years in speaking with investment officers suggests that their biggest challenge is convincing investment committees to commit to this cost and risk underperformance relative to their peer group. This defensive paradigm of portfolio hedges hides the fact that severe market crises (as in 2007 and 2008) create opportunities for investors who have access to liquidity. The purpose of this chapter is to illustrate that the opportunity to increase risk exposures in a tail event improves the return distribution of most investment portfolios; in other words, tail risk management is not only risk-reducing but also return-enhancing. This chapter produces a simple model to support the concepts. More precisely, we show that the "shadow value" of a tail-hedging program is positive.

In thinking about the added benefits from tail hedging, one must conduct a relative-value exercise whereby the implicit value of the tail hedge depends both on its explicit price in the market and on the subjective expected return[2] on the portfolio. As a simple example, consider the case of an investor who finds the risk versus reward of a 60 percent stock, 40 percent bond allocation to be optimal with given risk preferences. This investor has made, via actual allocation, a statement about the amount of risk he is comfortable with in his portfolio. Long-term equity volatility in the developed market (as measured by the Standard and Poor's 500 Index) has averaged about 18 to 20 percent, whereas the volatility of a 60/40 mix has been in the 8 to 12 percent per annum range.

Application of a tail hedge to this portfolio will likely reduce overall volatility because the hedge truncates a portion of the return distribution. Comparing the original 60/40 portfolio with the tail-hedged 60/40 portfolio places the two on different scales because the tail return profile of the two asset allocations will be different. An investor who is comfortable with the risks in the unhedged 60/40 portfolio also should be comfortable with a riskier portfolio, say, 70/30, if it incorporates the right amount of tail hedges. Although both portfolios display similar behavior on the downside, the 70/30 portfolio takes more equity risk and, thus, is positioned to harvest more equity-risk premium. Thus the investor's asset allocation and attitude to risk imply a fair value of a tail hedge to the investor, and this implicit value should be compared with the market value. We will outline the computations for this valuation here, leaving discussion of the behavioral aspects to Chapter 7.

In the following example, we illustrate how the shadow value of the put option can be derived and the potential gains from combining a more aggressive portfolio with a tail hedge. Consider the two annual portfolio return probability distributions described in Exhibit 3.1. The first distribution is a fat-tailed distribution whose explicit shape is derived based on the assumptions that 60 percent of capital is allocated to stocks and 40 percent to Treasury bills and that the risk premium on equities is 5 percent per annum, a number broadly consistent with the 4 to 7 percent range found in surveys (e.g., Graham and Harvey 2005).

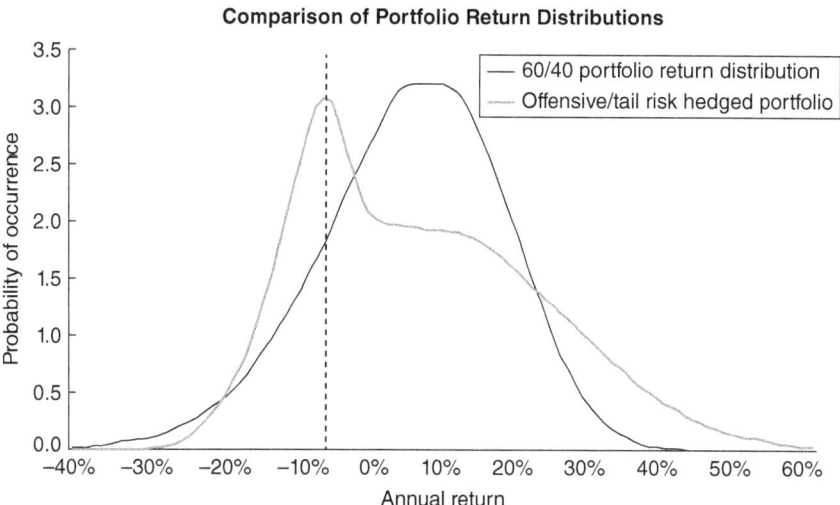

Exhibit 3.1 Comparison of unhedged and offensively hedged probability distributions. *Source: PIMCO.*

The second distribution is derived using the following assumptions: the investor cares about losses that exceed 5 percent, and he increases exposure to risk assets and finds an equity option that equates the expected value of losses greater than 5 percent in the second portfolio with the expected value of losses greater than 5 percent in the first portfolio.[3]

The important point here is that even though the median return of the offensive portfolio is lower, its expected return is higher (expectations require averaging over all outcomes, and the fatter right tail compensates for the shift of the median to the left). Intuitively, the value of a put option is equal to the probability of the loss times the severity of the loss. The 60/40 portfolio exhibits a larger tail than the more offensive, tail risk–hedged portfolio with a higher probability of more severe losses but compensates by a much lower probability of smaller losses. On average, these severities, weighted by the probability of occurrence, are the same. Here we are using the value of a put option, struck at a

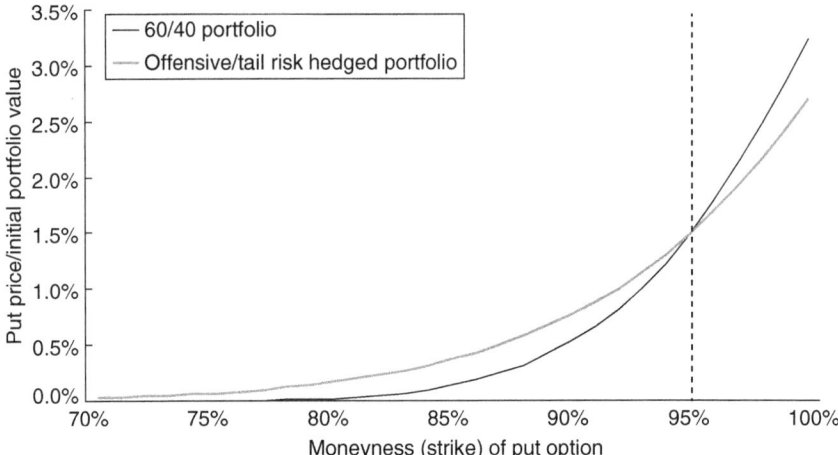

Exhibit 3.2a Theoretical price of a put option on the portfolios for different strikes. *Source: PIMCO.*

particular threshold. Exhibit 3.2 compares the implied values of put options on the two portfolios for different strikes, showing that the two portfolios have equivalent values for a put struck 5 percent below the initial value of the portfolio.

Exhibit 3.2b contrasts the statistical characteristics of the two return distributions. For the same level of risk, that is, when the value

	60/40 Portfolio	**Offensive / Tail Risk Portfolio**[1]
Expected Return	6%	7%
Volatility	12%	16%
Downside Volatility	8%	5%
Upside Volatility	8%	12%
10th Percentile	−11%	−11%
90th Percentile	21%	30%

Exhibit 3.2b Distributional statistics of 60/40 versus offensively hedged portfolio. *Source: PIMCO.*

of a put option on the two portfolios struck at initial portfolio value is equal, the offensive, tail risk–hedged portfolio offers greater expected return than the 60/40 portfolio. Although volatility of the tail risk–hedged portfolio is greater, this volatility is from the right side of the distribution. Downside volatility is much larger in the 60/40 portfolio. Upside volatility is much larger in the offensive, tail risk–hedged portfolio. The 10th and 90th percentiles of the two distributions are statistics that also tell an interesting story. The downside tail on the 60/40 portfolio is greater, whereas the upside tail on the offensive, tail risk–hedged portfolio is greater.

Note that the beneficial aspects of tail hedging we are trying to motivate using the simple toy model also have been borne out since the 2007–2008 crisis, although admittedly this is only one history of the markets. Since the lows in the Standard and Poor's 500 Index (S&P500) in the early 2009, the equity markets have more than doubled. Starting in 2008, the returns to this index were as follows: −38.49 percent in 2008, 23.45 percent in 2009, 12.78 percent in 2010, 0 percent in 2011, and 13.41 percent in 2012. Suppose that a portfolio each year spent 100 bp in premium, thus locking in a reduction of 1 percent in return from options expiring worthless (although I discuss how active management can actually reduce the hedging cost substantially). If the risk was increased, say, 10 percent, then the gains from the underlying market performance were sufficient to make up the premium cost. Thus, clearly, there is a premium per year that can be justified by the ability to increase exposure to risky assets. In other words, tail risk hedging not only can be risk-reducing, but if implemented as an asset-allocation decision, it also can be return-enhancing if hedges are purchased at a cheap enough price!

In the following section we make an apples-to-apples comparison by placing a tail-hedged asset allocation between stocks and bonds on the same risk-adjusted scale as a 60/40 portfolio. We then describe how to derive the implicit value of the tail hedge and compare this with observed market prices.

A Model to Compute the Value of Tail Hedging

To set up the problem, we first assume that assets follow both a real-world distribution that requires hedging of tails and a risk-neutral distribution on which options markets are priced. Start by assuming that log stock returns exhibit stochastic volatility (see, e.g., Heston 1993).

$$r_t \sim N\left[\left(r_t^f + rp_t\right)dt, \sigma_{t-1}\sqrt{dt}\right]$$

where r_t^f is the annualized short-term interest rate, rp_t is the annualized risk premium of the asset, dt is the amount of time over which the return is measured (in years, for example, $dt = 1/52$ for weekly spacing), and σ_{t-1} is the annualized volatility of the stock return conditional on the information at time $t-1$. Under this notation, the expected return of the asset over the horizon given by dt is approximately $\left(r_t^f + rp_t\right)dt$, and the volatility of that return is $\sigma_{t-1}\sqrt{dt}$. Note that when $\sigma_{t-1} \equiv \sigma$, a constant, this model exhibits constant volatility as in Black-Scholes.

What differentiates this model from the simple constant-volatility lognormal process underlying Black-Scholes is that the conditional volatility of the log stock return is allowed to vary. In particular, the annualized variance of the stock return is assumed to have the following dynamics:

$$\sigma_t^2 = \kappa\theta + (1-\kappa)\sigma_{t-1}^2 + \gamma\sigma_{t-1}\sqrt{dt} \times u_t$$

with the additional criteria that $\text{corr}(u_t, r_t) = \rho$ and $u_t \sim N(0, 1)$. The correlation between the stock's return and the stock's return volatility allows the model to match the negative skewness of the observed stock return distribution. This negative skewness is an important feature to include in accurately modeling portfolio tails because it implies that larger negative outcomes are more likely than larger positive outcomes. Furthermore, the fact is that the time variation in the volatility of stock returns allows the model to exhibit excess kurtosis relative to a constant volatility distribution, a feature consistent with empirical return distributions, whereby large outcomes are more likely relative to the normal distribution.

In addition to the preceding assumptions about the true log stock return process, we allow for options on the stock to be priced using the risk-neutral distribution. The risk-neutral distribution is the probability distribution *implied by the market*, which makes the assumption that the risk premium on all assets is zero. In essence, the risk-neutral distribution implies that the expected return on the stock is equal to the risk-free rate. This is important for deriving option prices that are consistent with the absence of arbitrage opportunities and for assuming that option returns can be dynamically replicated by trading in other instruments such as the underlying stock and a risk-free asset.

Under the risk-neutral distribution, option prices behave as though stock returns and return volatility behave differently than under the true distribution, which includes a risk premium. Instead, they behave as follows:

$$\tilde{r}_t \sim N\left(r_t^f \, dt, \tilde{\sigma}_{t-1}\sqrt{dt}\right)$$

$$\tilde{\sigma}_t^2 = \kappa^* \theta^* + (1-\kappa^*)\tilde{\sigma}_{t-1}^2 + \gamma \tilde{\sigma}_{t-1}\sqrt{dt} \times u_t$$

where $\kappa^* = \kappa + \lambda$ and $\theta^* = \kappa\theta/(\kappa+\lambda)$ are the necessary adjustments for pricing in terms of the *risk-neutral distribution*. In the Heston model, the additional parameter λ pertains to the risk premium on volatility. For simplicity, we will assume that $\lambda = 0$ so that the analysis focuses solely on the risk premium as it relates to the expected return on the asset.

Model Calibration

We now describe a calibration of the model to match the characteristics of historical equity returns based on a weekly return frequency.

To begin, we assume that $\sqrt{\theta} = 20$ percent and $\sigma_0 = \tilde{\sigma}_0 = 20$ percent, which implies, along with the following parameters, that at-the-money equity put options trade at 19 percent volatility, a value close to the long-run average of the Volatility Index (VIX). The correlation parameter between equity returns and changes in equity volatility can be roughly calibrated by comparing returns on the S&P500 Index and the changes in the VIX (squared). Because implied volatility and realized volatility generally track one another well over time, this should provide a reasonable approximation to the correlation and volatility of volatility parameters.

$$\sigma_t^2 \approx \left(\text{VIX}_t / 100\right)^2$$

$$u_t \approx \frac{\sigma_t^2 - \sigma_{t-1}^2}{\gamma \sigma_{t-1}}$$

$$\gamma \approx \text{stdev}\left(\frac{\sigma_t^2 - \sigma_{t-1}^2}{\sigma_{t-1}}\right)$$

Here the parameter describing the volatility of $\gamma = 0.057$, and the correlation is found to be $\text{corr}(r_t, u_t) = \rho = -0.75$. Finally, a simple regression using the squared VIX reveals that the parameter describing weekly frequency is $\kappa^* = 0.0653$.

The annual return distribution on the simulated stock process based on the preceding calibration can be seen in Exhibit 3.3. This chart contrasts this more realistic model with a simple constant-volatility lognormal stock return process (which sets $\gamma = 0$). This simpler distribution is characteristic of those used in mean-variance portfolio optimization because only the mean and the variance matter in that framework. One can see that whereas the mean and variance here are similar, the more elaborate stock return process displays negative skewness and excess kurtosis, two features important in highlighting the true tails of the equity return distribution.

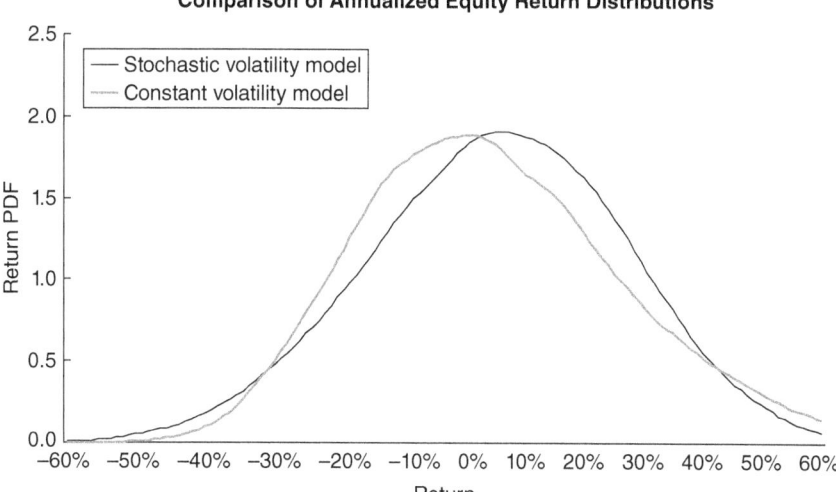

Exhibit 3.3 Annual return distributions simulated under constant volatility and stochastic volatility models. *Source: PIMCO.*

Exhibit 3.4 shows the model's implication for the difference between the risk-neutral market price of a put option for different strikes compared with the fair price based on the expected return of the put option (under the "realized" distribution). The difference between the two lines can be interpreted as a risk premium for our calibration, which is driven by the assumed risk premium on equities, here assumed to be 5 percent.

Finally, we cast the model's calibration in terms of Black-Scholes implied volatilities. To do this, we find the implied-volatility parameter needed in the constant-volatility lognormal Black-Scholes option-pricing model that allows the Black-Scholes put price to match the model price. Exhibit 3.5 shows that the calibrated model is qualitatively consistent with the equity put option volatility skew.

To begin the analysis of the value of tail hedging, we start with a baseline 60/40 stock/T-bill allocation. The core intuition behind the marginal valuation of tail hedging can be built from a hypothetical example. Here we assume that the T-bill return is 3 percent per annum.

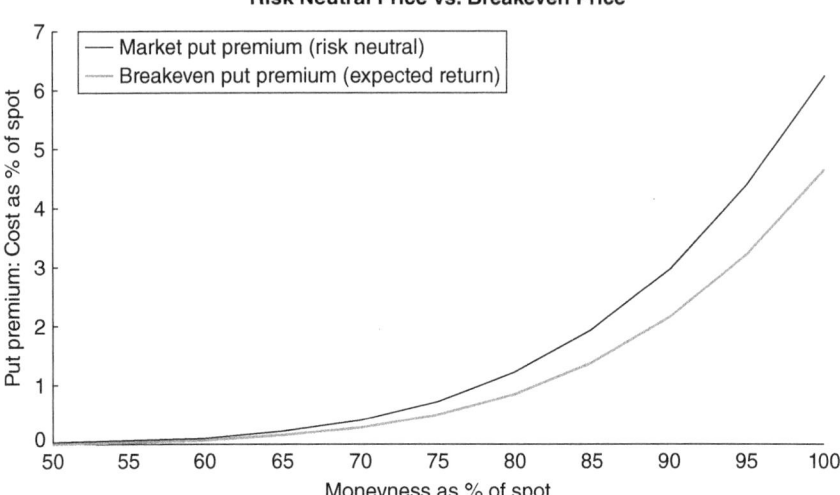

Exhibit 3.4 Put premium for various strikes under constant volatility and stochastic volatility models. *Source: PIMCO.*

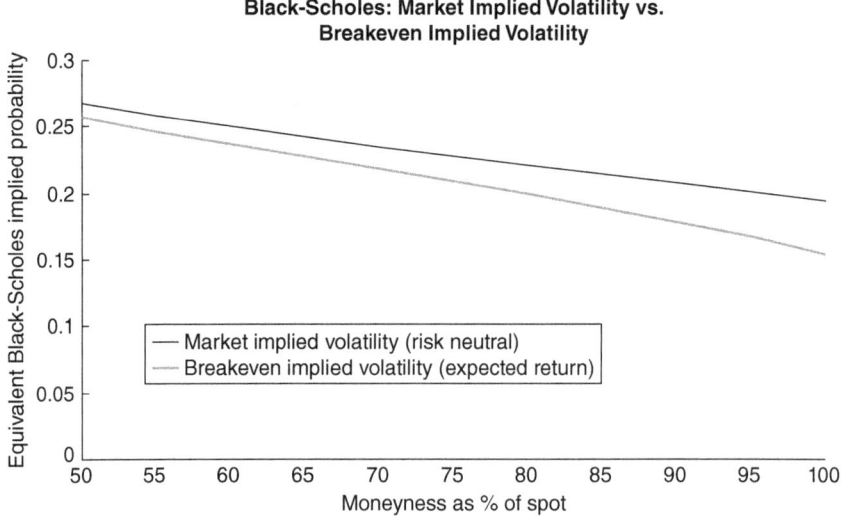

Exhibit 3.5 Volatility skew under stochastic volatility model. *Source: PIMCO.*

Offensive Tail Risk Hedging

To derive the implicit value of the tail hedge, consider an investor comparing two different asset allocations:

1. 60 percent in stocks, 40 percent T-bills
2. (1 − x percent) in stocks + tail hedge

Here the tail hedge is assumed to have a fair-value cost of x percent and a hypothetical return that equalizes the return between the two portfolios whenever the return on 60/40 is below some threshold. As an example, setting $K = 0$, the probability distribution of returns for the two portfolios will be exactly the same for returns that are less than or equal to zero.

This example is instructive because it places the riskiness, here measured by the probabilities below the threshold K, on the same scale. Because portfolio 2 is more heavily invested in stocks, which return, on average, more than T-bills owing to the assumed risk premium, we can derive the implicit value of the hypothetical tail hedge as the cost that could make the expected return of the two portfolios the same.

Exhibit 3.6 shows the value the investor would pay for a tail hedge that equalizes the expected returns on the two portfolios as well as the risk of returns below a given threshold K. This exhibit shows how much an investor would pay for a tail hedge under different equity risk premium assumptions. When the return threshold K is set to zero, this

Return Threshold K	Stock Excess Return over T-Bills				
	1%	2%	3%	4%	5%
0%	5.31%	5.44%	5.59%	5.71%	5.85%
−5%	4.10%	4.26%	4.45%	4.62%	4.79%
−10%	3.04%	3.26%	3.44%	3.65%	3.85%
−15%	2.17%	2.41%	2.67%	2.93%	3.18%
−20%	1.54%	1.82%	2.09%	2.38%	2.68%

Exhibit 3.6 Shadow value of tail hedge for various thresholds. *Source: PIMCO.*

tail hedge ensures that the probability distribution of returns is exactly the same for the two portfolios whenever returns are less than zero. Thus the two distributions are set to be on the same risk scale and have the same expected returns. These two criteria fix the value of the tail hedge based on the other parameters. Moving from left to right in the exhibit, one notices that as the expected return on stocks moves up, the value of moving into stocks moves up, implying that the amount the investor would pay for a hedge that maintains the same downside riskiness as a 60/40 also should move up.

Now, moving from top to bottom in the exhibit, one sees what an investor would pay if the measures of riskiness of the portfolios were equated at some threshold K. For example, an investor may care little if returns fall between −10 percent and 0 percent, but may care a lot if returns fall below −10 percent. In this sense, the investor cares more about outcomes in the far left end of the return distribution and seeks a hedge that equalizes the left tail of the riskier portfolio beyond a certain threshold to the tail behavior of the 60/40 portfolio. Moving K to increasingly more negative thresholds implies that the tail hedge pays off less frequently, suggesting that the price one would pay for such a hedge declines.

Next we apply the same relative-value approach as we did with the hypothetical tail hedge from the preceding section but instead use simple equity put options. The advantage of the hypothetical tail hedge from the preceding section is that it allowed the probability distributions of portfolios 1 and 2 to match exactly below the threshold K. By making the two returns have the same downside risk and expected returns, we were able to back out the implicit value of a tail hedge that would make the investor indifferent between the two allocations.

In the hypothetical example, the expected return on the tail hedge itself was zero, so the tail hedge was priced at a fair value on an absolute basis. In reality, tail hedges include a risk premium, so the expected return on, for example, equity put options is less than zero. Having a negative expected return implies that as a standalone allocation in a portfolio, the tail hedge is a poor choice because it has a negative expected return. However, on a relative basis, the tail hedge allows the investor to scale up her exposure to risky assets, which also have a risk premium. Thus, in the context of the overall portfolio, it makes sense. The investor should compare the relative risk premia gained from investing in the risky asset with that lost from investing in the tail hedge subject to maintaining an overall risk target.

Investor risk preference ultimately pertains to the impact from the severity of negative returns. Different metrics have been derived to measure this riskiness:

1. *Downside volatility.* This is the standard deviation of return distribution conditional on the returns being negative.
2. *Value-at-risk (VaR).* This is the probability that losses in the portfolio, over a given time horizon, exceed a threshold value.
3. *Conditional VaR (cVaR).* This is the expected loss on a portfolio conditional on the loss exceeding a particular VaR threshold value.
4. The fair value of a put option purchased on the portfolio struck at K percent moneyness. Such a security would completely protect an investor's portfolio value below K percent.

Here we will focus on the fourth measure, the price an investor would pay for hedging beyond some threshold K. This metric measures the tails of distributions in terms of a commonly traded asset that is familiar to investors. However, when measures such as cVaR are used for capturing expected tail loss, most of our conclusions regarding the value of tail hedging still hold true.

We now set out to determine the value of options struck at different levels on different portfolios. We derive put option values for a

60/40 portfolio, assuming that it is rebalanced weekly, and for a portfolio invested in equities, a risk-free asset, and a tail hedge composed of equity put options. The expected returns on each portfolio can be expressed as

$$E[r^1] = 0.6(rp + r^f) + 0.4r^f$$
$$E[r^2] = (1 - \text{TailCost})[w^s(rp + r^f) + (1 - w^s)r^f] + E[\text{TailPayoff}]$$
$$- \text{TailCost}$$

Defining Port^1 as the value of the 60/40 portfolio in one year with initial value of \$1 and Port^2 as the offensive, tail risk–hedged portfolio in one year with initial investment of \$1, the constraint on the offensive, tail risk–hedged portfolio can be expressed as

$$E\left[\max(K - \text{Port}^2, 0)\right] \leq E\left[\max(K - \text{Port}^1, 0)\right]$$

Stated otherwise, the value of a put option on the offensive, tail risk–hedged portfolio must be less than the value of a put option on a 60/40 portfolio (for a given strike with moneyness K).

Exhibit 3.7 provides the intuition of how the risk measure places portfolios on the same "risk" scale. For different risk thresholds K, the offensive, tail risk–hedged portfolio is sized to match the value of an equivalently priced put option on the 60/40 portfolio. Smaller thresholds indicate that an investor is willing to take more risk. The exhibit shows the value of put options on various portfolios assuming a risk premium of 5 percent on equities for thresholds $K = 85$, 90, and 95 percent.

The overall expected return to the tail hedge is the sum of the explicit expected return $E[\text{TailPayoff}]$ and the "shadow" expected return $E[r^2] - E[r^1]$, which is the gain the investor expects from investing more heavily in risky assets and earning a greater risk premium.

Offensive Tail Risk Hedging

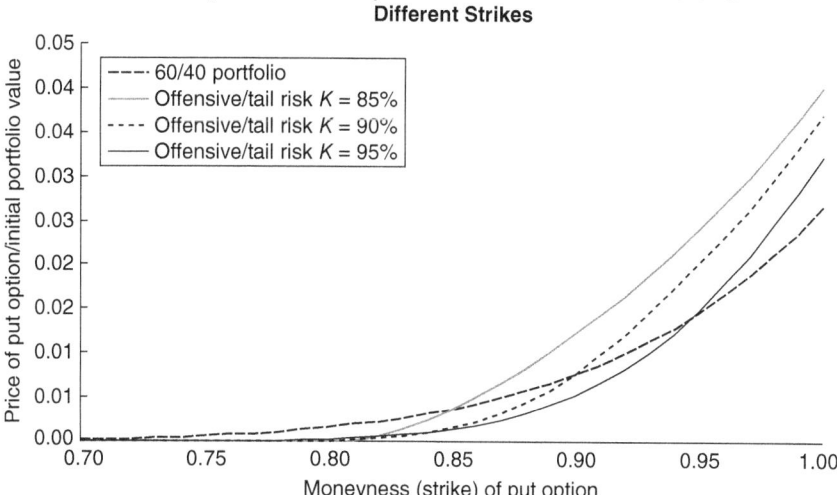

Exhibit 3.7 Comparison of put option values on different portfolios for different attachment levels. *Source: PIMCO.*

Without the addition of the tail hedge, the investor could not increase the allocation to risky assets and still hold the overall risk the same, as measured by value of the put option with strike K. Thus this shadow return should be incorporated when thinking about the overall value added of a tail hedge. Exhibit 3.8 breaks down the expected return to the tail-hedged portfolio into its component returns.

This demonstrates that tail hedging has a utility beyond simple defense and can allow for better risk positioning in attractive assets. Tail hedging has the potential to improve the return profile of portfolios. Tail risk–hedging strategies may impose deadweight costs, but they permit investors to implement strategies that more heavily weight risk assets that presumably have higher expected returns. On balance, hedges offer the chance of improving the overall return profiles of return distributions.

Expected Return on Tail Hedges

Moneyness of Put K	Equity (S&P500) Risk Premium				
	1%	2%	3%	4%	5%
80	0.88%	0.87%	0.83%	0.78%	0.72%
85	1.47%	1.35%	1.27%	1.18%	1.10%
90	2.23%	2.02%	1.89%	1.77%	1.63%
95	3.01%	2.90%	2.66%	2.54%	2.37%
100	4.07%	3.92%	3.72%	3.58%	3.43%

Shadow Value of Tail Hedges

Moneyness of Put K	Equity (S&P500) Risk Premium				
	1%	2%	3%	4%	5%
80	1.14%	1.52%	1.91%	2.30%	2.69%
85	1.10%	1.48%	1.87%	2.24%	2.64%
90	1.05%	1.42%	1.80%	2.17%	2.55%
95	1.00%	1.35%	1.72%	2.08%	2.45%
100	0.92%	1.26%	1.61%	1.95%	2.29%

Market Cost of Tail Hedges

Moneyness of Put K	Equity (S&P500) Risk Premium				
	1%	2%	3%	4%	5%
80	1.09%	1.15%	1.18%	1.19%	1.19%
85	1.79%	1.76%	1.77%	1.76%	1.77%
90	2.69%	2.58%	2.59%	2.58%	2.55%
95	3.59%	3.65%	3.58%	3.61%	3.60%
100	4.84%	4.93%	5.00%	5.10%	5.21%

Expected Net Benefit of Tail Hedges

Moneyness of Put K	Equity (S&P500) Risk Premium				
	1%	2%	3%	4%	5%
80	0.93%	1.24%	1.56%	1.89%	2.22%
85	0.78%	1.07%	1.37%	1.66%	1.97%
90	0.59%	0.86%	1.10%	1.36%	1.63%
95	0.42%	0.60%	0.80%	1.01%	1.22%
100	0.15%	0.25%	0.33%	0.43%	0.51%

Exhibit 3.8 Summary of results on shadow value of hedging discussed in the text. *Source: PIMCO.*

Simulation of a Stochastic Volatility Model

Here we show how to simulate the simplest stochastic volatility model, known as the *Heston model*, in *Mathematica*, Version 9 and above. In the Heston model, the stock process and volatility process are correlated.

```
numpaths=100;

cW[ρ_]:=ItoProcess[{{0,0},IdentityMatrix[2]},{{w1,w2},
{0,0}},t,{{1,ρ},{ρ,1}}];
```

These two lines of code define the number of paths and a two-dimensional Ito process. The next line defines the stock process and the Heston variance process:

```
hm=ItoProcess[{ds[t]==μs[t]dt+Sqrt[r[t]]s[t]dw_s[t],
dr[t]==κ(θ-r[t])dt+ξSqrt[r[t]]dw_v[t]},{s[t],r[t]},
{{s,r},{s_0,r_0}},t,{w_s,w_v}≈cW[ρ]];
```

Next we generate the matrix of random paths denoted by `td` using the function `RandomFunction`:

```
td=BlockRandom[SeedRandom[1];RandomFunction[hm/.
{μ→0,κ→1.5,θ→0.2,ξ→0.8,ρ→-0.8,s_0→100,r_0→0.18},
{0,1,0.01},numpaths,Method→"StochasticRungeKutta"]];
```

We can now plot the paths for the underlying:

```
ListLinePlot[td["PathComponent",1]]
```

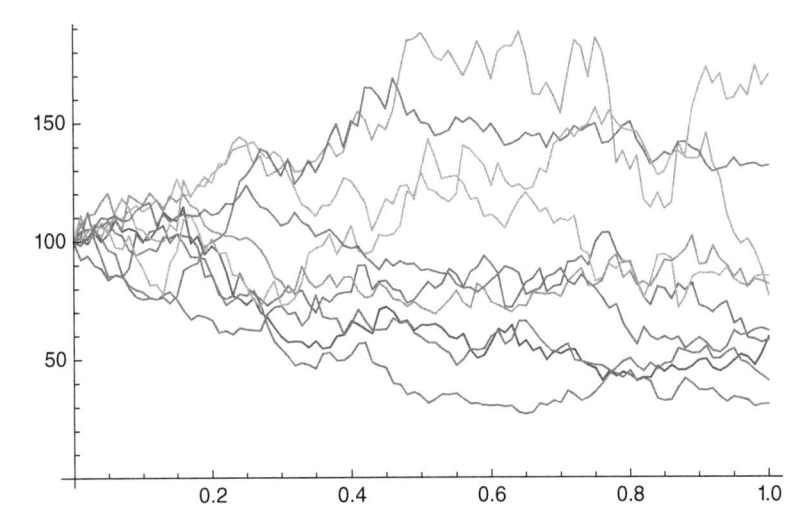

And for the volatility:

```
ListLinePlot[td[PathComponent,2]]
```

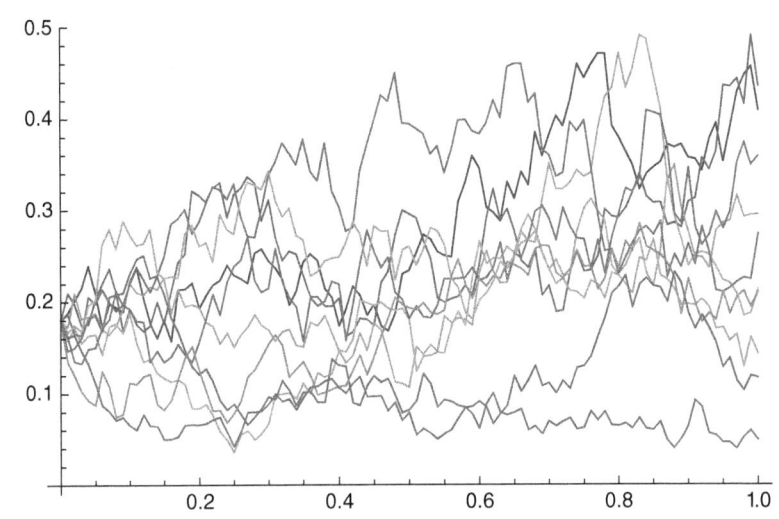

Now we can compute the probability of breaching a barrier labeled attach in the context of the stochastic volatility model given by

Offensive Tail Risk Hedging

```
PBreach[attach_,time_]:=N[Probability[x
<attach,x~Re[Transpose[td["SliceData",time]]][[1]]]]

PBreach[75,0.5]
```

which yields 0.282.

Finally, we can create the slice distributions for different horizons:

```
SmoothHistogram[{Re[Transpose[td["SliceData",0.08]]
[[1]]],

Re[Transpose[td[SliceData,0.25]]][[1]]],
Re[Transpose[td[SliceData,0.5]]][[1]]],
Re[Transpose[td["SliceData",0.75]]][[1]]],Re[Transpose
[td["SliceData",1]][[1]]]}]
```

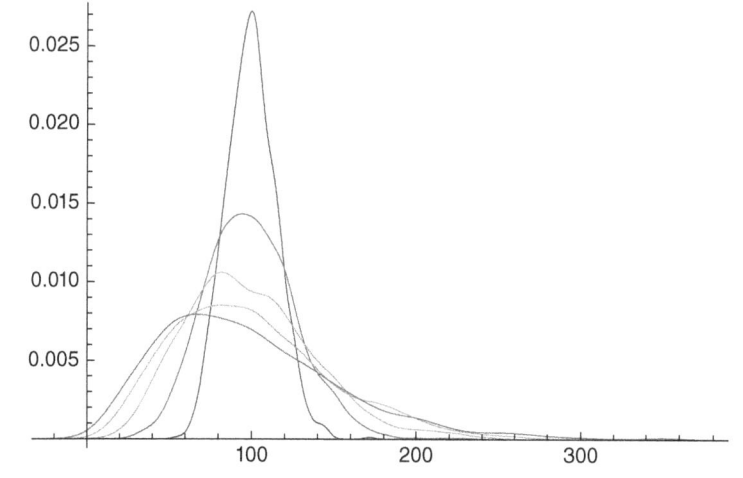

4

Active Tail Risk Management[1]

In Chapter 3 we discussed one aspect of what we have called *offensive risk management*, that is, how using tail hedges in a portfolio might permit investors to increase returns and the right-side convexity of returns while also looking to mitigate the risk of large investment losses. We demonstrated that if the hedge is purchased at the right price, the portfolio with tail risk hedges might have a more attractive risk-return profile ex ante than a buy-and-hold portfolio. We also mentioned that active monetization of hedges may provide liquidity that might be used to purchase cheap assets in periods of crisis, thus further improving the ex ante long-term return potential of the portfolio, but we did not discuss monetization rules in detail.

This chapter addresses the second point and shows that indeed in the context of the 80-year history of Standard and Poor's indexed market data, (as represented by S&P 500, and prior to March 4, 1957, the S&P 90) one can justify intuitive rules of thumb for monetization that are consistent with the cyclical behavior of the economy and the markets.

We find it comforting that the ex post analysis discussed in this chapter is both complementary to our previous work and produces commonsense results that investors might want to apply in their offensively risk-managed portfolios. Note that our analysis can easily be, and should be, extended to other risk factors as well. In particular, if we believe that risk factors such as the duration of fixed-income instruments are a potent portfolio risk, then the approach should extend to managing interest-rate risk through interest-rate options.

We have found four levers that we can pull on while managing a tail risk–hedging portfolio actively. They are

- Monetization
- Extension
- Conversion
- Rotation

This chapter will focus on quantifying the long-term historical payoffs of rules based purely monetization strategies that may be suitable for an equity index portfolio. We discussed the benefits of opportunistically changing maturity earlier and will discuss rotation and conversion in Chapter 5. Given the dominance of the equity risk factor across asset classes, we expect to find similar results for other mixes of risky and riskless assets, so do not consider the focus on equity indices as a limitation. Also, in practice more active management using the other three levers to make tail risk hedging more efficient can supplement the rules. *Extension* is an approach that uses the term structure of volatility and underlying asset forward prices to take advantage of opportunities. If we have "always on" version of tail risk hedging in the portfolio, then it makes sense to extend hedges when the extension is cheaper for each unit of desired protection (please see the discussion on rolling hedges for more detailed description of what tradeoffs this entails). If there is a short-term shock in the market, the volatility curve flattens and inverts because the demand for shorter-term hedging exceeds the demand for longer-term hedging. This can be used as an opportunity to reduce shorter-expiry hedges and extend them out to reduce the cumulative long-term cost of hedging. *Conversion* is a technique that exchanges direct option purchases for spreads, for example, exchange of puts for put spreads and vice versa. We discuss the tradeoffs of such a strategy more formally in Chapter 5, but for the present purpose, note that when there is a market shock, the price of put options rises, and at a higher volatility, both the time decay and the potential losses of puts exceed those of put spreads. Thus the rule of thumb is that when volatility is low, prefer straight puts (because they are more volatility sensitive), and for higher volatilities, prefer put spreads. *Rotation* refers to the exchange of direct hedges in one market for indirect hedges in other markets. For instance, if we can identify that the equity risk factor is responsible for the drawdown in many assets simultaneously, we want to sell options on assets that are more expensive and replace them with relatively cheaper options on other assets. Immediate examples would be replacing equity put options with credit-default swaps or puts on carry currencies.

To set the stage for the benefits from active monetization, we will compare a passive buy-and-hold strategy to a naive, actively managed alternative in which the tail hedge is liquidated whenever its value hits an arbitrary multiple of its initial value any time before expiry. Our interest is in estimating the empirical performance gains from selecting various monetization multiples. This chapter analyses the benefits from simple, transparent, and quantifiable rules. In practice, supplementing the rules with valuation considerations can improve the performance of tail hedges further.

As mentioned, we believe that a tail-hedging strategy should be thought of not as a high-frequency trade or even a passive buy-and-hold but rather as an asset-allocation decision. The immediate benefit of looking at the strategy from an asset-allocation perspective is that all the knowledge of asset allocation and rebalancing gained by practitioners over the years applies to this (hedging) asset. Also, monetization rules become less a function of time elapsed and more a function of high-severity, low-probability events that happen rarely but have the potential to cause significant damage to portfolios. In other words, the monetization rules are event-driven, not time-driven. The potential gain from the hedges comes not from the options "going in the money," which is rare given that we are working with catastrophic events, but from the value of the hedges rising as the market bids up the price of hedges. If we believe that falling values of the risky asset results in increased volatility and risk aversion, then it is the mark-to-market value of the hedge that makes the hedge potent. The crisis demonstrated this in many guises. For instance, even though the SPX Index never fell below 500, implied volatilities and hence the value of such out-of-the-money tail options soared.

Thus a well-managed tail-hedging strategy is far from passive. The investor has to first purchase the hedge when it is cheap, both in terms of its real-world value in the context of possible scenario shocks and with reference to other hedges from related markets. Second, the investor has to actively monetize and swap for other hedges when the hedge already in the portfolio pays off and becomes relatively expensive. Unless this is done, the hedge rapidly loses its value. In the extreme, when held to maturity, the value of the hedge goes to zero if it is still out of the money, so a purely passive tail-hedging strategy would contribute nothing more than a one-for-one reduction of potential return of the same magnitude as the premium paid for the hedge.

To illustrate these results numerically, let us first consider an investor who purchases a tail risk hedge on a security whose current spot price is $100. Let's also assume that the investor wants to buy a hedge against losses beyond 15 percent for the following year. The option the investor is seeking to buy will have a strike of $85 and a maturity of one year. Assume that the deposit rate is 5 percent and that the Black-Scholes implied volatility is 20 percent. The price of the 15 percent out-of-the-money "put" in the Black-Scholes world is $1.32.

In order to see the effects of market risk aversion on the value of the option, assume that a minicrisis occurs before expiration of the option. Suppose that one month following the purchase of the option, the equity market trades down to $90. In addition, because the market becomes increasingly risk averse as the equity market sells off, assume that the implied volatility parameter rises from 20 to 30 percent. Following this equity market shock, assume that the market settles down at $90 for the remainder of the year, so the put option expires worthless. Furthermore, because the equity market is assumed to settle at $90, assume that the implied volatility of the option slowly reverts back to its initial value of 20 percent.

Exhibit 4.1 shows the value of the option through time, with and without the contribution from the change in implied volatility. Notice that the effects from implied volatility can be extremely large depending on the time left to maturity, in this case doubling the value of the put option relative to one where implied volatility is held at a constant 20 percent throughout. As the implied volatility slowly reverts to the initial level of 20 percent, the value of the put option decays rapidly and converges to the value of the constant 20 percent put option.

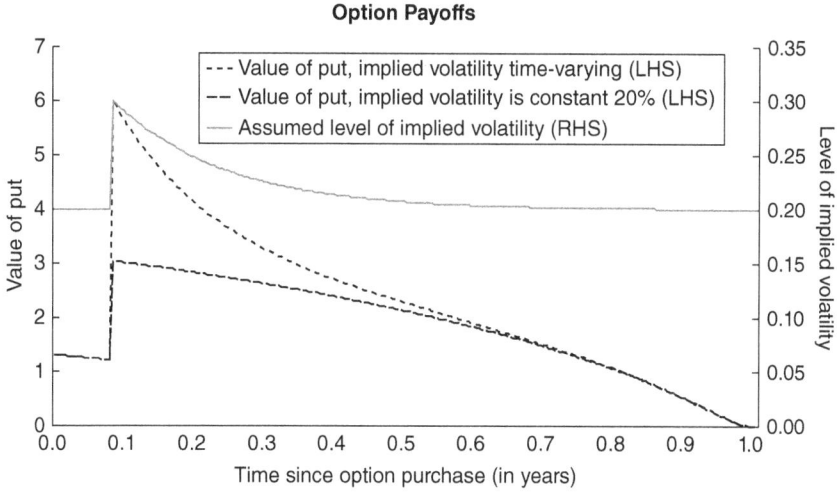

Exhibit 4.1 Value of a one-year put option at assumed historical values. *Source: PIMCO.*

Finally, given that the option expires out of the money, the value of the option converges to zero despite having been worth more than five times the purchase price within the year. It could have made sense for the investor to sell the option when it was priced high and invest part of the proceeds in another option and the remainder in the now "cheaper" market.

Although this stylized example is extremely simple, it highlights the core ideas behind why active monetization of the put option has the potential to significantly outperform a passive buy-and-hold strategy. The buy-and-hold strategy returns zero because the market settles at $90, above the $85 strike of the put option purchased by the investor. By holding the put option to maturity, the investor was able to lessen mark-to-market gains and losses within the year and also was able to hedge against movements of the equity price below $85. As the equity market fell from $100 to $90 and the level of implied volatility rose from 20 to 30 percent, the value of the hedge provided by the put option increased significantly even though it ultimately expired worthless. By selling the hedge back to the market when it was priced at a much higher price, the investor could have profited from the put option position intrayear. These profit opportunities are often short-lived because the value of the hedge decays with the time left to expiration and the rate of mean reversion in the implied volatility underlying the option. Furthermore, on monetization, the investor must weigh the benefit of selling this position back to the market at a profit against the cost that it no longer hedges the investment portfolio from market declines below $85.

Subsequent results in this study are based on daily data from April 2, 1928, through March 2010. Because we do not have option implied-volatility data for most of the long-term history (we employ actual data only for the period January 2005 to March 2010) we first had to develop a method for estimating the volatility surface using a simple model. Because the severity of a tail risk event is inversely related to the probability of its occurrence, accurate estimation of the proper monetization rule requires a very long history. To see this, assume that stock returns are normally distributed with a 5 percent annual expected return and 16 percent annual volatility. Under these distributional assumptions, the probability of a 50 percent or more decline in the stock market, roughly the decline of the Standard and Poor's 500 Index (S&P500) from November 2007 to November 2008, is 0.003, occurring on average once every 333 years. Thus, when analyzing the payoff to tail-hedging strategies, one would like to look out beyond the 30 years or so of history on which most modern investment studies are based.

In order to make inferences about the long-run historical performance of active tail-hedging strategies we build a parametric model of implied volatilities and use it to interpolate based on realized equity market returns and realized equity market volatility. Exhibit 4.2 uses our model to show the value of a one-year tail hedge, which initially costs 1 percent of the value of the S&P500. It is purchased in April of 1928 using the implied-volatility model we develop in the next section. Between April and October of that year, the S&P500 rallied more than 25 percent, driving the strike of the tail hedge very far out of the money. At the peak in September, the value of the tail hedge is less than 5 basis points (bp). The following month the market fell more than 45 percent from the September peak, driving the tail hedge from 5 bp to more than 1,110 bp in November. Following these traumatic market events the S&P500 rallied back to end the following April near its starting point the preceding year. The tail hedge expired out of the money, having done its job to hedge the S&P500 during the onset of the Great Depression. Despite this, investors looking at year-to-year returns would find that this tail hedge had little to no value, expiring worthless and costing 1 percent of the value of the S&P500. Indeed, if the option and the portfolio were held to expiration of the option, the net result would have been a reduction in returns of the portfolio

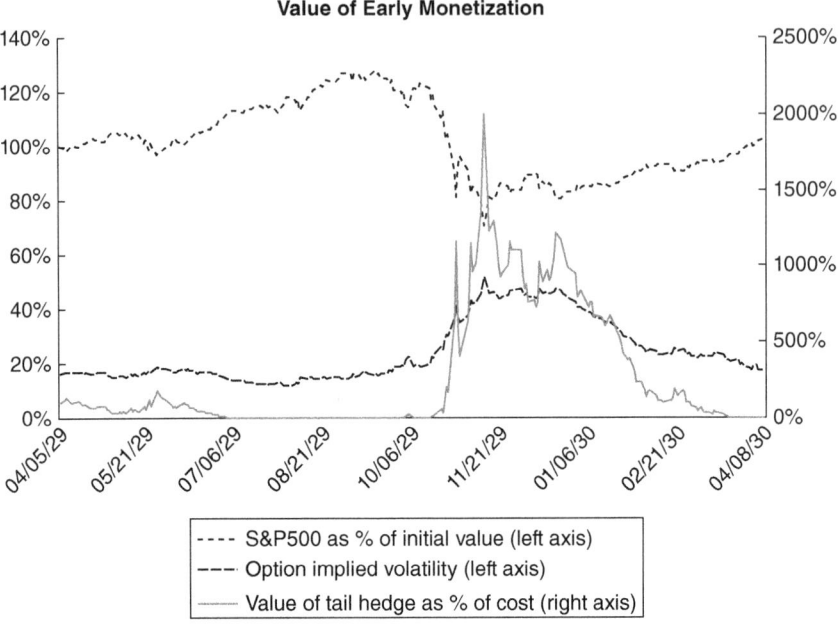

Exhibit 4.2 Value of a one-year put option from April 1929–April 1930.
Source: PIMCO.

by exactly the premium paid! It is thus not surprising that academic studies and traditional lore conclude that there can be no net benefit from buying options. One can easily see why the conclusion is too extreme—clearly, if an option is bought for a low enough price, there is a high probability that during the life of the option its mark-to-market price will exceed the price at which it was bought. If this value is monetized, on balance, the option will add positive value to the portfolio.

Creating a Long History

The goal of this section is to build a robust and dynamically consistent model of implied volatilities interpolated from observable market information. We impose three simple requirements on the model that can be motivated by relationships observed in the middle of April 2005 to March 2010. First, implied volatilities track realized volatilities (of course, there is an excess risk premium in some maturities and strikes due to an embedded crash premium). Second, implied volatilities show clustering; that is, higher volatilities are followed by higher volatilities. Third, and most important, the level of implied volatilities is very sensitive to the high-frequency movement of the underlying market, rising when the market falls and falling when the market rallies. This third assumption (illustrated in Exhibit 4.3) drives the turnaround in the volatility, resulting in a sharp rise or fall after a sustained grind in the same direction.

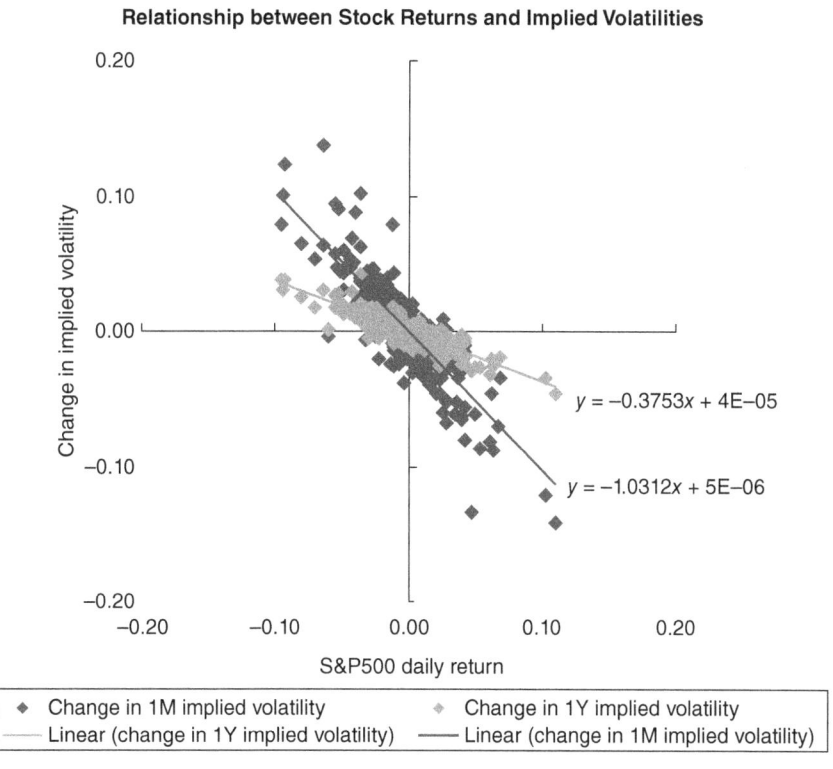

Exhibit 4.3 Data from April 1, 2005–March 31, 2010. *Source: PIMCO.*

Thus the model interpolates implied volatilities based on both endogenous and exogenous market factors. The exogenous factors driving the changes in interpolated volatilities are realized stock price volatility and daily stock returns. The endogenous component is the lagged values of the model's interpolated volatilities, allowing the model to match the persistence exhibited by implied volatilities of different maturities. In order to maintain robustness of the results over longer-term history, we place a boundary on the minimum value that can be achieved by the implied volatilities. We require that the interpolated values cannot fall below the actual levels reached in the historical data on which the model was estimated. This restriction does not affect the qualitative results of this chapter but makes the practical implications more conservative because it prevents the model from buying large amounts of cheap options during the "quiet" of the post–World War II boom and overstating the benefits of hedging.

Exhibit 4.4 shows that one-month and one-year implied volatilities are closely related to trailing realized volatility. We use this feature to relate implied volatilities in the option markets to realized three-month volatility, a series for which there is a long history of daily levels. Exhibit 4.4 also illustrates other well-known features of implied volatility that are captured by our model. On average, implied volatility is above realized volatility; one-month implied volatility is, on average, below one-year implied volatility; implied volatility and realized volatility are very persistent; and one-month implied volatility moves more with realized volatility than one-year implied volatility does with realized volatility.

To capture the impact of the realized volatility, the past implied-volatility surface, and the equity market's performance on the current implied-volatility surface, we use a threshold factor–augmented vector autoregression model (threshold FAVAR) to describe the dynamics of the implied-volatility surface. This is sensible because we want to simultaneously capture the impact of the three "factors" driving today's volatility surface (hence *factor-augmented*), and we want to relate the

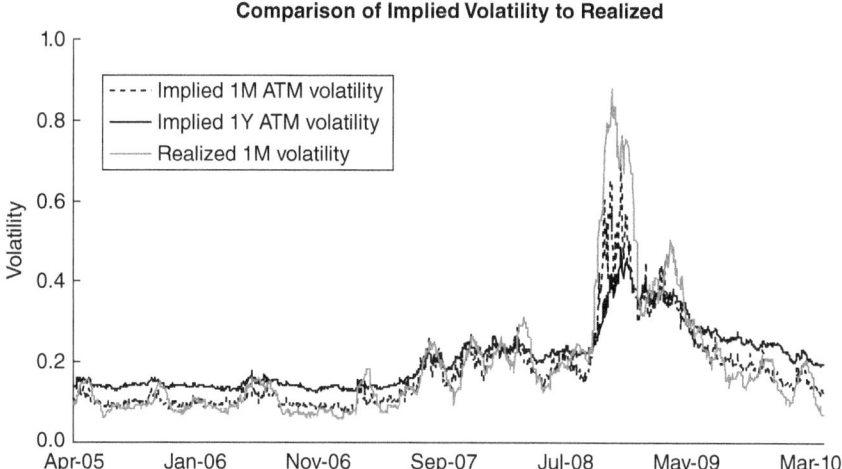

Exhibit 4.4 Data from April 1, 2005–March 31, 2010. *Source: PIMCO*.

dependencies of each maturity to every other maturity (hence, the *vector autoregression*, or VAR). We also want to differentiate between regimes of high volatility and low volatility; hence we pick the long-term average of realized volatility, 20 percent, as a threshold for differentiating between the two different model estimates.

Thus our threshold FAVAR model can be expressed as set of two simple regression models, where the regression is run conditional on the level of realized volatility

$$y_t = \begin{cases} X_t \beta_l + u_t^l & \sigma_{rlzd}^{1M} < 20 \text{ percent} \\ X_t \beta_h + u_t^h & \sigma_{rlzd}^{1M} > 20 \text{ percent} \end{cases}$$

Here y_t represents a $1 \times N$ vector of implied volatilities, X_t is a $1 \times M$ vector of factors and lagged implied volatilities y_{t-1}. The residuals u_t^l and u_t^h are assumed to satisfy the usual assumptions of being mean zero and uncorrelated with the regressors. To be explicit, the y_t consists of one-, three-, and six-month and one-year implied volatilities with deltas of 0.1, 0.5, and 0.9 at each maturity for a total of $N = 12$

implied volatilities total. For each maturity we include three different strikes, denoted by the delta, in order to capture skew effects, which will affect the pricing of the put options.

$$y_t = \begin{bmatrix} \sigma_{10d}^{1M} & \sigma_{50d}^{1M} & \sigma_{90d}^{1M} & \sigma_{10d}^{3M} & \sigma_{50d}^{3M} & \sigma_{90d}^{3M} & \cdots & \sigma_{10d}^{1Y} & \sigma_{50d}^{1Y} & \sigma_{50d}^{1Y} \end{bmatrix}$$

For clarity, $X_t = \begin{bmatrix} \sigma_{rlzd}^{1M} & \ln(S_t/S_{t-1}) & y_{t-1} \end{bmatrix}$ is the vector of factors and lagged implied volatilities. As mentioned earlier, we also "penalize" our results by requiring that volatilities stay above the minimum value that each realized during the 2005–2010 period. Volatility fell to historically low levels in 2005–2007. Constraining the data to remain above these levels ensures that tail hedges are never bought at historically cheap levels. Removing this restriction would make my results even stronger.

We use simulated implied-volatility levels derived from this model whenever actual volatility surface data are not available. For each put option of interest, the volatility surface data are interpolated to find the corresponding volatility at that put's strike and maturity. The Black-Scholes model is then applied to these estimated implied-volatility levels, as well as the prevailing spot equity levels and interest rates in the market to determine the market value on that date.

Exhibit 4.5 compares model-derived interpolated implied volatilities and true implied volatilities. The model-derived implied volatilities are obtained by iterating the model forward at the daily frequency, starting on April 2, 1928, with the initial implied-volatility surface simply set to be equal to the level of one-month realized volatility at that time. The model updates at each date based on realized one-month volatility, one-day spot returns, and lagged levels of the model's estimated implied volatilities. We compare the model results for the period beginning in January 2005 and ending March 2010 with the volatilities implied by the market.

Note that the model accurately captures the increase in implied volatilities at both the short and long maturities through the crisis of

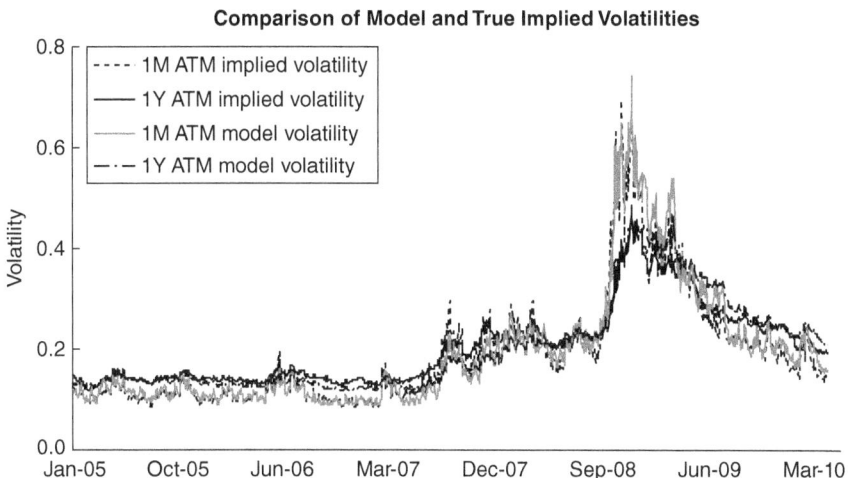

Exhibit 4.5 Data from January 1, 2005–March 31, 2010. *Source: PIMCO.*

2007–2008. Prior to the crisis, when market implied volatilities were low and stable, the model's estimate of implied volatilities are very close to those observed in the market. This implies that put options were purchased when the price of hedging portfolios was relatively low. We emphasize that the model estimates the volatility surface based only on realized and past implied volatilities and the recent behavior of the market, but it has limited or no power to forecast volatilities because such forecasts would depend on forecasts of realized volatility and returns of the equity market itself.

We also looked at the model's volatility for one-month 10-delta options and at-the-money (ATM) options throughout our sample period. We confirmed that the volatility skew gets much larger in episodes when the market "crashes." We also compared short- and long-term options and confirmed that the shape of the volatility skew is consistent with what is observed (i.e., short-term skew is steeper than long-term skew). Although the one-year results are qualitatively the same as the results for one-month options, the magnitude of the one-year option skew is much smaller. This is consistent with our observation that shorter options have lower total premium than longer options, so the market charges a higher premium for crash risk. Also as observed, the model replicates volatility-curve inversion when crashes happen.

Active Monetization Rules

Armed with a robust model to describe and capture the implied-volatility surface of the equity market to backfill history that precedes the advent of liquid options markets, we can now quantify how different tail risk hedge monetization strategies would have performed in a long-term historical backtest. We used the Black-Scholes parametric model described in the preceding section to relate the prices of options at different strikes and maturities to the market environment at the time. The risk-free rate is also an input to the Black-Scholes model. We assume this rate to be the one-month U.S. Treasury-bill rate, which is available at a monthly frequency for the entire simulation period.

We first test simple rule-of-thumb monetization strategies based on different budget levels that we have used in the recent crisis. Given an initial budget, a risk-free rate, and the implied-volatility surface on a particular date, we find the strike of a one-year option with cost exactly corresponding to the budget. In the hypothetical backtest, the whole annual budget is spent on an option at the purchase date. The option is sold whenever its value reaches a particular multiple, for example, five times the cost of the initial annual budget. Often the put options never reach the required multiple for monetization. In these cases, the options expire, and a new one-year option is purchased. This new option is struck again at a level that exhausts the annual budget on that date. If the option does exceed the multiple for monetization, it is sold on that date, and a new option is purchased with one year to expiration and with a strike dictated by the annual tail risk hedging budget.

Active Tail Risk Management

All options are purchased and sold taking into account the market environment on that date. These conditions include the spot level of the S&P500, the risk-free rate, the time left until maturity of the option, and the implied volatility of the option, all monitored daily, with trades executed at the end of the trading day. This simulation is particularly involved because we must interpolate the implied-volatility surface at each point in time to find the implied volatility corresponding to the particular maturity and strike of the option being valued.

Exhibit 4.6 summarizes the average times to payout (in years) of a tail hedge given a budget (down the rows) and a monetization multiple (across the columns). Whenever the average time period from purchase to monetization is less than the monetization multiple, the simple tail hedge monetization strategy implied by rule of thumb would have been profitable based on data for the period 1928–2010. For example, an investor spending 1 percent per year of her overall portfolio value on tail risk hedges who also followed a five times monetization rule would have monetized, on average, every 4.01 years. Thus, on average, every 4.01 years the investor would have paid out a total of 4.01 percent consistent with the budget but would have received at least 5 percent back for the tail hedge investment. The realized average value the investor would have paid to break even is 80 bp, more than a 25 percent discount from the annual budget.

		Monetization Multiple			
		2.5	5	7.5	10
Annual Budget (bps)	50	1.16	2.68	4.23	5.36
	100	1.52	4.01	6.69	8.92
	150	1.91	3.83	7.30	8.93
	200	1.96	5.35	8.93	14.64

Exhibit 4.6 Average time to payout for given initial tail hedge budget and monetization multiple.

This exhibit illustrates the power of early monetization strategies. Often a simple rule of thumb that actively trades the tail hedge is superior to a naive strategy of buying, holding, and allowing to expire. The tendency of implied volatility to mean revert further compounds this effect. Mean reversion in implied volatility implies that spikes in implied volatility are followed by a fall in implied volatility toward historical averages. Thus the mark-to-market value of tail hedges typically peaks prior to expiry. Further evidence of these dynamics is that active monetization rules are profitable historically, whereas buy-and-hold strategies are not. Indeed, every asset class empirically has an optimal monetization multiple that we can use to set guidelines for when to monetize.

By looking at the distribution of the years between monetization events for a 100-pb annual budget, we find some interesting results. First, crises and volatility tend to cluster in time. Also, in two instances, the strategy took more than 10 years to pay out. A pragmatic investor could easily have been tempted to abandon a systematic hedging program in the middle of such a long period of "drag" on portfolio returns. The results support taking a long-term asset-allocation approach to tail risk hedging.

The active strategy does force the investor to restrike the hedges on monetization at implied volatility levels that are "high." In these cases, the strike of the new option will be further out of the money, and thus the portfolio will be less insured than prior to monetization. Thus the approach also suggests care in selecting hedges and, when direct hedges are expensive, examining indirect hedges in related markets. As discussed in subsequent chapters, the additional basis risk of indirect hedges becomes largely irrelevant as correlations rise in crises.

We finally compare how three various tail-hedge strategies, combined with an investment in the S&P500 Index of stocks, would have performed in 1928, the beginning of our simulation period. The first strategy employs no tail hedge and simply invests in the S&P500 Index. The second is a naive strategy that involves purchasing a tail hedge for 100 bp/year and holding the put option until it expires. The third also spends 100 bp annually but monetizes the tail hedge whenever it moves beyond five times the purchase price of the option. The last strategy follows a rule that generates liquidity by selling options at their mark-to-market value when the returns to selling liquidity are high. The last strategy also involves spending the proceeds of option sales on replacement hedges and stocks.

Exhibit 4.7 compares the performance of each strategy beginning in January 1988, following the large market tail event of 1987, placing all strategies on an equivalent playing field in a time familiar to many modern investors. Notice that the naive strategy that monetizes only at expiration and rolls into new options performs the worst. The performance of this strategy is consistent with most investors' intuition, that the amount one pays for tail hedging is, on average, more than the amount one receives in return over a long period of time. Any difference

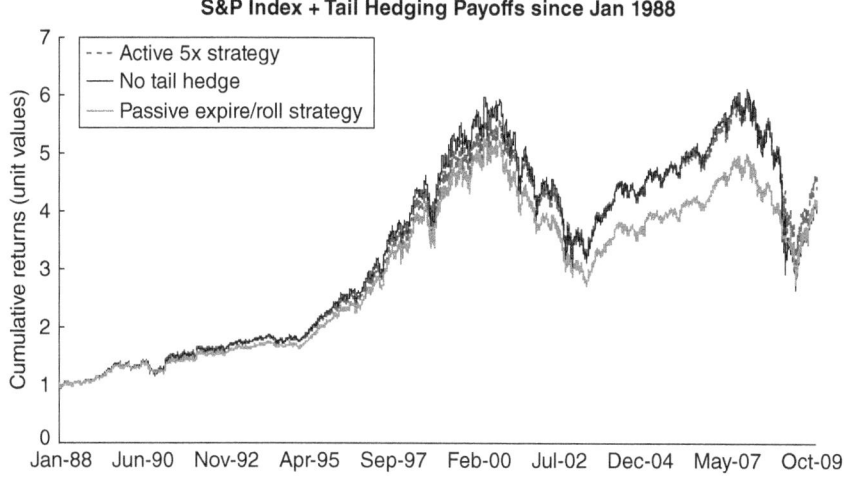

Exhibit 4.7 Data from January 1, 1988–October 9, 2009. *Source: PIMCO.*

is a risk premium attributable to the value of the hedge against catastrophic events. Investors might be unable to adjust their portfolios for several reasons. For example, prior commitments to meet capital calls on illiquid investments potentially could absorb all liquidity from appreciated hedges. However, recent and past crises have shown that hedge markets remain relatively liquid, that hedges themselves can be sold, and that cash can be raised.

The effects of this hedge performance can be seen toward the end of the crisis of 2007–2009. The performance of the passive strategy catches up with the performance of the unhedged strategy precisely at the time when investors would have wanted the tail hedge to pay out. The investor in the passive strategy would have generated greater returns simply by investing in the S&P500 without a tail hedge. However, the simple, robust monetization strategy provides a different perspective on tail hedging. Moving from passive to active management of tail hedging, even under simple rules of thumb, can potentially make tail hedging profitable over short periods of time.

The simple rule-of-thumb strategy performs well because of the dynamics of the risk premium in the stock market. It creates a commitment to a strategy that allows "buying on dips" by monetizing an option or selling a hedging asset that has increased in value. As volatility subsides, the equity market tends to rise, and the risk premium embedded in the equity market also falls to normal levels. By rolling the profits from the tail hedge into the underlying equity market, the *investor can turn a defensive strategy into an offensive strategy* by taking profits from hedges, thus harvesting the benefit of the increased risk premium.

When we extend the history of these strategies back to January 1950, a period of dramatic growth in the U.S. economy, the same patterns emerge (see Exhibit 4.8). Again, the passive strategy that spends 1 percent each year and holds the tail hedge to expiration performs the worst. Over the 60-year period it returns 16 percent less than the buy-and-hold strategy with no tail hedge, a loss of approximately 27 bp/year.

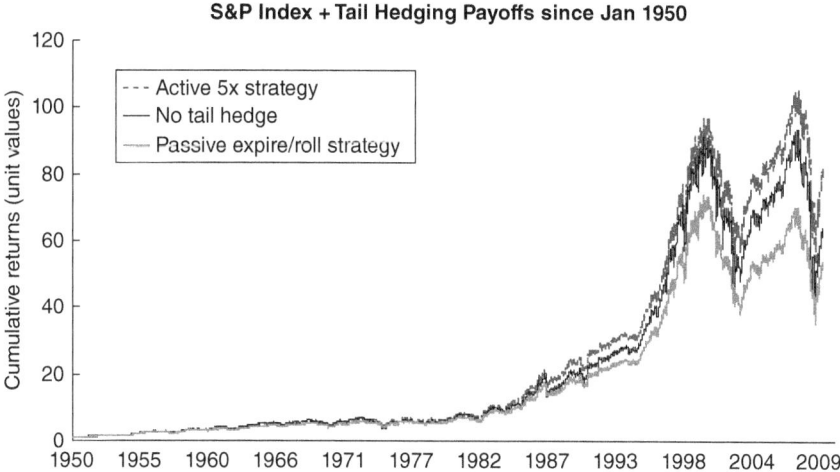

Exhibit 4.8 Data from January 1950–October 9, 2009. *Source: PIMCO.*

For long-term investors who can withstand the downside volatility in the stock market, a buy-and-hold tail-hedging strategy is a losing proposition unless the horizon is extremely long—long enough that a catastrophic event such as the Great Depression may be needed to justify many years of spending for the hedge. Turning to the active tail-hedge strategy, we again see the opposite outcome that active management of the tail hedge may lead to significant outperformance for even the long-term investor. Over the same time horizon, the simple five multiple rule nets a 30 percent greater return than the unhedged S&P500. This corresponds to an extra 50 bp/year of return.

Exhibit 4.9 presents results extending the three strategies back to April 1928. The long-term nature of the passive buy-and-hold tail-hedging strategy becomes apparent over the full simulation period. In an event such as the Great Depression, when the stock market fell more than 85 percent in fewer than five years, the tail hedges provided by simply holding the options until expiration would have paid out far more than the simple monetization strategy. In the simple strategy,

Exhibit 4.9 Data from January 1, 1928–December 31, 1949. *Source: PIMCO.*

the investor sells too early, not realizing the ultimate gains that would have been realized had the tail hedges been held to maturity or at least until a greater monetization multiple was reached. The simple strategy still performs better than the unhedged strategy, a consistent and robust result that holds across the relevant time periods sampled in this chapter.

The outperformance of the passive buy-and-hold tail-hedging strategy is so significant during the Great Depression that an investor who had followed that strategy until 2010 still would have outperformed the active tail-hedging and unhedged strategies despite underperformance following the Great Depression. The value gained from hedging the portfolio against severe and rare events such as the Great Depression can far outweigh the small losses an investor experiences for buying this hedge. "Great depressions" do not occur that often, so investors following the passive tail-hedging strategy will often spend more on hedges than they earn from the hedges in return. However, a short-term cost creates the potential for increased excess returns over a longer-term holding horizon.

Our results from this study depend critically on our model for estimating the equity option volatility surface going back to 1928. The results also depend on being able to trade hypothetical options with transactions costs that mirror the ones available in the markets of the last 20 years. That said, our results suggest that systematically allocating capital to tail-hedging strategies during long periods of market stability would have resulted in potentially superior multiperiod performance for equity index portfolios.

Building on previous chapters, this chapter discussed the empirical evidence on the potential performance benefit for investment portfolios in the period from 1928 to the present in following an active tail-hedging strategy. Chapter 3 discussed the ex ante reason to tilt portfolios when tail hedges are presented. Here we supplemented it by simple empirical results. We found that an active tail-hedging strategy that follows a simple "monetize and reinvest" strategy can potentially outperform both unhedged buy-and-hold strategies and passively hedged strategies. We believe that in an environment of uncertainty and increasing possibility of dislocation across and between markets, the case for active tail risk hedging for modern investment portfolios is stronger than ever before.

For readers who are interested in the episode by episode payoffs for tail hedges and waiting times for such payoffs to occur, we point them to the Journal of Portfolio Management article where this study was initially published.

5

Indirect Hedging and Basis Risk[1]

In previous chapters we discussed our macro approach to tail risk hedging, the gains to portfolio performance from tilting the hedged return distribution toward a slightly more aggressive posture, and the critical role of active tail risk management. In this chapter we extend this work to an understanding of indirect strategies and the tradeoff between cost savings and basis risk such strategies entail.

To motivate this, note that because credit and equity are fundamentally related by virtue of their dependence on the profitability of the company issuing them, a catastrophic sell-off of a firm's equity would result in increasing leverage of the company's balance sheet. This increased leverage would result in a higher probability of default, which, all else being equal, should result in widening credit spreads. If we aggregate all the companies in an economy, we can expect that broad equity-market indices would be correlated with credit-market indices, which is what is found empirically. For large, systemic shocks, we should expect the correlations between companies and sectors to increase. Thus, in the limit, when correlations increase, which usually occurs during periods of systemic risk, we should expect diverse hedges to perform similarly with little basis risk. Similar increases in correlations are observed when we look at other assets that show common exposure to risk, for example, carry currencies, certain commodities, and volatility instruments. However, knowing this qualitatively is not enough. We will develop a framework to quantify the basis risk in this chapter.

For simplicity and transparency, let us assume that the investor holds a simple portfolio that consists of 100 percent exposure to a broad liquid index, for example, the Standard and Poor's 500 Index (S&P500). The approach and results are not specific to this portfolio and can be generalized to any mix of assets. Assume that the tail-averse investor is concerned with hedging all losses beyond 25 percent for the next year, which we call the investor's *attachment point*. As discussed earlier, to achieve this, the investor can purchase a *direct* hedge on the underlying index, corresponding to a put option struck at 75 percent, which for this simple portfolio provides a low basis-risk hedge that the portfolio will not lose more than 25 percent in one year. This portfolio and its hedge exhibit almost no basis risk by construction.

However, the cost of direct hedges can vary substantially with equity index option volatilities in the market. As Exhibit 5.1 shows, as the volatility rises or the attachment level becomes closer to spot, the price of the direct put option rises drastically. In particular, the purchase of deeply out-of-the-money puts and longer-dated volatility in the index options markets by tail hedgers can make those options quite expensive, with cheaper alternatives attractive.

Given the valuation concerns with direct equity hedges, the investor may be willing to look at alternative *indirect* hedges that cost less than the direct hedge yet are likely to be highly correlated with the payoffs of the direct hedge. Of course, nothing is free, and this discount to the cost of the tail hedge creates the risk that the indirect hedge may not perform as expected in a crisis. We refer to this slippage as *basis risk*.

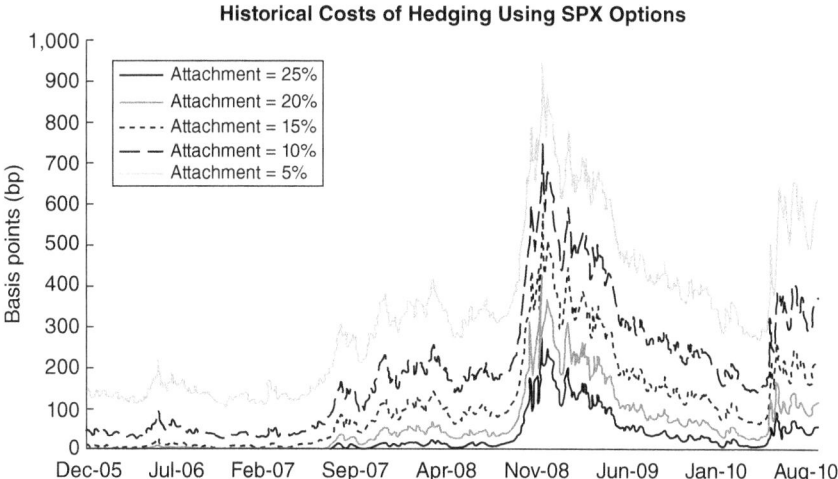

Exhibit 5.1 Price of SPX options as a function of volatility and attachment level.

Quantifying Basis Risk

Before jumping into the complexities of indirect hedges and the cost-versus-basis-risk tradeoff, we develop a framework for evaluating the implicit tradeoffs. The framework attempts to simplify the number of moving parts, reducing the analysis to an intuitive factor framework that improves transparency.

To begin, consider the price of a put option at some time in the future, as represented by the Black-Scholes option-pricing model

$$P(K, S_{t_1}, \sigma_{t_1}, T-t_1, r) = e^{-r(T-t_1)}KN(-d_2) - S_{t_1}N(-d_1)$$

where t_1 is the time (in years) from now until the portfolio hits the investor's attachment point, K is the strike of the option, S_{t_1} is the spot time t_1 price, T is the time (in years) to maturity of the option from now, r is the interest rate, and σ_{t_1} is the Black-Scholes implied volatility required so that the Black-Scholes put option price matches the market price. The implied volatility is the degree of freedom that may be solved for to make the model and market match; hence it serves simply as a quoting convention. The term $N(\cdot)$ represents the cumulative standard normal distribution function, and the terms d_1 and d_2 are given by

$$d_1 = \frac{\ln(S/K) + \sigma_{t_1}^2/2(T-t_1)}{\sigma_{t_1}\sqrt{T-t_1}}$$

$$d_2 = d_1 - \sigma_{t_1}\sqrt{T-t_1}$$

Now let us motivate the pricing of the indirect hedge in the context of the direct hedge example just given. We assume that the tail-averse investor wants to follow a trading strategy that allows him to purchase the direct equity hedge whenever portfolio losses hit the attachment point at the then-current price of the direct hedge. In order to finance the purchase of this hedge, the investor will have to set aside money in a "tail-hedge portfolio" today and invest in securities that are expected to be worth as much as the direct hedge when portfolio losses are equal to the investor's attachment point. The trivial trading strategy that satisfies the investor's criterion is to simply purchase the direct hedge today. Alternatively, and allowing for pricing variations across securities, the investor could purchase a portfolio of securities that may be cheaper today but in the scenario that portfolio losses are equal to the attachment point is equal to the value of the direct hedge. If there were no basis risk in this combination of indirect securities, then a lower cost for the combination of indirect securities would constitute an option market "arbitrage." Of course, in reality, there is basis risk, so there is no arbitrage, and our purpose here is to quantify this basis risk. In other words, we want to figure out how much risk there is that if the adverse event happens, there is not enough value in the indirect-hedge portfolio to *exchange* it for the direct hedge at that point in time.

Indirect Hedging and Basis Risk

As mentioned earlier, note that the value of a tail hedge is rarely from the underlying going "into the money." If one thinks of tail hedges as nonlinear assets, then the real value of the option-based tail hedge is driven by the change (typically an increase) in volatility as the underlying begins to move closer to the attachment point. Thus we can see that the relationship between the volatilities of the two instruments will play an important role in quantifying the basis risk.

To be specific, suppose that the portfolio losses hit the attachment point so that the strike $K = (1-A)S_0 = 0.75 S_0$ and $S_{t_1} = K$ in t_1 years from now.[2] Then, evaluating Black-Scholes, assuming dividends and interest rates are zero, we find that the inputs to Black-Scholes become

$$d_1 = \frac{\ln(K/K) + \sigma_{t_1}^2/2(T-t_1)}{\sigma_{t_1}\sqrt{T-t_1}} = \frac{\sigma_{t_1}}{2}\sqrt{T-t_1}$$

$$d_2 = d_1 - \sigma_{t_1}\sqrt{T-t_1} = -\frac{\sigma_{t_1}}{2}\sqrt{T-t_1}$$

These equations imply $N(-d_2) = N\left[(\sigma_{t_1}/2)\sqrt{T-t_1}\right]$ and $N(-d_1) = N\left[-(\sigma_{t_1}/2)\sqrt{T-t_1}\right]$. Application of symmetry of the normal distribution function $N(-x) = 1 - N(x)$, with the appropriate substitutions reduces the price of the option to the following expression:[3]

$$P(K, K, \sigma_{t_1}, T-t_1, 0) = 2(1-A)S_0\left[N\left(\frac{\sigma_{t_1}}{2}\sqrt{T-t_1}\right) - \frac{1}{2}\right]$$

If we focus on tail-hedge trading strategies that purchase the direct hedge whenever the portfolio losses hit the attachment point, we simply use the arithmetic for computing the value of the direct hedge in the scenario that matters to the investor. In this example, the investor needs to forecast only two variables, the at-the-money volatility and the expected time of hitting the boundary defined by the attachment point.

Thus the implied-volatility skew effects of at-the-money versus out-of-the-money options are eliminated.

Additionally, the market's risk-neutral expected hitting time of the boundary may be estimated by the current distribution of option prices (we can compute the expected value analytically when the underlying distribution is normal and by brute-force simulation when the distribution is more complex). If the investor assumes that the market distribution is wrong and instead prefers an alternative assumption, she is implicitly making a relative-value call on the richness/cheapness of option implied volatility and skewness. The interaction of the hitting time and implied volatility for the scenario of interest is critically important. In particular, if the time expected for hitting the boundary is near the expiration of the option, then the option price will not be largely affected by implied volatility or option vega. However, if the boundary is expected to be crossed well before expiration, the assumptions for implied volatility will have a much larger impact on the value of the direct hedge. Thus, in formulating a trading strategy, the expectation for the amount of vega left can play a large role in determining alternative approaches.

Hedge Matching at the Attachment Point

In order to make the ideas concrete, we'll present an example of how the framework can be used in practice. Consider first the value of a direct hedge initially purchased with a strike at 750 when spot is 1,000. Exhibit 5.2 displays the value of the option for various hitting times and various levels of implied volatility. Recall that the boundary in this example is at 750, so at the time of hitting the boundary, the options are at the money.

The investor purchasing the direct hedge alternatively can purchase an indirect hedge in other markets or at other points on the volatility surface. For simplicity, let's suppose that the investor wants

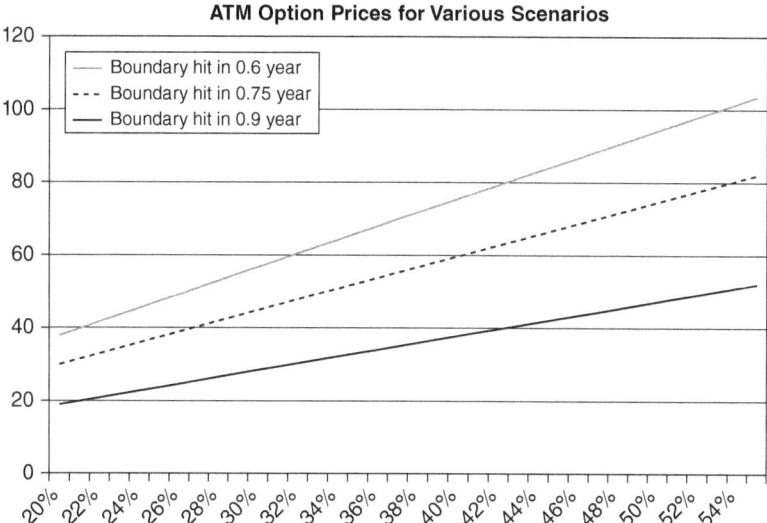

Exhibit 5.2 Value of a 750 strike option when spot is at 1000, for different hitting times and volatilities.

to compare the payout of an at-the-money put struck at 1,000, which is at the money now, with the direct hedge struck at 750. In the scenario where portfolio losses hit the attachment point, the direct hedge becomes an at-the-money option, and the indirect hedge, here struck at 1,000, is deeply in the money.

For the deep in-the-money option, the contribution of volatility is negligible because it roughly trades as the difference between spot and strike, that is, intrinsic value. In the scenario where the spot is 750, the strike is 1,000, so this option is worth at least $250. In order to purchase the direct hedge (struck at 750) when portfolio losses hit the attachment point, the investor would need to purchase the following amount of the indirect hedge

$$w_{\text{ATM}}(\sigma_{t_1}, t_1) \approx \frac{P(\sigma_{t_1}, T - t_1)}{AS_0} = 2 \times \frac{(1-A)}{A} \left[N\left(\frac{\sigma_{t_1}}{2}\sqrt{T-t_1}\right) - \frac{1}{2} \right]$$

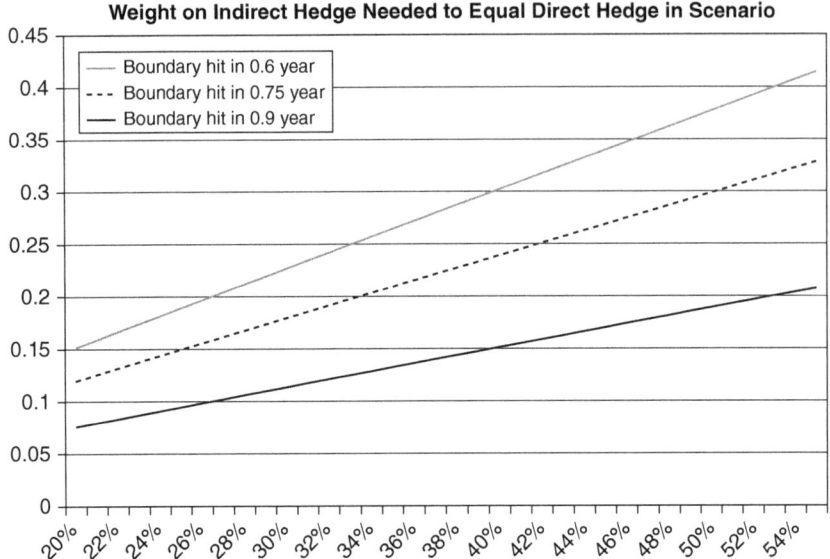

Exhibit 5.3 Amount of indirect hedge needed to equal direct hedge at crossing threshold.

The weights on the indirect hedge that equalize the value to the direct hedge for different boundary-hitting times and levels of volatility are given in Exhibit 5.3. The reason the lines shift down as the hitting time moves further into the future is simply that there is less time value left in the deeper out-of-the-money options, and to match the performance of the out-of-the-money option, a smaller intrinsic value of the at-the-money option is needed.

The matching condition we have just described fixes how much of the indirect hedge the investor *would need* to purchase the direct hedge when portfolio losses are at the attachment point. Now we can ask how much the direct and indirect hedges would cost at inception.

Suppose that at inception the direct hedge, an out-of-the-money one-year option with a 750 strike trades at 30 percent implied volatility, and the indirect hedge, an at-the-money 1,000 strike, trades at 25 percent implied volatility. Exhibit 5.4 compares the upfront cost

Indirect Hedging and Basis Risk

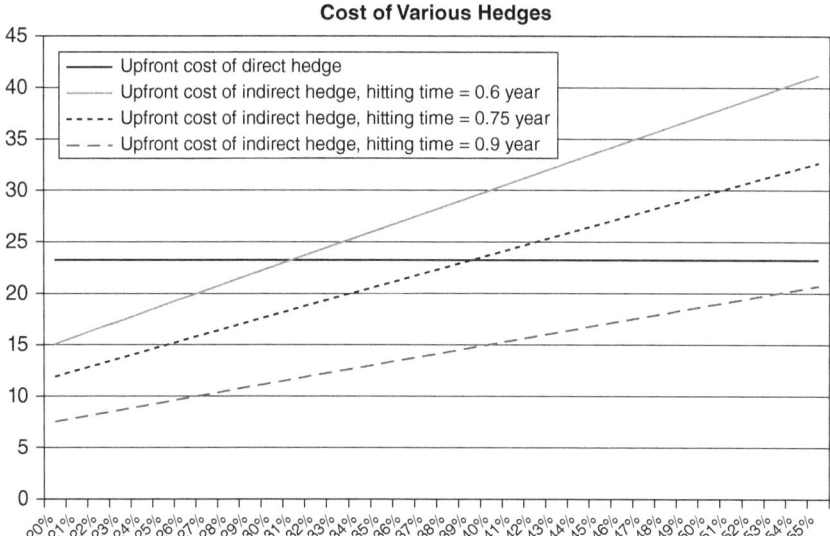

Exhibit 5.4 Comparison of direct and indirect hedges for different times for reaching the attachment point.

for the indirect and direct hedges, with indirect hedges weighted to be equal to the direct hedge in the scenario of interest.

Exhibit 5.4 reveals the relative value of the indirect and direct hedges for the scenarios of interest. The direct hedge costs a constant amount at inception because it is ex ante determined by fixing the strike and corresponds to the heavy horizontal line. The indirect hedge costs various amounts at inception, the variation due to the different weights needed for each of the scenarios. It is clear that based on the investor's priors, the direct hedge can be more or less expensive than the indirect hedge. Generally, when the attachment point is closer to the current value of the portfolio, indirect hedges are cheaper than direct hedges. Similarly, as the potential for breaching the attachment level moves out in time, indirect hedges become relatively cheaper. In the case where the attachment point is reached very far in the future, the indirect hedge can be cheaper than the direct hedge for all attachment points, as illustrated by the line corresponding to the 0.9-year crossing of the attachment point. This result is due to vega decay in the direct hedge; as time passes, the implied volatility plays an increasingly smaller role.

We can also see a direct relative-value implication between strikes as a function of volatility and expected breach time. Suppose that the investor believes that portfolio losses, conditional on the portfolio losing more than the attachment point, will hit the attachment point in 0.6 year of maturity; then at-the-money implied volatility would be 30 percent. In this scenario, the investor is indifferent between purchasing the two hedges because this corresponds to the intersection of the heavy horizontal and light solid lines. Thus, to derive equivalence between different hedges, both expectations of attachment level crossing and expected volatility have to be forecast. This requires active monitoring of the market's valuation of the volatility surface relative to the investors' own forecasts.

As another illustration, suppose that instead the investor believes that volatility will be 35 percent at the attachment point and that the hitting time is the same as earlier. In this scenario, the direct hedge would offer cheaper pricing than the indirect hedge, the solid horizontal line below the light solid line. The weight on the indirect hedge needed to equate the direct and indirect hedges at the attachment point makes the total cost of the indirect hedge relatively expensive. The increased weight in the indirect hedge is needed to offset the vega in the direct hedge, the interaction of higher volatility, and hitting time, making the value of the direct hedge expensive when portfolio losses hit the attachment point.

For the special case of comparing the hedge struck at the money at inception, with price given by P_0^{ATM}, and the hedge struck at the attachment point, with price given by P_0^A, the approximate breakeven implied volatility for a given hitting time, as a function of current option prices, turns out to be

$$\sigma_{t_1}^{B/E} \approx \frac{2}{\sqrt{T-t_1}} N^{-1}\left[\frac{1}{2}\left(\frac{P_0^A}{P_0^{\text{ATM}}}\right)\left(\frac{A}{1-A}\right)+\frac{1}{2}\right]$$

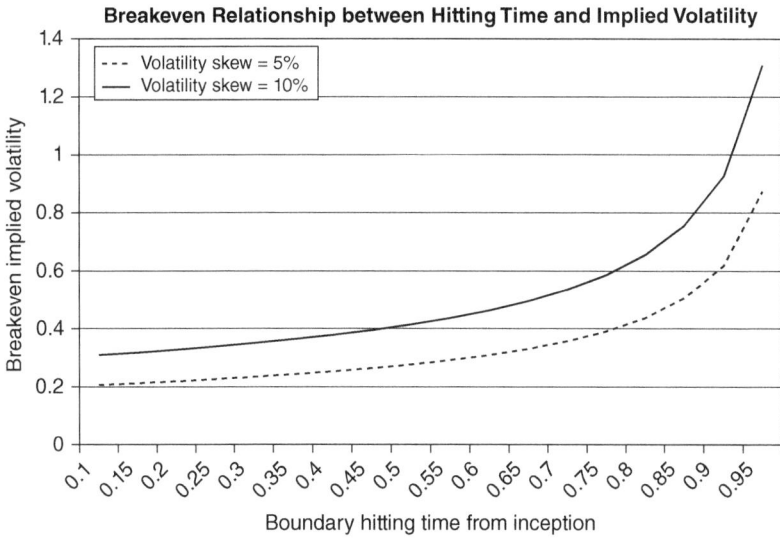

Exhibit 5.5 Breakeven volatility for different starting skew levels for different threshold crossing times.

Exhibit 5.5 plots the breakeven volatility as a function of portfolio hitting time given in the preceding formula. The formula needs additional input, the current ratio of the out-of-the-money (OTM) option, struck at the attachment point, and the at-the-money (ATM) option, both prices at inception of the hedge. In order to show the importance of skew and how it affects the breakeven relationship, we plot two versions where the implied volatility of the OTM option is 5 and 10 percent above the ATM option. As the premium for the OTM option moves up relative to the ATM option, the breakeven volatility required at a particular hitting time needed to justify the OTM option over the ATM option increases.

As an example, if the investor believes that the attachment point will be struck in 0.6 year, he would need to also believe that the ATM implied volatility of the direct hedge will be below 30 percent for the case of 5 percent volatility skew. The closer the investor believes the hitting time will be to the maturity of the option, the less volatility is

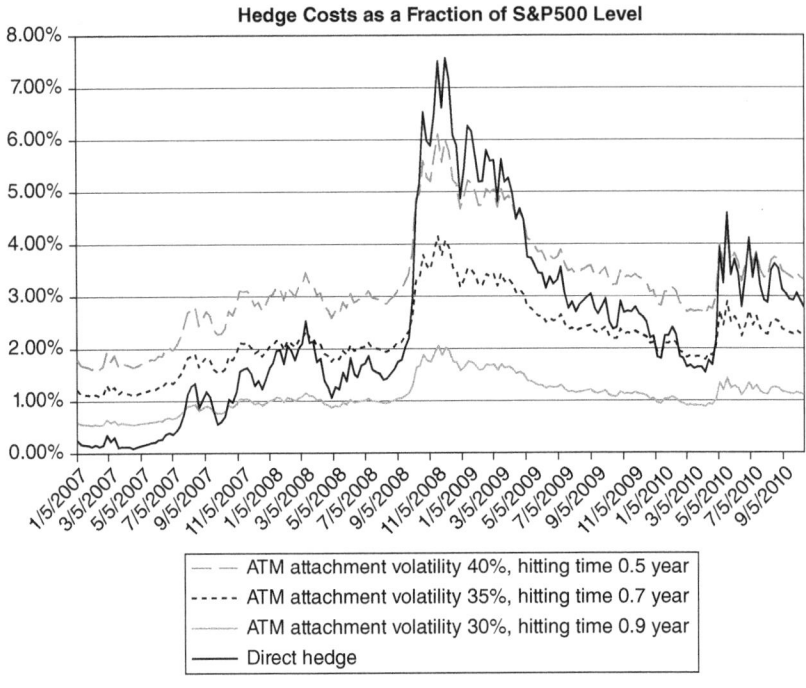

Exhibit 5.6 Hedge cost over time for various ATM volatility assumptions.

needed to justify the direct hedge over the indirect hedge. Again, this is just a variation on the idea that the exposure to implied volatility of the direct hedge becomes less important as the hitting time moves further into the future. Exhibit 5.6 gives a historical account of the direct hedge with one-year maturity and strike 25 percent OTM versus an ATM strike sized for various assumptions on ATM volatility at the attachment point and boundary hitting times.

"Soft" Indirects: Comparing Puts versus Put Spreads

As mentioned earlier, when volatility is low, we would naturally prefer outright put options because the potential gain from volatility rising is substantial. On the other hand, when volatility is high or the skew in OTM put options is steep, we can use put-option spreads (buying a close to ATM put and selling a deeper OTM put) to essentially obtain the same profile of protection but with an added benefit from "selling the skew." Also note that put spreads are less sensitive to volatility (see details on comparison of the Greeks later in this chapter). In our framework, we can consider put spreads without adding additional factors to the scenario analysis. Here the put spreads are structured to be long an option that is ATM at inception and short an option that is ATM at the attachment point. To a close approximation, the weight on the put spread needed to match the value of the direct hedge is given by

$$w_{\text{SPD}}(\sigma_{t_1}, t_1) \approx \frac{P_{\text{Direct}}(\sigma_{t_1}, T - t_1)}{AS_0 - P_{\text{Direct}}(\sigma_{t_1}, T - t_1)}$$

$$= \frac{2 \times (1-A)\left[N\left(\frac{\sigma_{t_1}}{2}\sqrt{T-t_1}\right) - \frac{1}{2}\right]}{A - 2(1-A)\left[N\left(\frac{\sigma_{t_1}}{2}\sqrt{T-t_1}\right) - \frac{1}{2}\right]}$$

The point at which the investor would rather purchase the put spread in lieu of the outright put is when the upfront cost of the put package is less than the outright put, sized for the appropriate scenario

$$w_{\text{SPD}}(\sigma_{t_1}, t_1)\left(P_0^{\text{ATM}} - P_0^A\right) < w_{\text{ATM}}(\sigma_{t_1}, t_1)P_0^{\text{ATM}}$$

Letting

$$x = 2 \times (1-A)\left[N\left(\frac{\sigma_{t_1}}{2}\sqrt{T-t_1}\right) - \frac{1}{2}\right]$$

the equation can be written as

$$\frac{x}{A-x}\left(P_0^{\text{ATM}} - P_0^A\right) < \frac{x}{A}P_0^{\text{ATM}}$$

implying that

$$x < A \frac{P_0^A}{P_0^{ATM}}$$

Solving for implied volatility as a function of hitting time, we get that the put spread is optimal over the outright ATM put whenever

$$\sigma_{t_1} < \frac{2}{\sqrt{T-t_1}} N^{-1}\left(\frac{1}{2}\left(\frac{A}{1-A}\right)\left(\frac{P_0^A}{P_0^{ATM}}\right) + \frac{1}{2}\right)$$

Notice that this result is the same as the breakeven volatility on the ATM put. This result implies that the investor should only consider either the direct hedge or the appropriately sized put spread for tail hedging; the appropriately sized ATM put will always be more expensive than the cheapest of the other two options.

Exhibit 5.7 shows the relative value of the direct hedge, the appropriately sized ATM put, and the appropriately sized put spread.

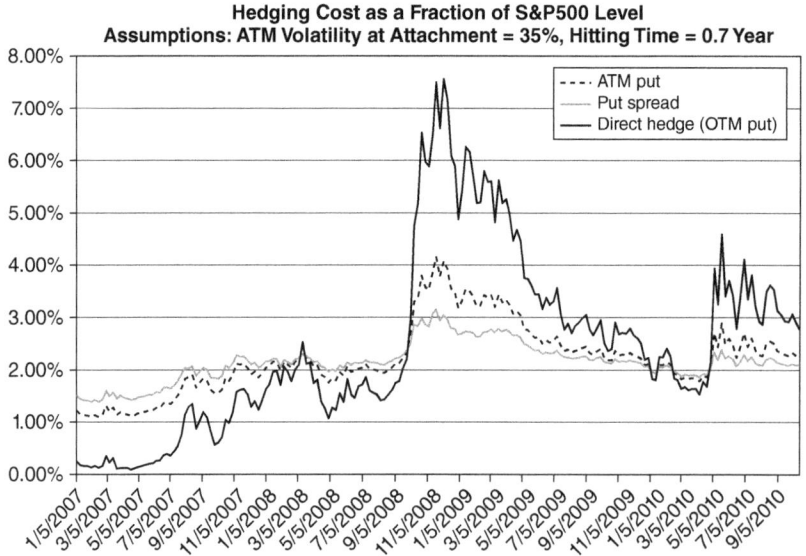

Exhibit 5.7 Comparison of hedging costs of puts vs. put spreads.

This exhibit reveals the intuition of the formula: the ATM put always costs more than lesser of the direct hedge or the put spread. Notice that the points at which the put spread and direct hedge cross, the ATM put also crosses.

Basis Risk from Correlated Asset Classes

The preceding section laid out the intuition for purchasing hedges for ATM strikes versus OTM strikes. Now we turn to the analysis of hedges that take positions on other asset classes. This might be relevant if all points in the equity volatility surface are expensive relative to other asset classes. For instance, credit is closely related to equities, and synthetic credit-default swap index positions can be constructed to replicate the performance of equities in severe downturns. Similarly, carry-currency pairs such as the AUD/USD and AUD/JPY cross are tightly correlated with the behavior of equity and other risk markets.

To begin, let σ_{IND} represent the annualized volatility of the indirect asset, σ_{DIR} represent the volatility of the direct asset (in our working example the S&P500 volatility), and ρ represent the correlation between the two assets. The *beta* of the direct hedge to the indirect hedge allowing for equal strike points across markets is defined as usual by

$$\beta = \frac{\sigma_{IND}}{\sigma_{DIR}} \rho$$

As an example, suppose that the direct hedge is a one-year S&P500 put option struck 25 percent OTM at 750, assuming that spot at inception is 1,000 and the S&P500 volatility is 25 percent. Suppose that the indirect hedge of interest is the AUD/USD exchange rate, which for simplicity we'll assume has a correlation of 0.9 with S&P500 returns and a volatility of 17.5 percent. Of course, one has to have reasons to believe that the structural relationships between AUD/USD and the equity market will persist. Because both investments are driven primarily by risk aversion and macroeconomic volatility, the investor can have some confidence that the indirect hedge will perform on the tails (for a discussion of the relationship between volatility and currency carry, see Bhansali [2007]). The return on AUD/USD consistent with a 25 percent loss on the S&P500 is given by

$$\tilde{K} = \tilde{S} \times \exp\left[\beta \ln\left(\frac{K}{S}\right)\right]$$

where $\tilde{K}$ is the strike of the indirect hedge, a function of the spot of the indirect hedge $\tilde{S}$ as well as the strike of the direct hedge K and underlying spot of the direct hedge S.

Thus, a 25 percent loss on the S&P500 corresponds to a 16.5 percent change in the AUD/USD exchange rate. This calculation determines the strike needed to size consistent linear moves across alternative hedging assets. If we assume that spot AUD/USD is at 1, then the OTM strike of interest is 0.834. Notice that as correlation rises in absolute value to 1, the OTM strike needed on the indirect hedge moves further away from spot, making it cheaper. Furthermore, the amount of the OTM indirect hedge that is purchases is inversely proportional to correlation; as correlation rises in absolute value to 1, less of the indirect hedge needs to be purchased. Thus the forecast correlation affects the sizing of an indirect hedge in two ways, via strike and allocation.

Extending the argument of the preceding section, the notional weight on the OTM indirect hedge, which becomes an ATM option in the scenario of interest, needed to equalize the value of the indirect hedge to the direct hedge in the scenario of interest can be written as

$$w_{\text{IND}}(\gamma) = \frac{P(K, \sigma, t_1)}{P(\tilde{K}, \tilde{\sigma}, t_1)} = \frac{K\left[N\left(\frac{\sigma}{2}\sqrt{T-t_1}\right) - \frac{1}{2}\right]}{\tilde{K}\left[N\left(\gamma\frac{\sigma}{2}\sqrt{T-t_1}\right) - \frac{1}{2}\right]} \approx \frac{1}{\gamma}\frac{K}{\tilde{K}}$$

where $\gamma = \tilde{\sigma}/\sigma$ is the ratio of the indirect to direct ATM volatility when portfolio losses are at the attachment point, K is the strike on the direct-hedge asset, and $\tilde{K}$ is the strike on the indirect-hedge asset. This equation has several important lessons for indirect hedging that aren't obvious at first glance. In sidebars 5.1 and 5.2, we show that the weight on the indirect hedge is largely independent of both σ and t_1, eliminating the need to forecast these factors for the scenario of interest. Instead, γ, the ratio of the ATM volatilities, and ρ, the correlation between the assets determining the corresponding location of the OTM strike of the indirect hedge, are the key factors determining relative value. The sidebar derives the approximation using a Taylor expansion and may be useful for further intuition, that is,

$$\tilde{w}(\gamma) \approx \frac{1}{\gamma} \times \frac{K}{S} \times \exp\left[-\beta \ln\left(\frac{K}{S}\right)\right]$$

The ratio of volatilities and correlation determine the strike via the beta and the weights. Given these predictions, the investor can compare the cost of the indirect versus direct hedge today by taking into account the current volatility skew.

To give an explicit example of how this framework can be used, Exhibit 5.8 shows the historical ATM implied-volatility ratios for one-year AUD/USD to S&P500.

Exhibit 5.9 displays the historical cost of the premium spent on the indirect hedge $\tilde{P}_0^A \tilde{w}(\gamma)$ to the cost of the direct hedge P_0^A under the assumptions that the realized ATM volatility ratio is 0.6 at the attachment point and that the correlation is 0.9 between the assets (recall that correlations rise in tail events). Using the volatility ratios and correlation as input, the strike of the indirect hedge and its weight are determined. The exhibit plots the total cost of the indirect hedge, that is, the weight multiplied by the price, versus the total cost of the direct hedge. For scaling purposes, both quantities are presented as a percentage of

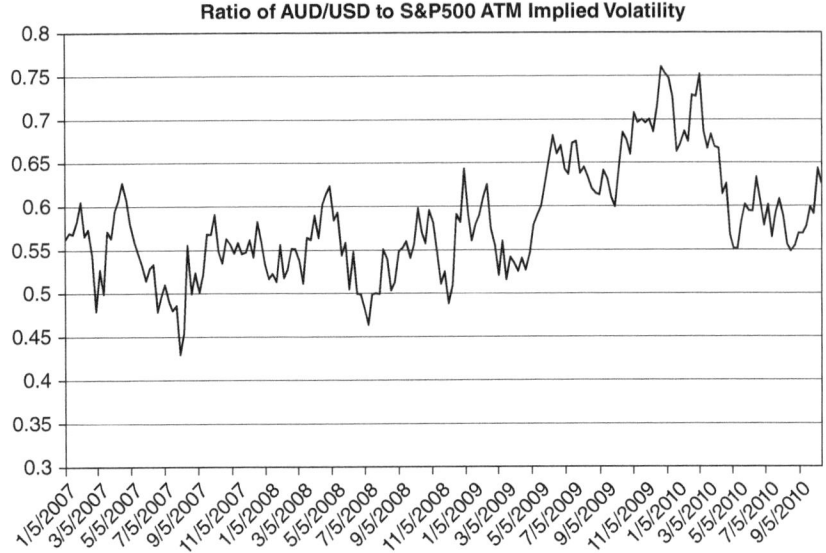

Exhibit 5.8 Ratio of AUD/USD implied volatility to S&P 500 at the money options with one year left to expiry.

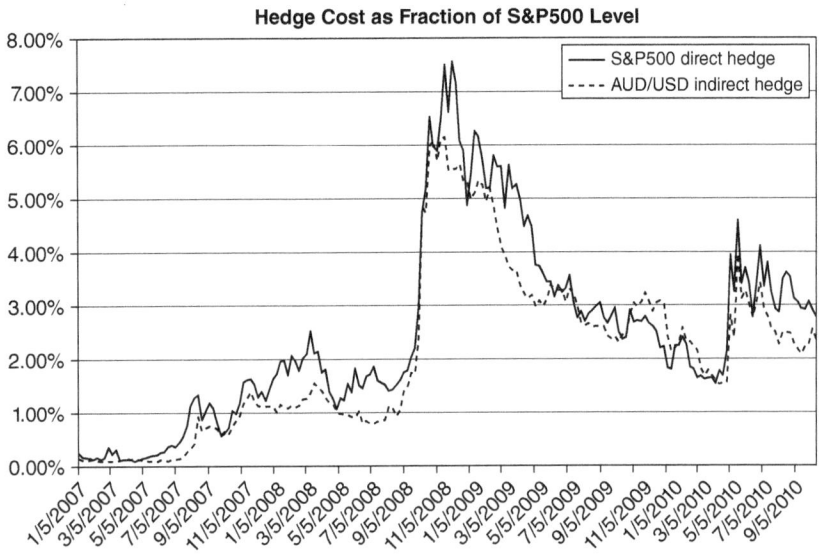

Exhibit 5.9 Hedge cost comparison of direct hedge on S&P 500 and indirect hedge using AUD/USD puts.

Indirect Hedging and Basis Risk

S&P500 spot level, translating the quantity into a premium. Of course, the main risk here is that the forecast correlations turn out to be very different from the ones assumed in the calculation. But combined with a scenario analysis and sensitivity tests for the assumptions, we believe that a diversified portfolio of actively managed tail hedges suffers little from correlation forecast errors.

In previous sections we've reduced the complications of option pricing across multiple assets to a few simple inputs: hitting times, ATM volatilities, correlations, and ATM volatility ratios at the attachment point. These factors can be used to determine the sizing and relative value of ATM strikes on indirect hedges.

The sizing for the ATM put needed to equal the OTM put on the indirect hedge at the attachment point is given by

$$\tilde{w}(\tilde{\sigma}_{t_1}, t_1) \approx \frac{P(K, K, \sigma_{t_1}, T-t_1)}{\tilde{S} - \tilde{K}} = \frac{2K\left[N\left(\frac{\sigma_{t_1}}{2}\sqrt{T-t_1}\right) - \frac{1}{2}\right]}{\tilde{S} - \tilde{K}}$$

Plugging in the formula for the indirect strike as a function of the direct strike and spot and beta of the indirect-to-direct assets, we get the following weight as an expression of the fundamental inputs:

$$\tilde{w}_{\text{ATM}}(\gamma, \sigma_{t_1}, t_1) \approx \frac{2\times(1-A)\times S\left[N\left(\frac{\sigma_{t_1}}{2}\sqrt{T-t_1}\right) - \frac{1}{2}\right]}{\tilde{S}\times\{1 - \exp[\beta\ln(1-A)]\}}$$

Exhibit 5.10 gives a historical account of the direct hedge with one-year maturity and strike 25 percent OTM versus an ATM strike on AUD/USD sized for various assumptions on ATM volatility at the attachment point and boundary hitting times. For this example we have used the assumption of a beta of AUD/USD to S&P500 of 0.54.

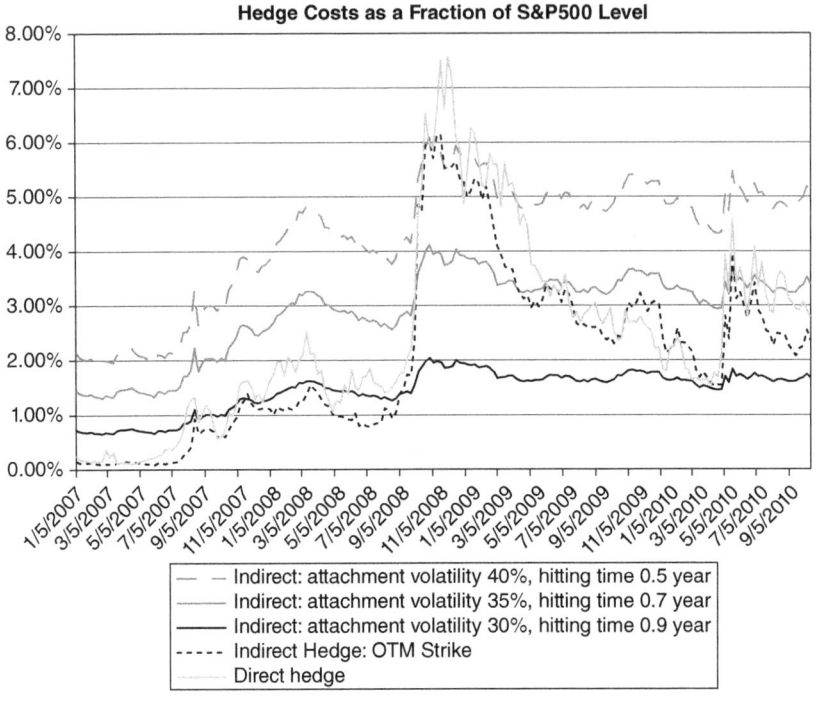

Exhibit 5.10 Comparison of direct and indirect hedge costs over history.

Faced with all the choices for efficient hedges by exploiting relationships between different points within the same asset's volatility surface and across assets, the investor should prefer the one that is the lowest cost from all the alternatives.

Exhibit 5.11 collects the various strategies, giving a complete picture of the historical costs of various strategies with some simple assumptions. The assumptions underlying the exhibit are that the ATM volatility at the attachment point of the direct hedge is 35 percent, the time to hit the attachment point is a constant 0.7 year, the ATM volatility ratio between the direct and indirect hedge is 0.6, and the correlation is 0.9.

The lower envelope of the exhibit, the minimum of the four lines over time, displays the cost of the cheapest hedge. Exhibit 5.12 shows this cost as a percent of the cost of the direct hedge, highlighting the discount

Indirect Hedging and Basis Risk 113

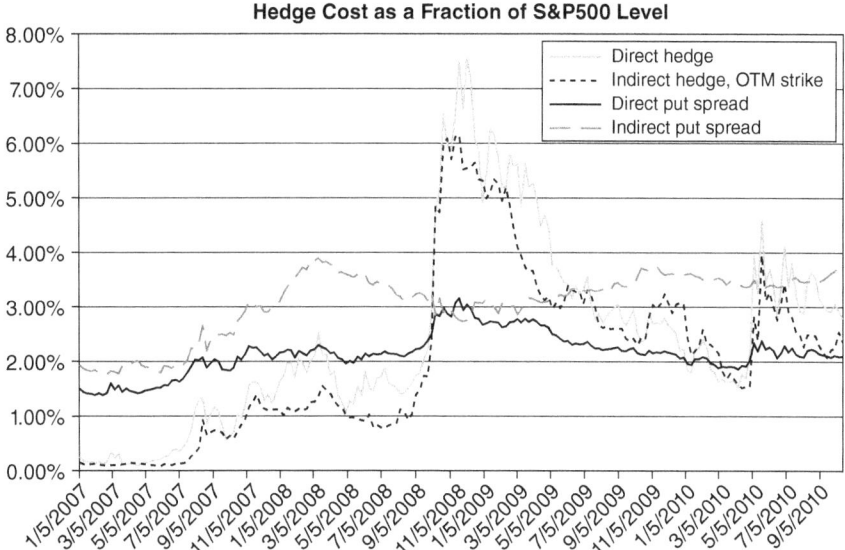

Exhibit 5.11 Hedge cost as fraction for direct and indirect hedges.

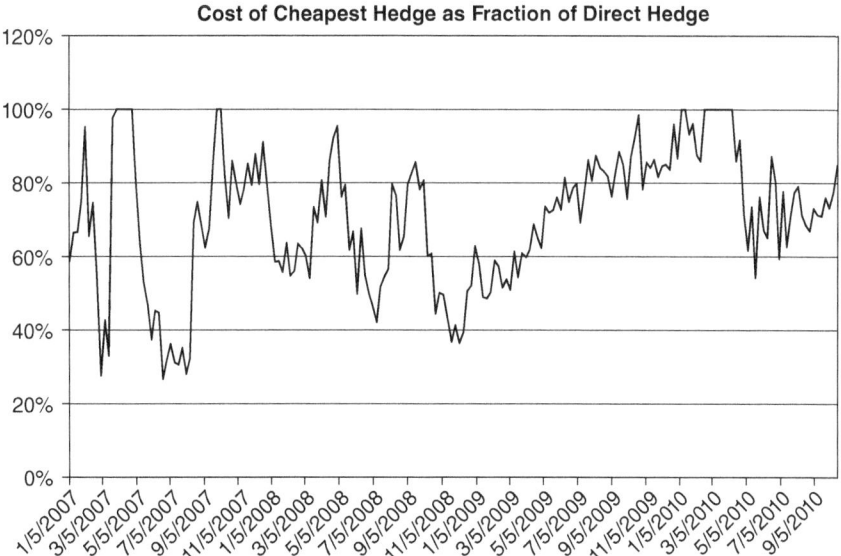

Exhibit 5.12 Cost of cheapest indirect hedge as a fraction of the direct hedge.

that one could obtain if the assumptions were true over time. What we want to emphasize is that just as active monetization of hedges is required to extract the most value out of a hedging program (see Bhansali and Davis 2010), active rebalancing between hedges across asset classes is just as critical for maintaining an effective hedge program.

The framework presented herein describes a methodology for appropriately sizing options of various strikes on both direct and indirect hedges under a particular set of investor expectations. In reality, the investor has a range of expectations, resulting in a range of plausible portfolio values at the attachment point for a given sizing of the portfolio. Aggregating over these ranges and taking into account the allocations to each indirect hedge, the investor can arrive at a complete picture of basis risk. Exhibit 5.13 displays simulated results for three different tail-hedge portfolios sized for 25 percent attachment on the S&P500, each corresponding to different levels of basis risk. In this exhibit, the low-basis-risk portfolio is the minimum-cost portfolio of tail hedges purchased across a wide range of assets and subject to the constraint of having only a 10 percent probability that the tail-hedge portfolio will be less than 90 percent of the value of the direct hedge at the attachment point. The exhibit simulates the value of an investment in the S&P500 accompanied by the tail-hedge portfolio. The medium- and high-basis-risk tail-hedge portfolios are defined analogously, differing only in the percentage of the direct hedge that the tail-hedge portfolio value can be less than at the attachment point with 10 percent probability, these being 70 and 50 percent, respectively. All portfolios are expected, on average, to be equal to the value of the direct hedge at the attachment point. They differ only in the variation around this expectation. By targeting greater basis risk, there is both a greater risk the tail-hedge portfolio will outperform and underperform the direct hedge in the tail event.

It is obvious that the high-basis-risk portfolio has more dispersion than the low- and medium-basis-risk portfolios. The costs associated with the various levels of basis risk for the Exhibit 5.13 are given in the

Indirect Hedging and Basis Risk 115

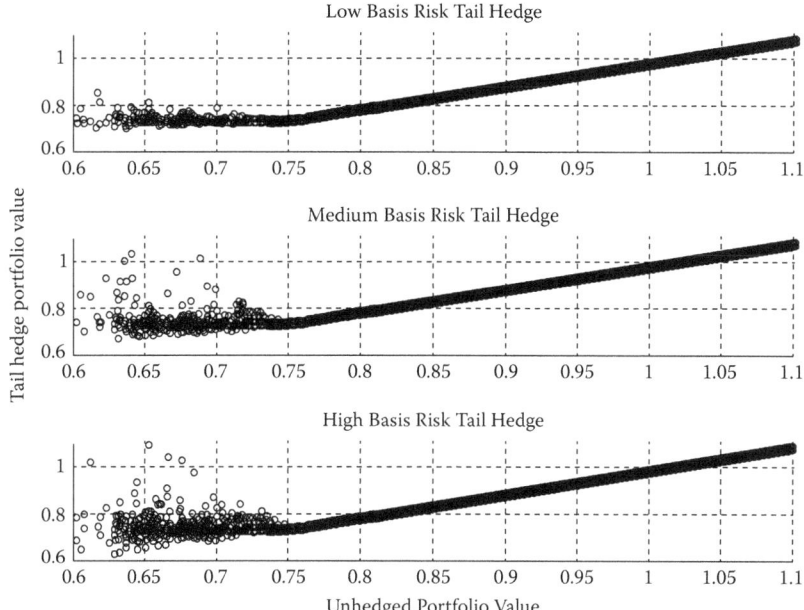

Exhibit 5.13 Basis risk dispersion for high, medium, and low basis risk portfolios.

following table. The direct hedge is the most expensive; by moving to indirect hedges, the investor could nearly halve the budget. By accepting basis risk, the investor is explicitly trading off dispersion of the possible outcomes versus a cost reduction.

Equity beta	1
Attachment point	25%
Total cost (bp): direct-hedge cost	292
Total cost (bp): low-basis-risk portfolio	257
Total cost (bp): medium-basis-risk portfolio	184
Total cost (bp): high-basis-risk portfolio	154

In conclusion, this chapter has continued our previous work by taking a closer look at the basis-risk-versus-cost tradeoff in tail risk hedging portfolios. We systematically evaluated basis risk from within assets by exploiting relative value in the volatility term structure and across assets by exploiting correlation opportunities. Given the rich and dynamic nature of volatility skews and term structures as well as cross-market relationships, we believe that an active tail risk management approach that broadens the assets under consideration with a targeted level of basis risk may indeed be superior to a single-asset tail-hedge or passive approach.

5.1 Derivation of Formulas

The weight on the OTM indirect hedge, sized for the scenario of interest, is

$$w(\gamma) = \frac{P_{\text{Direct}}(K_{\text{DIR}}, \sigma_{\text{DIR}}, t_1)}{P_{\text{Indirect}}(K_{\text{IND}}, \sigma_{\text{IND}}, t_1)}$$

$$= \frac{K_{\text{DIR}}\left[N\left(\frac{\sigma_{\text{DIR}}}{2}\sqrt{T-t_1}\right) - \frac{1}{2}\right]}{S_{\text{IND}} \times \exp\left[\beta \ln\left(\frac{K_{\text{DIR}}}{S_{\text{DIR}}}\right)\right]\left[N\left(\gamma\frac{\sigma_{\text{DIR}}}{2}\sqrt{T-t_1}\right) - \frac{1}{2}\right]}$$

Recall that β determines the comparable strike across surfaces. Noting that $(\sigma_{\text{DIR}}/2)\sqrt{T-t_1}$ is small, the weight can be written as a simple and accurate approximation using the Taylor expansion.

$$N(D) = \frac{1}{2} + \frac{1}{\sqrt{2\pi}}D$$

$$w(\gamma) \approx \frac{1}{\gamma} \times \frac{K_{\text{DIR}}}{S_{\text{IND}}} \times \exp\left[-\beta \ln\left(\frac{K_{\text{DIR}}}{S_{\text{DIR}}}\right)\right]$$

The breakeven point is the point where the initial cost of both hedges, sized to have the same payouts in the scenario of interest, $P_0^{\text{IND}} w(\gamma) < P_0^{\text{DIR}}$. Thus

$$\gamma_{B/E} \approx \frac{P_0^{\text{IND}}}{P_0^{\text{DIR}}} \times \frac{K_{\text{DIR}}}{S_{\text{IND}}} \times \exp\left[-\beta \ln\left(\frac{K_{\text{DIR}}}{S_{\text{DIR}}}\right)\right]$$

5.2 Derivation of Formulas in Text

Using the same approach as used previously,

$$\tilde{w}_{\text{SPD}}(\tilde{\sigma}_{t_1}, t_1) \approx \frac{P(K, K, \sigma_{t_1}, T-t_1)}{(\tilde{S}-\tilde{K})-P(\tilde{K}, \tilde{\sigma}, t_1)}$$

$$= \frac{2K\left[N\left(\frac{\sigma_{t_1}}{2}\sqrt{T-t_1}\right)-\frac{1}{2}\right]}{\tilde{S}-\tilde{K}-2\tilde{K}\left[N\left(\gamma\frac{\sigma_{t_1}}{2}\sqrt{T-t_1}\right)-\frac{1}{2}\right]}$$

A historical comparison with the OTM and ATM indirect hedge is provided in Exhibit 5.14.

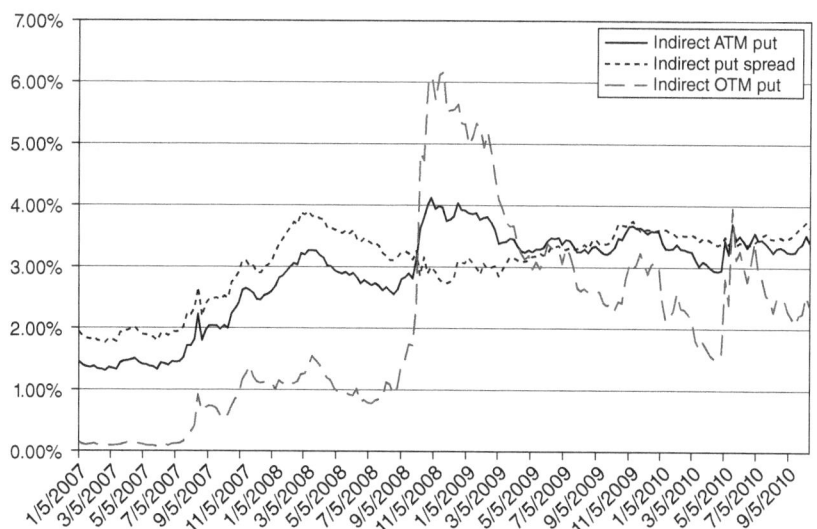

Exhibit 5.14 Hedging cost as a fraction of S&P500 level. Assumptions: ATM volatility at attachment = 35%, hitting time = 0.7 year

5.3 Sensitivities of Puts versus Put Spreads

Here I show how the pricing and sensitivities (Greeks) of puts and put spreads allow one to make tradeoffs by moving from direct hedges to the simplest indirect hedges. One can think of put spreads as relatively more attractive hedges when the skew is higher than normal and puts as relatively more attractive hedges when the absolute level of volatility implied in option prices is low.

For this example, we assume that the spot index is at 1,450, and we compare a 1,087.50 strike one-year put (25 percent out of the money) against an 1150/850 put spread. We use 27.6 percent implied volatility for the 1,087.50 put, 26.16 percent volatility for the 1,150 put, and 32.4 percent for the 850 put (to capture skew). At inception, the prices of the put and the put spread are identical (29 points or 2 percent approximately), and the delta is almost the same as well (−12.5 percent). The vega (sensitivity of price to volatility changes) of the put is 2.98 (price change for 1 percent volatility change), and the vega of the put spread is 2.36. Generally, put spreads are less vega-sensitive than puts. The time decay (theta) of the put is −0.12 per day, whereas the put spread has a time decay of −0.08.

Impact of Changing Underlying (Spot) Prices

Value of Put versus Put Spread

The obvious and important thing to note here is that as spot falls, the put continues to increase in value, whereas the put spread starts to reach its maximum value out at the width of the spread (i.e., 300 points in our example).

Indirect Hedging and Basis Risk

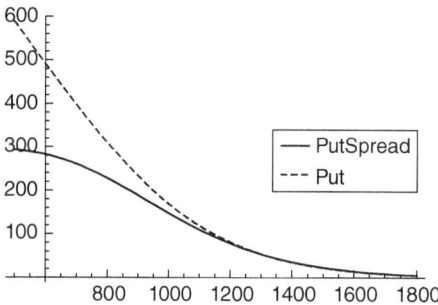

Delta

The important thing to note here is that the puts delta keeps increasing, whereas the put-spread delta stops increasing after the upper strike is breached and indeed starts to fall somewhere in the middle of the strikes.

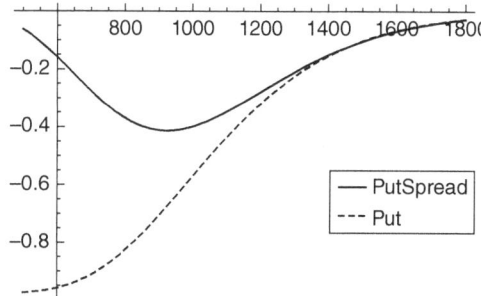

Gamma

Again, the put-spread gamma tops off much quicker than the put. Thus the convexity of a put spread is always less than or equal to the put.

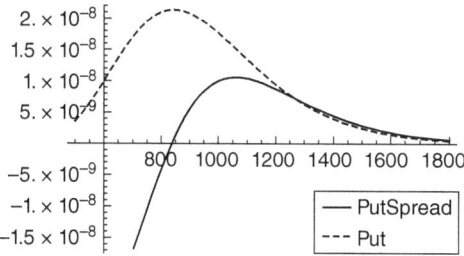

Put Theta

Interestingly, while the put always has negative time decay, the put-spread time decay is initially negative, but then turns positive as the lower strike is approached. This is so because the lower strike is the one we are short, and it has positive time value. Clearly, this is a tradeoff against the lower delta and gamma of the put spread.

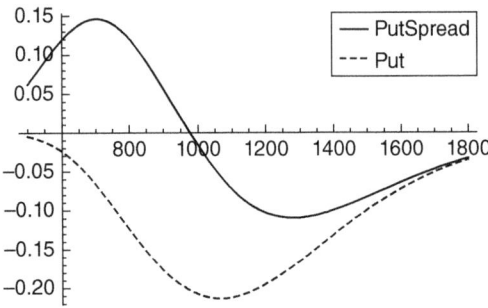

Vega

This is similar to gamma with spot variations. The put spread loses its sensitivity to volatility changes more quickly as the spot moves down compared with the put.

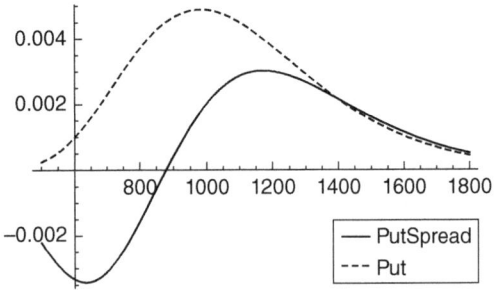

Vanna (Derivative of Vega with Respect to Spot)

Again, as spot falls, the put spread loses its vega much faster once the spot falls below the lower strike.

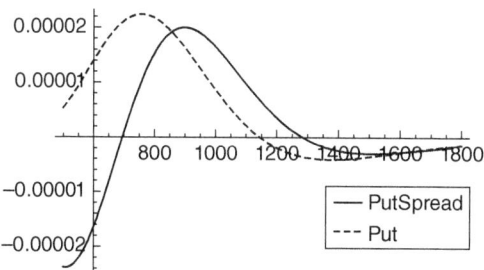

Volga (Derivative of Vega with Respect to Volatility)

Volga shows a relatively interesting and non-linear, non-monotonous behavior for both puts and put spreads.

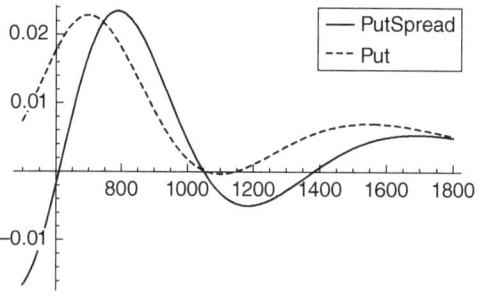

Charm (Delta Decay)

The put spread has lower delta decay as the lower strike is reached because the delta of the lower strike compensates for the delta decay of the higher strike. This is compensation for lower gamma on the put spread.

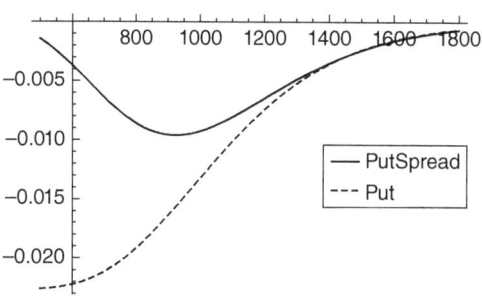

Impact of Changing Volatilities

Value

Note that as volatility increases, the put spread does not gain as much value as the put (here we are parallel shocking volatility, so any skew change effects are not being captured).

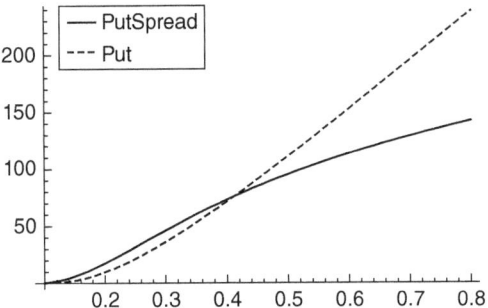

Delta

As volatility rises, the effective delta of the put rises, but the delta of the put spread rises and then falls as the lower strike becomes more valuable (the one we are short).

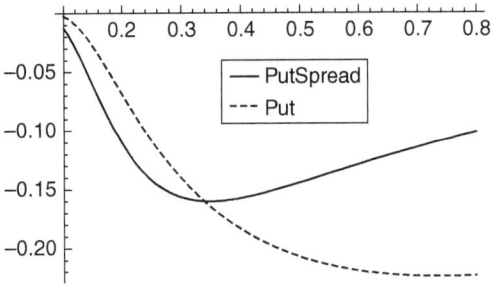

Gamma

The put spread has higher gamma for lower volatility levels compared with the put. For high volatility levels, the gamma is almost the same (and falling).

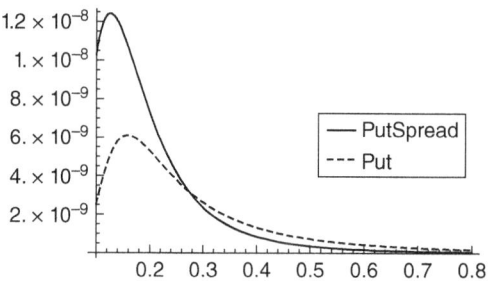

Theta

The put-spread time decay falls off rapidly as volatility rises because the time decay on the lower-strike put starts to compensate for the time decay of the higher strike. On the other hand, the time decay of the put increases rapidly. This is a good reason to actively monetize puts once volatility increases.

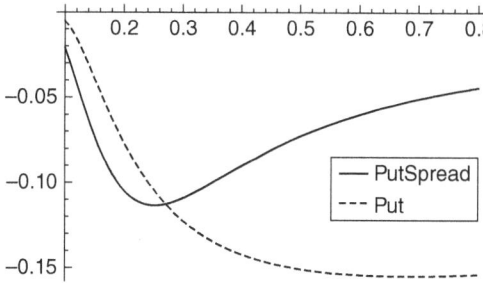

Vega

The vega of the put spread is higher than the put for low volatility levels (because the closer put has much higher vega), but it falls below the put as the volatility starts to rise.

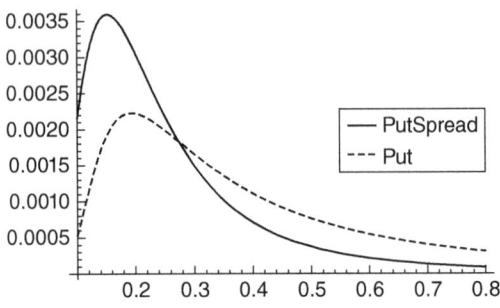

Vanna

The rate of vega sensitivity to spot of puts and puts spreads is significantly different for low volatility levels.

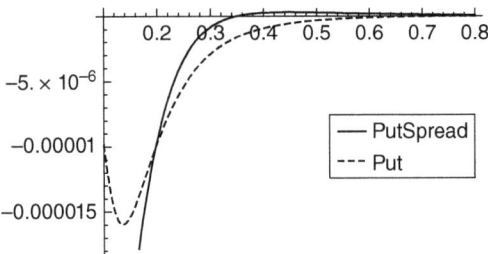

Volga

Puts and put spreads exhibit similar vega change with respect to volatility changing for low and high volatilities, but puts have higher Volga for middling vols.

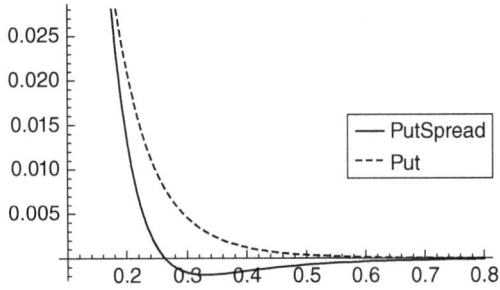

Charm

The rate of delta decay is higher for the put compared to put spread for higher volatility levels.

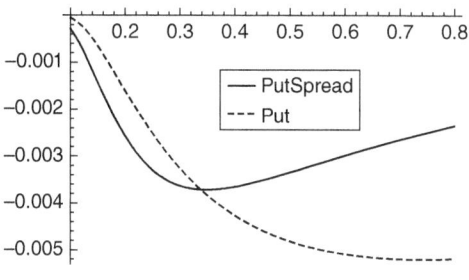

5.4 Generic Path Generation for Simulations

The piece of *Mathematica* code that follows comes in handy in simulating generic paths to test various thought experiments within a Black-Scholes type of environment:

```
genpath[S0_,mu_,sigma_,horizon_,numsteps_]:=
Module[{incr,deltat},
   deltat=horizon/numsteps;
     incr=Table[Exp[(mu-sigma^2/2)*deltat+_
         sigma*Sqrt[deltat]*Random[NormalDistribution
[0,1]]],{i,1,numsteps}];
FoldList[Times,S0,incr]
     ]
```

To generate the paths, use (see Exhibit 5.15):

```
ListPlot[Table[genpath[100, 0.10, 0.20, 1, 365],
{i, 1, 100}], PlotJoined -> True]
```

Now we can also use the generated paths for various thought experiments on the payoffs. It is easy to replace the normal distribution by sampling from actual history (*bootstrap*) or from other, fatter-tailed parametric distributions.

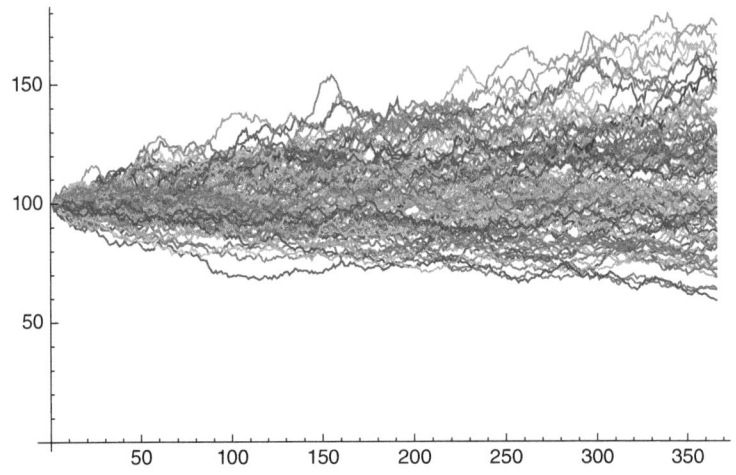

Exhibit 5.15 Generation of paths from simple *Mathematica* code.

5.5 High-Frequency Estimation of Stress Correlations

The mini tail event around 10 a.m. on April 23, 2013, was a statistical lab that showed the potential response of the market to stress events and where risk-off correlations should be expected in periods of shocks. The idea is that by looking at intraday mini stress events, we can tell where larger correlations might be hiding at lower frequency. Because tail events are rare, statistical analysis is harder, and looking at intraday experiments, we can basically expand our data set for the stress periods.

What I find interesting is that in almost all cases the correlations are much higher during the stress than excluding the stress period. Also, the magnitudes of stress changes shown in the next table dominate the overall daily magnitudes. This is some validation that markets are more likely to "jump" rather than "drift" if unforeseen news appears.

Max Move (max-min)	SPX Index	Emini future	AUD	JPY	EUR	30y Bond	10y Note	5y Note	2y Note	USA	TYA	FVA	TUA	RXA
Whole Day	1.05%	1.11%	0.34%	0.83%	0.18%	1.20%	0.57%	0.23%	0.02%	0.80%	0.39%	0.18%	0.02%	0.20%
Event Period	0.93%	1.01%	0.28%	0.62%	0.10%	1.09%	0.52%	0.21%	0.02%	0.74%	0.35%	0.16%	0.02%	0.12%
Day without Event Period	0.41%	0.44%	0.19%	0.32%	0.18%	0.46%	0.18%	0.06%	0.01%	0.25%	0.13%	0.06%	0.01%	0.10%

6

Other Tail Risk Management Strategies

So far in this book I have focused on explicit options based tail risk hedging. Clearly, spending premium is not the only way to manage tail risks. In this chapter, I will discuss some other methods for tail risk management. First, I look at the qualitative tradeoffs between explicit dynamic asset allocation against explicit tail risk hedging. Next, I take a look at alternative betas such as momentum and trend following for tail risk mitigation. These strategies notably did well in the crisis of 2007–2009 as the bounds of mean reversion broke, and large trends were observed across markets. Next, I take a look at "zero premium" strategies such as costless collars and evaluate their costs and benefits. Direct volatility-based hedging such as variance swaps are explored next. Finally, I take a look at dynamic overlay strategies such as option replication via derivatives.

Tail Risk Hedging versus Asset Allocation in a Multimodal World

For many years, market participants have confidently relied on a modeling framework that considered a single "equilibrium" when constructing portfolios. The most popular assumption under such a model has been a probability distribution for asset returns that is unimodal (i.e., has only one peak) and a mean that coincides with this single peak. Indeed, many mechanical asset-allocation strategies use the assumptions of stable asset class returns, volatilities, and correlations estimated over long history; many of these assumptions should be questioned (see Bhansali et al. 2012). A key impact of the recent bout of crises hitting global markets has been the possibility of the emergence of multiple equilibria, which might occur if one or another competing force takes the upper hand.

For example, the policy risk that pervades the markets in the aftermath of the 2007–2009 crisis caused high correlations among asset classes and a temperament of "risk on/risk off" among investors. This phenomenon can be traced to the connectedness of markets, the ease by which market participants can access these connected markets, and the speed of assimilation of information in response to political events. This environment creates the possibility of multiple equilibria in the market, as well as trends that move markets between these equilibria and, once settled, restraining forces that may trap markets locally.

Even though predicting which force will win is next to impossible given the real-time evolution of the interaction between markets and policy, we can still ask an important question: How should the framework for asset allocation be modified if the distribution of returns from a hypothetical portfolio look more like the one shown in the chart on the right of Exhibit 6.1, that is, a bimodal distribution with more than one peak? The bimodal distribution has two peaks, and interestingly, even though it is generated as the result of mixing two normal distributions, each from a different regime, it can exhibit both fat tails (a higher probability of larger losses due to unusual events results in a fat tail on the left side of the distribution curve) and skewness (a lack of symmetry between the left and right

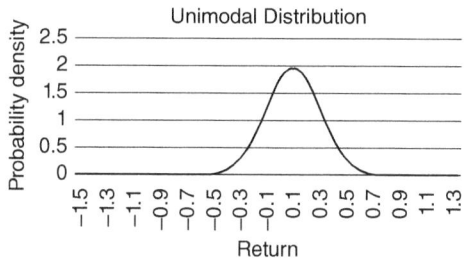

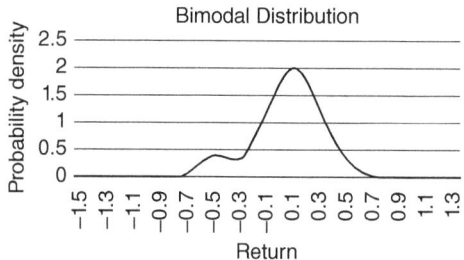

Exhibit 6.1 Unimodal versus bimodal distributions.

sides of the peak). Thus variance is not necessary and sufficient as a metric for the risks.

When constructing the "normal" returns chart, we used the long-term history of the Standard and Poors' 500 Index (S&P500) as a proxy to approximate the stock market (1951–2010) and assumed a normal distribution: 10 percent average annual return and 20 percent volatility, as measured by standard deviation. For the bimodal distribution, we assumed that there were two regimes: the first is the one shown in our normal distribution (10 percent average return and 20 percent volatility), but the second "bad" regime is one in which equities go down 50 percent and then become trapped in that new scenario.

We assumed for our example that there was only a 10 percent chance of the second regime happening, but once it happens, the environment is a sticky local equilibrium—a "hole that is hard to climb out of."

The interested reader can make up an infinite number of plausible scenarios such as these and is encouraged to question accepted lore of asset allocation and portfolio construction when faced with multimodal distributions. In this section we will attempt to do one such exercise. Some of the effects of higher moments in asset allocation are discussed in published papers (e.g., Bhansali and Wise 2002).

For the bimodal distribution that results from combining the normal and bad regimes, the average return is 4 percent, and the volatility is 26 percent (versus a 10 percent average return and 20 percent volatility for the unimodal normal distribution).[1] This is simply because the bad regime has sufficient weight to reduce the overall returns. There is also negative skewness (of -0.58) in the bimodal curve versus zero skewness for the normal distribution and excess kurtosis (a measure of whether data are peaked or flat) of 0.19 over the normal distribution, reflecting the magnitude of unlikely outcomes or how fat the tails are. All these statistics are not too far from what one could glean from looking at the implied distributions from option prices in broad equity indices during stress periods, but with the important difference that traditional option pricing models get their fat tails and skewness from building in the skew ex post on top of a unimodal distribution, with volatility that is assumed to vary with the option strike.

None of these observations should seem surprising if one realizes that a mixture of two normal regimes can yield a result that is not normal. Fat tails and negative skewness can arise from even the mere *possibility* of multiple equilibria, even though both equilibria in themselves are normal. This practice of generating very complex distributions from mixtures of simple, normal distributions is well known among statisticians and has applications in many fields of practical import: medicine, astronomy, and casino gambling, to name a few. In the present context, the two "normals" are the mixture of the "old normal" and the "new normal" with higher sensitivity of markets to policy action and economic shocks.

How does this bimodality apply to portfolio construction? Here is what we find when we apply it to two problems: optimal asset allocation and option pricing.

Optimal Allocation to Risky Assets and Tail Risk Management by Derisking:

If we start with an assumption that we would allocate 50 percent of the portfolio to equities in the unimodal case, what would the optimal allocation be in the bimodal case, assuming that our risk preferences are unchanged? By following a very traditional portfolio optimization exercise, which involves a little bit of math (maximizing an expected utility function as the allocation changes),[2] the answer turns out to be that the optimal allocation would be only 10 percent! In other words, one would have to derisk by almost 80 percent from the unimodal optimal allocation to arrive at the mathematically optimal result. Clearly, this is a substantial derisking of a portfolio, which could result in significant underperformance if indeed the risky assets in the portfolio outperformed. Thus, the shadow cost of modifying asset allocation needs to be compared with the explicit cost of option purchases.

If we started with an assumption of unimodality and the real distribution turned out to be the bimodal one, how mispriced would put options on the tails be in retrospect? My research shows that a typical unimodal distribution just cannot be tweaked large enough to make it come out with the price of a put option one would likely get if the real world turned out to be bimodal. A portfolio manager pricing such tail options armed with traditional unimodal distributions would wrongly think that the tail options were "expensive" (tail options generally will tend to be underpriced when based on a unimodal distribution but significantly higher when derived from bimodal distributions). I priced the options by mathematically summing the put payoff over all the probability-weighed outcomes from the two distributions. This comparison shows that the very possibility of a bimodal outcome forces you to derisk directly, that is, by reducing the allocation to risky assets, with the inherent costs of doing so, or by building in explicit tail hedging, which might look expensive by traditional measures but may turn out to actually be "cheap" in a bimodal world.

The Hedging Value in Trends and Momentum

Investing in momentum is not something that we are used to doing because we have grown up in a world of unimodal normal distributions. In a unimodal normal distribution, markets spend most of their time in the middle of the probability distribution because the thin tails at either end imply that mean reversion forces the probability to be highest close to the middle. In a bimodal world, the middle of the distribution is where the markets will spend the *least* of their time, and they will traverse between either end of the probability distribution. The dynamics of this traversal are exactly the opposite of mean reversion and are accompanied by momentum in markets. In other words, trending forces that create fatter-tailed distributions replace the same mean-reverting forces that create the normal distribution.

Exhibit 6.2 shows the correlation of various hedge fund strategies with the Chicago Board Options Exchange Volatility Index (VIX), which measures the volatility of S&P500 options. The VIX is a good measure of the turbulence in the equity markets, so negative correlation with the VIX (as exhibited by most of the strategies shown below) shows that market turbulence may result in destructive forces on typical mean-reversion-based portfolios. On the other hand, the momentum strategy ("Managed Futures" in Exhibit 6.2) and the short-bias strategy both exhibit zero to positive correlation with this turbulence, with the correlation rising in periods where the turbulence is especially bad. While reducing risk helps to cushion against market downdrafts,

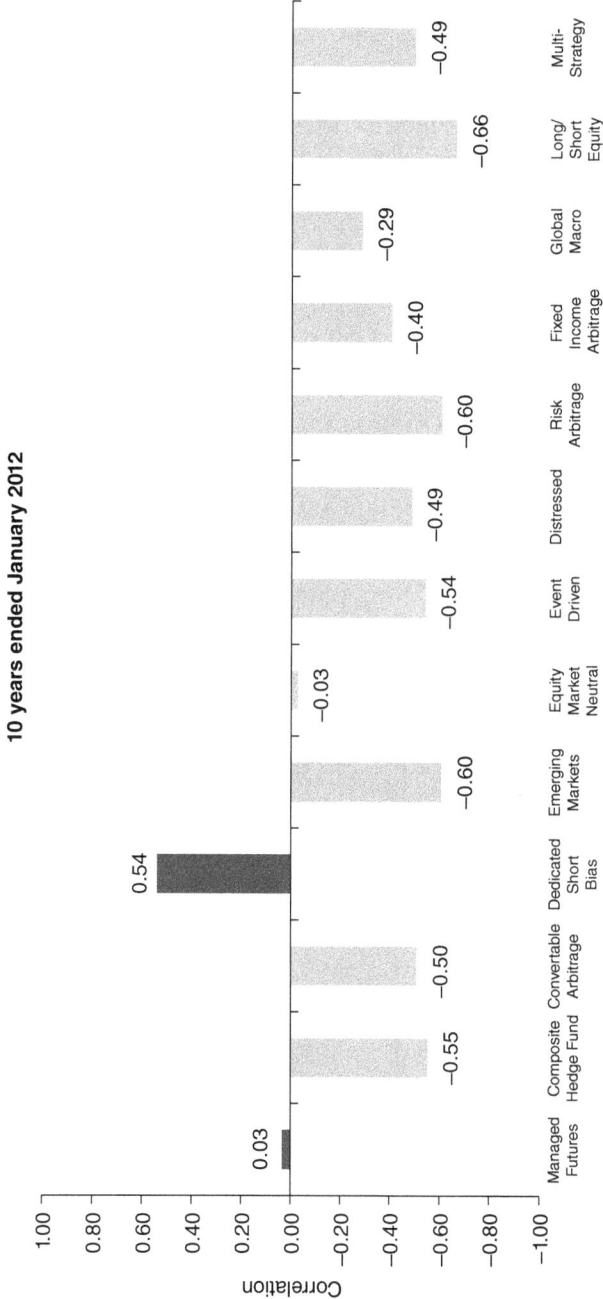

Exhibit 6.2 Correlation of hedge fund strategies with the VIX.

it may be expensive in terms of opportunity costs to not hold risky assets with their risk premium for an extended period of time. On the other hand, a small allocation (3 to 5 percent) to momentum-based strategies may provide significant risk-mitigation benefits. This is so because of the asymmetry and option-like behavior of the momentum factor returns: it tends to pay off large when the bounds of mean reversion break and effectively helps to provide portfolio diversification against large movements in asset prices.

For an illustration of how momentum can be a source of positive returns, see Exhibit 6.3. It shows that the BARRA momentum-style factor has demonstrated significant cumulative positive returns over more than 15 years.[3]

Obtaining exposure to momentum is not that hard, but it forces one to think very differently about markets and investing. The momentum strategy consists of (1) buying what is going up and selling what is going down, (2) buying more of what is going up more and selling more of what is going down more (called *pyramiding*), and (3) stopping the buying and selling at predetermined position sizes for risk management. This is the perfect antithesis of value investing, where "buy low,

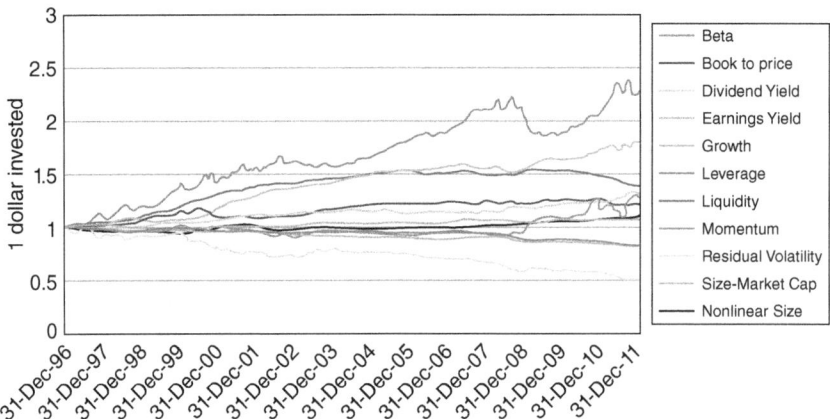

Exhibit 6.3 BARRA factor returns.

sell high" is the mantra, yet there is value in this style of investing as a tail risk hedge if (1) done cost-efficiently and (2) in a controlled fashion.

In a set of illuminating papers analyzing hedge-fund returns written over a decade ago, academics (Fung and Hsieh 2001) demonstrated that this strategy is theoretically and empirically the same as buying an *option straddle* (a call and a put) and hence offers exposure to rising market volatility. The potential benefit of the strategy is that by following a limited set of transparent rules, it can avoid high option premiums that one would pay in a straddle. When implied volatilities are high, such dynamic strategies can indeed become cost-efficient.

This equivalence of momentum or trend-following strategy actually can be demonstrated mathematically. To motivate this, note that when one buys an option straddle, the delta of the straddle at inception is zero because the call option and put option deltas cancel each other out. As soon as the market starts to move in one direction or other, the delta increases. Now, if one starts to replicate this option strategy with the underlying, then clearly one has to buy or sell more units as the delta increases. In other words, in a delta-replication strategy, one would continue to add to the existing position as the market moves further in the same direction—exhibiting a trend-following strategy, which is replicating an option's delta.

The same also works in reverse. A trend-following strategy looks at current prices relative to historical averages (either by looking at past prices at a specific point in history, at moving averages, at breakouts, or at regression lines). If the strategy is to add to the position as the current price deviates further and further away from the average (let's say by making the size proportional to the z-score or price difference from the mean adjusted for volatility), we are again replicating the delta of an option. In this sense, trend following is nothing but tail hedging or a long-volatility position without actually buying the volatility explicitly.

Of course, the implementation is not free—if markets do not trend but mean revert repeatedly, the "whipsaw" can cause the strategy to buy high and sell low continuously, creating losses that can add up. Empirically, these whipsaw effects have been relatively low compared with the potential for attractive gains as in 2008. This is no different from the time decay of non-delta-hedged options if the markets oscillate about a fixed value. Thus trend following as a tail risk hedge mitigation strategy pays the implicit cost from selling low and buying high if markets mean revert.

Other researchers have shown that *time-series momentum* is not limited to any one market but is actually everywhere, and thus the strategy is best implemented across all asset classes (i.e., stock indexes, bonds, commodities, and currencies). In addition, the momentum factor tends to do better when there are periodic bouts of illiquidity, as is typically the case when risk aversion rises. Because all these markets have liquid futures contracts, the momentum strategy actually can be implemented very cost-efficiently as a collection of long and short positions in futures contracts.

In a world of zero interest rates, the potency of bonds (or duration) to provide diversification-based hedges is very limited (e.g., at a 2 percent yield, the maximum capital gain if 10-year yields fall to 1 percent is only about 15 percent). Permanent derisking and holding excess cash also have a high real cost. In this world of low, pegged interest rates, an investor who is going to take risk needs every means to make the portfolio more inured to unforeseen shocks and market storms. In my opinion, one potent way for investors to hedge tail risks cheaply is via alternative beta strategies, such as momentum, that can be implemented efficiently.

A Look at the Risks and Rewards of Costless Collars

Investors are averse to paying for tail risk hedging. Our research shows that (1) cost-effective tail hedging allows one to build more efficient portfolios with higher ex ante long-term expected returns, (2) tail hedging

Other Tail Risk Management Strategies

allows defense while allowing offense when its most productive, and (3) the ex post returns to active tail-hedged portfolios have been superior to passive buy-and-hold portfolios. However, the temptation to "get something from nothing" is too much to turn away, and this motivates the interest in zero-cost or zero-premium options strategies.

The zero-cost option collar has been sold as a cheap way to buy tail hedging without spending premium upfront. Exhibit 6.4 shows the payoff to a portfolio with and without a simple zero-cost option structure. The solid line shows the payoff to a portfolio hedged with a zero-cost collar, where an out-of-the-money (OTM) put is bought to cut off downside risks, financed by selling an OTM call option.

Some things to note:

1. The zero-cost structure gives up some upside gains in order to protect the downside: The exhibit shows that a one-year put option at 85 percent can be combined with a call option sold at 107 percent to create a zero-cost collar. This protects the portfolio against falls

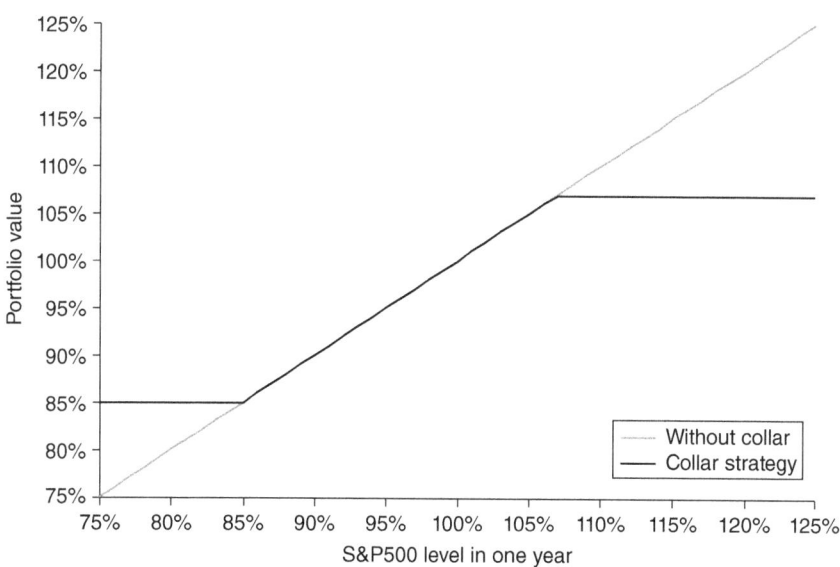

Exhibit 6.4 Payoffs with and without a zero-premium put-call collar.

in the S&P500 in excess of 15 percent over a one-year horizon, but pays away returns in excess of 7 percent to finance the put option protection. In recent experience, the rally in the stock market has made many of the sold calls go into the money, with the result that investors are finding that the sold call options are creating a negative performance relative to their benchmarks. Further, as the market rallies close to or through the sold call strike, the risk profile of the overall portfolio becomes harder to manage because market variations cause the delta, gamma, vega, theta, and so on to vary rapidly and create a lot of additional nonlinear risks.
2. The volatility skew penalizes the zero-cost structure. Downside puts are priced at a higher volatility than the upside calls. As a matter of fact, the skew between deeply OTM puts and OTM calls has become structurally high since the crisis, and zero-cost structures pay the skew, so OTM puts are half the distance of the OTM calls.

Here is some typical pricing math from a period when such structures were popular (S&P500 at 1,320), with one-year at-the-money (ATM) volatility at 20 percent (roughly equal to long-term realized levels). A 25 percent OTM put is at 28.5 percent implied volatility (option price 2 percent), and the one-year 25 percent OTM call is at 14.5 percent (price 0.31 percent). Thus the cost of the skew is 14 percent volatility points or 1.7 percent price points. Another way to look at this is to look at not the moneyness but at the delta. A 0.25 delta put at the same time is struck at 1,150 (170 points or 12.75 percent away) and costs 4.29 percent, whereas a 4.29 percent price call is around 1,400 (only 80 points or 6.23 percent away). Thus the market has to move twice the distance down as up for the put option to go in the money as compared with the call option.

The actual realized results may be even worse when one looks at the *skew roll-up*. What I mean here is that as the market rallies, the sold call becomes closer to at the money, and because ATM calls are

Other Tail Risk Management Strategies 141

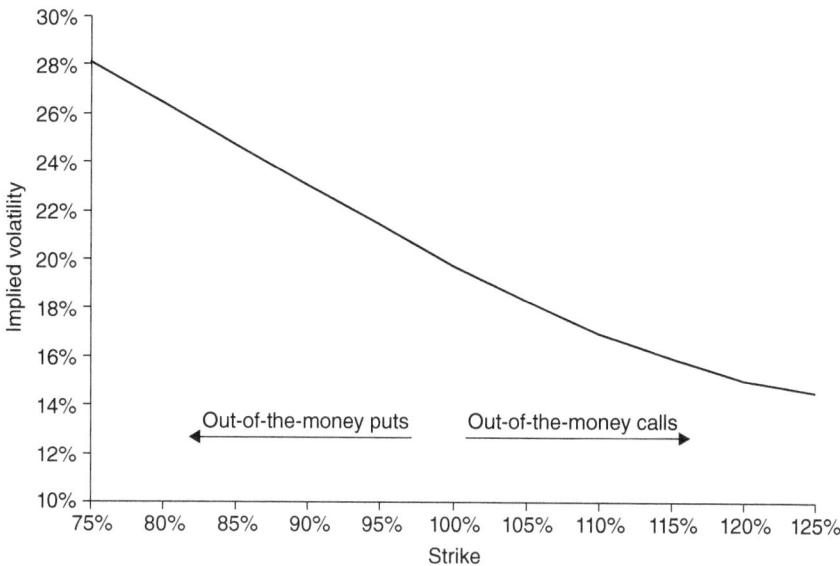

Exhibit 6.5 Implied volatility skew.

priced at a higher volatility than OTM calls, the sold call actually gains value because of the increasing implied volatility. It's as if a rallying market penalizes the structure twice: once from the rally and once from increasing call volatility as a result of skew roll-up (see Exhibit 6.5).

Variance Swaps and Direct Volatility-Based Hedging

With the advent of volatility instruments such as VIX futures, some systematic tail-hedging approaches use the direct purchase of such instruments for hedging. Indeed, there are exchange-traded instruments that allow one to obtain levered exposures to volatility futures. The design of these products is based on the observation that if equity markets fall, the level of volatility rises. We will not spend much space on a detailed exploration of these strategies, except to note some key facts.

SUMMARY OUTPUT

Regression Statistics

Multiple R	0.761309253
R Square	0.579591779
Adjusted R Square	0.579249148
Standard Error	1.841287652
Observations	1229

ANOVA

	df	SS	MS	F
Regression	1	5735.071816	5735.072	1691.59183
Residual	1227	4159.947448	3.39034	
Total	1228	9895.019264		

	Coefficients	Standard Error	t Stat	P-value
Intercept	0.110938783	0.052599455	2.109124	0.035136034
X Variable 1	−91.59331229	2.226978248	−41.129	3.9618E-233

Exhibit 6.6 The regression of changes in VIX on the percent changes in the S&P500.

First, empirically, it is observed that for every 1 percent fall in the equity markets, the VIX index moves roughly by 1 percent (see regression in Exhibits 6.6 and 6.7, which shows a −0.91 regression coefficient when weekly changes in the VIX are regressed against weekly returns of the S&P500). Thus, whereas an outright option profits mainly from the underlying equity index falling and volatility rising, the VIX makes it's gains from volatility rising. To compare the two, we need to figure out the equivalent vega risk of an outright option position and its change as a function of the movement in the underlying.[4]

Unfortunately, it is not possible to invest in the VIX directly. However, VIX futures that cash settle on the VIX do trade (and even

Other Tail Risk Management Strategies

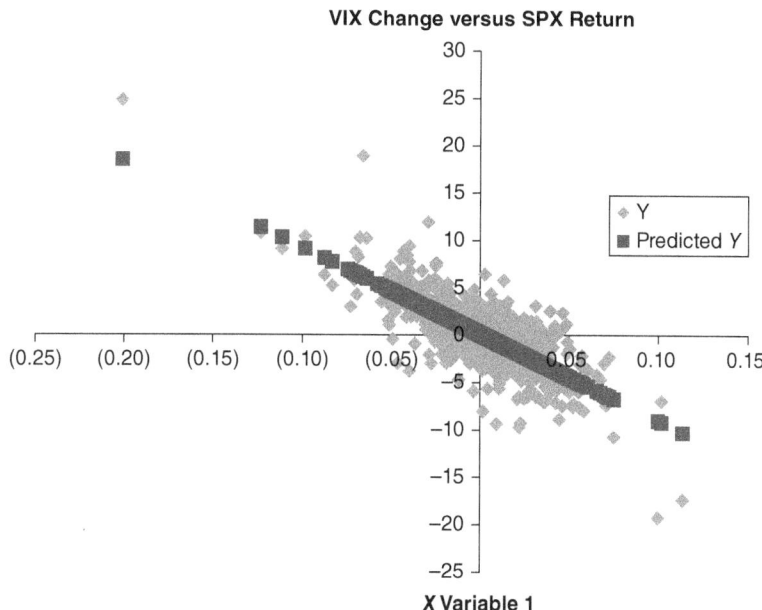

Exhibit 6.7 VIX change (vertical axis) versus SPX return (horizontal axis), weekly data from 1990.

exchange-traded funds and derivatives such as options on the VIX). The VIX futures market shows a distinct term structure that is normally upward-sloping. The buyer of the VIX future essentially pays for the premium by incurring a negative carry from holding a futures contract that converges to a lower-valued index. Occasionally, this curve and the negative carry can become quite large. On the other hand, when there are shocks to the risk markets, the demand surge for hedging can lead to short-term options rising much more rapidly than long-term options, resulting in an inversion in the VIX futures curve. Whereas, one would like to invest in volatility directly, the more liquid instrument that is traded is a variance swap, which is on the variance (or squared volatility). The reason is that variance can be hedged using a static portfolio of options, whereas volatility cannot.

Variance swaps are roughly a generalization of the VIX to longer maturities. For the S&P500 as the underlying index, a variance swap pays off according to the following formula:

Final payment = variance amount × ((final realized volatility)² − strike²)

Here the final realized volatility is computed using actual closing prices on the S&P500 employing

$$\text{Final volatility} = \sqrt{\left[252 \times \sum (\ln P_t/P_{t-1})^2 / N\right]} \times 100$$

The payoff is in terms of dollars per volatility, or vega for example, 1 million per volatility difference from the strike. The quotation can be in terms of vega or the variance amount. The variance amount is computed from the vega using the formula

$$\text{Variance amount} = \frac{\text{vega amount}}{2 \times \text{volatility strike}}$$

Thus, if the vega amount is $1 million, and the volatility strike is 20, then the variance amount is $25,000.

The variance swap, as a result of the quadratic computation, exhibits convexity with respect to the volatility. Given the presence of skew in the computation of the variance swap, the volatility corresponding to the variance swap is higher than the ATM forward volatility. Exhibit 6.8 shows the importance of skew as an independent and additional factor for the pricing of tail hedges beyond volatility. A good rule of thumb is that the variance swap volatility is roughly the same as the 10 percent OTM put (of course, this varies as the skew changes). Possibly the biggest advantage of using variance swaps to hedge is that the swaps do not expose the buyer to delta hedging, and as long as the volatility realized is higher than the variance strike, the swap will make profits. One thing to remember about variance swaps is that as

Other Tail Risk Management Strategies

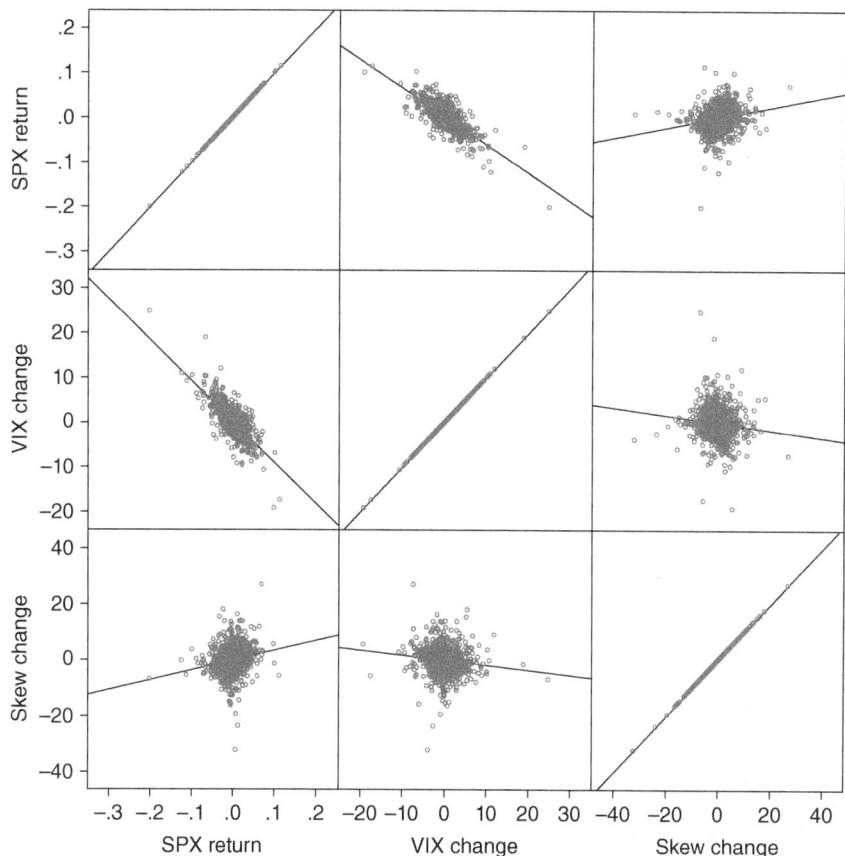

Exhibit 6.8 Relationship between S&P500 weekly returns versus VIX changes and implied skew changes. Note that while negative returns are associated with increases in the VIX, volatility is not empirically correlated with implied skew, and implied skew is not strongly correlated with the change in the S&P500.

time passes, the sensitivity of the variance swap to implied volatility decreases linearly with time. Also, the variance swap is sensitive to the steepness of the skew (even though the swap itself is on the variance). This is so because the hedging of a variance swap theoretically requires a static position in options of all strikes (see Carr and Madan 1998); thus, it picks up the skew of OTM options.

Dynamic Hedging[5]

When I first discussed the pros and cons of relying on dynamic, that is, delta, hedging of risks, I did not explore the comparison with static hedging thoroughly. Using overlays (e.g., S&P500 or other equity index futures) is an alternative way to manage the risks of a portfolio. The tradeoff between static and dynamic hedging is incurring the cost of hedging upfront or "as you go." The difference in performance arises from the difference in realized and implied volatilities and transactions costs. More precisely, the profit or loss of a dynamically hedged portfolio arises from the cumulative effect of the change in gamma of the option multiplied by the return in the underlying. If the gamma of the option is high (which can happen when a tail hedge becomes suddenly valuable or when the option is close to at the money), the cost of a static option can turn out to be much cheaper than the cost of dynamic replication. As a matter of fact, the variance swap discussed in the preceding section can be thought of as an instrument that hedges this risk of mishedging. A trader who sells an option and delta hedges it essentially replicates the payoff of a weighted variance swap, where the squared returns are weighted by the gamma times the underlying price squared (known as *dollar gamma*). Now, as discussed earlier, for deeply OTM puts, which form the basis for tail hedging, the option gamma can change very rapidly and increase multifold as either the spot price moves or volatility changes. If a dynamic hedging strategy tries to replicate this, it can become exposed to substantial transactions costs.

In *static hedging*, the buyer of protection buys a contractual obligation that if a particular event were to happen, the seller of the protection would pay according to a predefined formula. By contrast, in *dynamic hedging*, the protection seeker uses some algorithm to create the payoff he would have as if he had actually purchased the static hedge but without actually paying for the hedge now.

Other Tail Risk Management Strategies

In other words, static hedging is *outsourcing* of risk management to the options markets, whereas dynamic hedging is doing option replication *in-house*. In practical terms, static hedging consists of buying options, for example, S&P500 put options or indirect options, whereas dynamic hedging is done by replicating the option using the underlying instruments, for example, by selling and buying S&P500 futures.

The comparison depends on three factors: relative costs, access, and accounting constraints. In theory, with continuous trading and no market frictions, the dynamic and static approaches to hedging should be equivalent. The justification of the equivalence of the two hedging methods was provided by the approach of Black, Scholes, and Merton for option pricing. They showed over 30 years ago that under fairly crude assumption of normally distributed returns with constant volatility, the return of a European option on a stock can be approximately decomposed into a portion due to the return on the underlying stock as follows:

$$P(T,K,S_{t+1},\sigma,r) - P(T,K,S_t,\sigma,r) \approx \Delta(T,K,S_t,\sigma,r) \times (S_{t+1} - S_t)$$

where $P(T, K, S_{t+1}, \sigma, r)$ represents the price of a European option on stock S at time $t + 1$, expiring at time T, the stock having annualized volatility given by σ and a risk-free interest rate given by r. The term $\Delta(T, K, S_t, \sigma, r)$ is the delta of the European option, also known as the *hedge ratio*. Black, Scholes, and Merton determined a complex formula for $\Delta(T, K, S_t, \sigma, r)$ based on a set of simple assumptions.

The static approach to tail risk hedging involves simply buying the option, and the gains and losses are a result of the left-hand side of the equation. The gain and loss of this approach can be directly measured by the change in the value of the option. The dynamic approach to tail risk hedging uses the right-hand side of the equation to synthetically replicate the payoff of the option until expiration, that is, by trading the underlying itself, and adjusting the position up and down continuously with a weight in the stock determined by $\Delta(T, K, S_t, \sigma, r)$. If the equation were an identity that could be implemented perfectly in real markets, we would have one, not two, approaches. Static and dynamic hedging would be the same, and there would be no options markets.

The static approach is simple and does not require continuous trading or the approximations needed to determine the payoff at expiration (because it is contractually guaranteed). So what does dynamic hedging offer and at what cost? The market crash in 1987 is a textbook example of the difference between dynamic replication and the simple purchase of a direct hedge. To quantify the costs, suppose that an investor is pursuing a tail risk hedging strategy that requires either the direct purchase or dynamic replication of a one-year ATM European put option on the S&P500 beginning on December 31, 1986. The hedging mandate expires on December 31, 1987. Let's look at the value of the put option over time using a simple dynamic hedging methodology. Exhibit 6.9 shows the time value of the two approaches.[6]

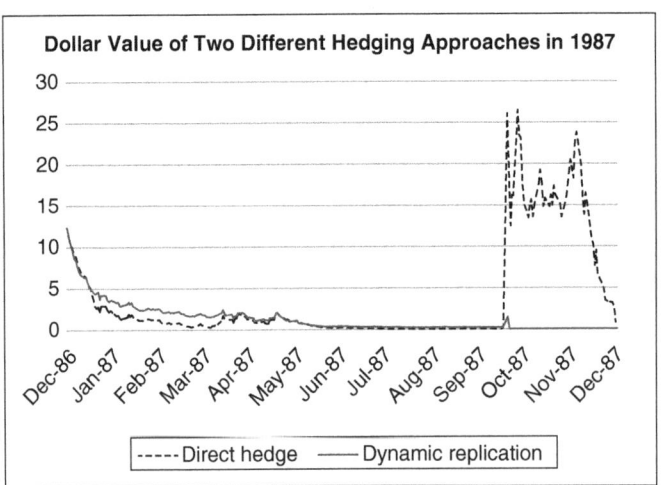

Exhibit 6.9 Comparison of static and dynamic hedging approaches around 1987 crash.

Leading up to Black Monday on October 19, 1987, which corresponded to a daily loss of 22.6 percent, equities had risen significantly, and options became further and further OTM. The dynamic-replication approach outperformed the static hedge as equities moved upward during the year, although both hedging approaches decayed to nearly zero value. At that point, the direct S&P500 hedge, while deeply OTM, became essentially a "lottery ticket" that, while valued near zero, contained a lot of hidden risk from jumps. The dynamic hedge cannot match this convexity profile in a crash.

According to common lore, a reinforcing spiral of falling equity prices forced market participants to liquidate an ever-increasing amount of equities as the put options being replicated got further into the money, requiring increased selling using cash and derivative instruments. This behavior can create momentum in price movements, as I discussed earlier.

The analysis of this 1987 event contains key elements about the two approaches to tail risk hedging. Proponents of dynamic replication often speak to the better "time decay" profile of dynamic hedges relative to static options-based hedges, as evidenced by the outperformance of the dynamic hedge in the early part of that year. Time decay is simply the cost of paying for the hedge now and seeing it bleed as time passes and bad events don't happen. The improved performance of the dynamic hedge in the absence of a tail comes at the cost of worse performance in the presence of a tail, the time when the investor is most concerned about the hedge working correctly. Finally, dynamic trading depends on the existence of many factors that are often absent or at least highly impaired in the presence of a tail. During tail events, bid/ask spread widens as liquidity falls, and market makers themselves are forced to deal with an unstable inventory. A dynamic-hedging approach relies on frequently rebalancing the hedges, and in a range-bound yet highly volatile market such as that in October and November 1987, the dynamic-trading approach requires rebalancing the hedge frequently, which leads to more transaction costs and basis risk between the dynamic portfolio and the target direct option hedge.

In other words, comparing the "pay as you go" dynamic hedge with the "pay now" static hedge, we see that the premium of the static hedge is proportional to the possible inability of the dynamic hedger to hedge in the presence of transaction costs, jumps, and fat tails. None of this is new discovery—the very fact that options markets exists suggests that the buyer of the option gets something that the seller considers valuable over and above the actuarially fair value of the option. But the important point is that it is entirely possible to miscompute the future uncertainty, and the premium that one pays for risk transfer via the options markets is proportional to the error of this forecast. Thus, the cost of paying now should be compared with the uncertain costs of hedging as you go. In an increasingly uncertain world, the error of forecasts is more likely to result in significantly higher future costs from dynamic risk management.

The financial crisis of 2008 is another laboratory for investigating the differences in the two hedging approaches during a time of significant market stress. Exhibit 6.10 documents the value of a 25 percent OTM put option purchased on December 30, 2007, and expiring on December 30, 2008.[7] This example represents the static tail hedging of deeply OTM options that offer a large payoff in a very severe event. The exhibit shows that, again, in a tail event not unlike the one experienced 20 years earlier, the direct option purchased outperformed the dynamic-replication strategy in a tail event. Also similar, leading up to the tail event, the dynamic-replication strategy had been outperforming the direct hedge, showing that the direct hedge offers more convexity and payoff when a tail event hits the market.

Perhaps the riskiest part of dynamic hedging is the potential for the replication to be force liquidated when the overlay strategies themselves are not fully collateralized, and mark-to-market volatility can result in margin calls. In this sense, knowing the potential cumulative premium

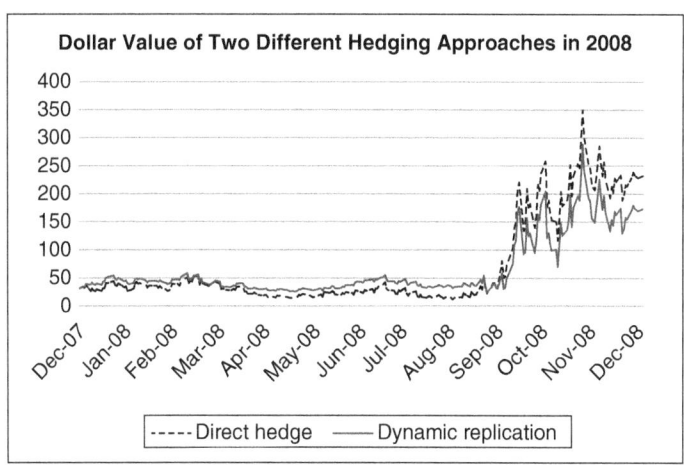

Exhibit 6.10 Comparison of static and dynamic hedging around the fall of 2008.

upfront can prove to be a benefit compared with the cumulative effect of unknown margin requirements.

We said that three things matter in comparing static versus dynamic hedges. Costs are first, and market access and accounting inconsistencies are second and third, respectively. We already identified the theoretical cost difference as a function of unforeseen jump risk and the added transaction costs this incurs. In terms of access, because not everyone has access to the options markets, static hedging using a wide variety of hedges might not be practical for everyone. In addition, many users of hedges have to realize the cost of hedging as an explicit loss today; that is, the way portfolio returns and hedges are accounted for might make it uneconomical to buy options-based static hedges. For both these reasons, we believe that though not perfectly optimal, dynamic hedging is here to stay for some time. But where it is possible to do efficiently, these access and accounting constraints ought to be removed in order to construct superior portfolios.

To summarize, we can think of the distribution of asset returns as composed of two distinct regions. In the middle part of the distribution, asset returns are nicely behaved, and there is ample liquidity to hedge using dynamic mechanisms. In traditional insurance, this is akin to managing a portfolio of automobile insurance policies. The price of insurance per car is low, and the average damage is relatively low and controllable. In this part of the distribution, endogenous means such as diversification and dynamic hedging work. On the other extreme are rare but severe hurricanes and earthquakes. There is really no way to hedge these tails dynamically because one does not know what the form and shape of the tail look like—there simply are very little data. For this part of the distribution, dynamic hedging cannot work because the probability and severity of losses can rise from nothing to a large value without warning. This is why even insurers reinsure. For this part of the distribution, static hedging is possibly the only robust way to manage tail risk.

So pay now for static hedges or pay as you go for dynamic hedges? It depends on what you are trying to hedge and how accurate the forecast of risk in the markets is. My view is to pay as you go for small losses using rebalancing and dynamic hedging, but to combine this strategy with sufficient static hedges on the tails to avoid the possibility of permanent losses from the rare but severe fat tails.

7

A Behavioral Perspective on Tail Risk Hedging

While there is no dearth of idealized analytical approaches to option pricing, no discussion of tail risk hedging can be complete without a discussion of investor behavior and how that behavior influences tail hedging. A behavioral approach necessarily takes us away from the idealized world of dynamically and continuously hedging of option positions, arbitrage, and fundamentally efficient markets that form the foundation of modern option pricing. Nonetheless, the significant structural changes in the behavior of market participants (both for intrinsic risk-management reasons and for extrinsic regulatory reasons) toward tail risk mitigation make it important for option participants to understand the real-world impact of investor behavior on option pricing and portfolio construction.

I will discuss the following main behavioral phenomena that are widely studied in the literature and their impact on tail risk hedging in this chapter:

1. Narrow framing and the proper accounting of hedges in the portfolio context

2. Behavioral explanation of the dynamic variation in the pricing of tail options and the volatility skew
3. Existence of rational multiple-market equilibria in markets with tail hedgers and nonhedgers
4. Time inconsistency in tail-hedging decisions

Narrow Framing and Tail Risk Hedging

In a recent survey, I asked participants the following question:

> Investor A invested 60 percent in equities and 1 percent in tail hedges.
> Investor B invested 50 percent in equities and nothing in tail hedges.
> The equity market rallied 10 percent.
> Investor A's tail hedges expired at 0 value.
> Who was happier?
> Choices:
>   Investor A
>   Investor B
>   No difference

Before I disclose the survey results, I would ask the reader to answer the same question. The question asks who was *happier*, not who was correct. The answer to this question has a deep connection to what perceived benefit tail hedging achieves. We know from experience that investors are acutely sensitive to the difference between an outcome that is unlikely and an outcome that is impossible. Tail risk hedging seeks to convert the unlikely to impossible, and as long as investors are exposed to low-probability events, however unlikely, we should expect that they will think of tail risk hedging strategies as adding value to their portfolios.

In the survey example, the expected (i.e., average) outcomes in the two cases are mathematically exactly the same (5 percent), so the "No difference" choice is clearly an acceptable answer. Note that from a traditional insurance perspective, one could make the argument that investor A was happier because "he could sleep better at night" knowing that he had protection on his portfolio. Equally soundly, we also can make the opposite argument that investor B was happier because he did not have to suffer the regret of "wasting" money on tail hedges that turned out not to be useful.

The answer one gives depends partly on whether or not the tail risk "gamble" is aggregated with the rest of the portfolio in the investor's mind. One could argue that whereas the outcome of an unhedged portfolio is hard to forecast with much accuracy, it is relatively easy to forecast the outcome for the tail hedge because its more binary. The outcome where the hedge would expire worthless is the more normal outcome, and hence its impact is more salient. Because the "loss" on the tail hedge is more accessible and quantifiable, the benefits from the aggregation will be ignored. This is so because the loss on the tail hedges is more salient and quantifiable and thus looms larger in the mind of an investor. A rigorous framework to establish this result uses a modification of the investor's utility function; the new utility function consists of both the utility as a function of total wealth and contributions from individual investments. If the individual investments are overweighted, then even though the contribution of the tail-hedging investments is to increase total utility for the overall portfolio, the individual investment itself will not be made. In other words, the choice to invest in the tail hedge will be evaluated on its own merits, apart from referencing the overall portfolio of which it forms a part. For a detailed discussion of the mathematical approach to utility theory with narrow framing, please see Barberis and Huang (2009).

Intuitively, we note that when a large gain arrives together with a small loss, the gain and loss are generally aggregated or combined. This is in contrast to gains—where we are happier if the gains are disaggregated or separated (receiving many small gifts in individual packages rather than all of them in one package). In my example, one could argue that for investor A, a gain and a loss cancel each other out (even though the magnitude of the final result was a gain), whereas for investor B, the gain, though small, stands out as a gain (nothing cancels it out). Thus, if one aggregates the tail hedges together with the portfolio benefits in the same account, then the cost of tail hedging appears very different from when the tail hedges are "segregated" from the underlying portfolio being hedged. Although we can argue that investors should aggregate and combine all the positions in their portfolios, if they exhibit narrow framing, they will actually evaluate that particular investment separately.

We also can approach the problem from the perspective of how people quantify the probability of rare events as compared with more likely events—called *probability weighting* in the literature. People generally tend to overweight the probability of rare events and underweight the probability of more common events. We could explain investor A's choices, regardless of his loss aversion, based on the realization of a potentially catastrophic event, in which case the tail hedge would protect him but not investor B. Further, if the equity market had a right-tail event that was larger than the 10 percent actually observed, one could see that investor A would have outperformed investor B. We will come back to the discussion of probability weighting more thoroughly in a later section. It has important consequences for the pricing of tail hedges, as well as for the actual behavior of participants in a repeated game of buying tail hedges.

For now, it seems easy to argue the validity of each one of the three positions in the example, and there is no "correct" answer. As the idiom goes, "there is no accounting for taste"; the taste for whether or not to buy hedges against portfolios is not something one can determine simply by doing a pure risk-neutral expected-return calculation. In other words, whereas Black-Scholes might be used as a calculator to translate implied volatility (a parameter) into a price for an option, it says nothing about whether the options so priced are expensive or cheap. The richness or cheapness of options has to be evaluated by applying an approach that can capture the variation in behavior and link the subjective probabilities to objective probabilities.

Thus, despite well-known empirical literature and the belief that, on average, investors pay too much for insurance (as do home owners, automobile owners, etc.), there seems to be no immediate and riskless way to take advantage of a bias for tail insurance even if it did exist. A systematic seller of tail options, the so-called risk-neutral investor, who is completely rational, would be buffeted by the impact of investor behavior on the pricing of options. Unless the investor has an infinite amount of capital and no sensitivity to mark-to-market losses, there would be limits to purely arbitraging out the perceived overvaluation of out of the money (OTM) options. This is clearly borne out in the market for equity index options, where deeply OTM puts have consistently traded at a higher implied volatility (and price) than a deeply OTM call the same distance away from the forward price. Since the 1987 "crash" when this smirk in the equity-volatility surface was discovered, many fortunes have been made and lost by trying to sell the skew as a "riskless" premium-gathering or "arbitrage" strategy. Selling of tail options is eventually exposed to whether or not tail events occur before the expiration of the option. Any strategy that benefits from the selling of the skew will need to know (1) on average how much is the current value of the skew higher or lower than its long-term fair value, (2) is there a reason to expect that historical estimates of what is average will not hold true in the future, and (3) is the structure of the market the same as the one that is used to calibrate the model? These are hard questions that cannot be answered in the risk-neutral framework because they require a calibration of investor behavior, which we know can be notoriously unstable.

Now let us look at the results of the survey. Of more than 250 respondents, almost 50 percent voted for investor A (equities plus tail hedge is happier), 30 percent for investor B (no tail hedge is happier), and 20 percent for answer C (no difference). Some critics suggested that knowing that the author has favored running tail-hedged portfolios, their opinions were swayed toward picking investor A in their response to the survey. Even if true, it is hard to believe that fully 30 percent more picked investor A over investor B based on this "bias," and in a separate blind survey where the author's identity was not revealed, we obtained broadly the same results. More surprisingly, the "economically rational" choice of "No difference" was an overwhelming *minority*, picked by only 20 percent of the respondents. Note that the survey population was investment professionals, so they are aware of and fluent with the concepts of utility functions, loss aversion, and distributions of returns. Again, to be sure, there is no clear and correct answer to the survey, but the consensus that the act of running a tail-hedged portfolio makes an average investor "happier" even in the face of the same returns with less complexity is telling. And it has consequences.

First, it points us in the direction of an alternative explanation of the volatility skew in option prices or the difference in the price of puts versus call options on risky assets. The skew refers to the fact that there are more buyers of downside insurance in the market than buyers of upside insurance (the lore is that markets do not "melt up," but they do "melt down").

The way market makers of options adjust for this has traditionally followed three valuation approaches. In the first approach, the classic Black-Scholes model is used for option pricing, but the volatility input in the model changes as the strike of the option becomes further out of the money. The traditional explanation is that the market maker, who is selling such a low-probability, high-severity option, needs to charge a substantial premium to do so because she is faced with potential catastrophe. The distribution of returns in such an approach, however, is still assumed to be normal, or bell-shaped, one for each strike, corresponding to a different implied volatility. Volatility, which is essentially the standard deviation of prospective return distributions, is sufficient for a complete description of the normal distribution, so this approach can rightly be viewed as compensating for a limitation of the underlying dynamics in the model.

In a more sophisticated approach, jumps in the stock price are introduced, and in an approach going back almost 40 years and pioneered by Merton, the skewness is explained as a function of the number and magnitude of the jumps that essentially results in a mixture of normal distributions (because a mixture of skewless normal distributions can exhibit a skew). The jump-based explanation of the skew is mathematically elegant, but it gives little direct insight into the behavior of participants that determines the shape of the volatility surface. It essentially ascribes the skew to illiquid, noncontinuous dynamics of the underlying processes.[1] In another class of models called *stochastic volatility models* (e.g., the Heston model), the level of the stock market and the volatility are correlated so that as the equity market falls, its volatility rises. By running a regression between the volatility index (VIX) and the Standard and Poor's 500 Index (S&P500), one can empirically observe that for each 1 percent decline in the stock market, volatility as measured by the VIX has risen approximately by 1 point. This class of models is elegant and widely used in practice because the models are intuitive and easy to simulate. They have become reference models for nonconstant volatility, which is needed to explain the skew. Yet again, it does not reference that the skew may exist because of investor behavior.

The three models mentioned so far to explain the skew assume that the true dynamics of the stock market are more complex than a simple normally distributed return distribution with constant volatility, as in Black-Scholes. They also assume that market participants are all completely economically rational and, in the parlance of economists, *risk-neutral*. This, as my survey illustrates, is not a completely fair characterization of actual behavior. What if we turned the approach upside-down and assumed that the dynamics of the market were simple (i.e., driven by the normal distribution) but allowed for the behavioral preferences to influence the pricing of options? We can, of course, make the analysis even more complicated and assume both complex dynamics of the underlying and complex behavior of option market participants, but I will not delve into that complexity in this chapter.

First, we will apply the main behavioral features to outline the pricing of put options, especially those on the tails. Behaviorally, as already previewed, three main concepts influence option pricing and have to be captured in a proper model: *framing, loss-aversion,* and *mental accounting.* For option pricing on the tails, the loss or gain relative to the status quo sets the frame. The important feature of framing is to evaluate outcomes relative to the current status quo, that is, losses and gains relative to the current endowment one possesses. And because different people have different current references, as well as different tolerances for risk, it is no surprise that their responses can be so different from each other. The price ascribed to an option from the perspective of a seller and buyer also can be different depending on who is setting the price and thus whose value function comes into play (I discuss value functions, which form the foundation of behavioral finance, in the sidebar in detail). The memory of the recent financial crisis makes the value of having tail hedges particularly vivid and hence creates a loss-averse value function. Mental accounting basically suggests that people compartmentalize their assets into different mental accounts that are nonfungible—we already previewed this in the section on narrow framing. For example, when purchasing tail risk hedges that enable them to keep or increase their risk to the market, some will account for the loss to the insurance as separate from the gains on the underlying investment account that is being hedged. Others will combine the gains and the losses. Narrow framing is really a form of mental accounting.

Pricing of Put Options on a Standalone Basis

When applied to the pricing of options, behavioral aspects follow Kahneman and Tversky's *cumulative prospect theory* and are quantified in terms of two input functions. The first input is a *value function*, which assigns a subjective value to the outcome and thus identifies the risk-seeking or risk-averse behavior as well as the relative weight assigned to gains versus losses. It is similar to the utility function of classical portfolio theory, but whereas the utility function refers to the total wealth of the investor in various states, the value function refers to the change of wealth from a reference point, that is, gains and losses. By doing so, it captures the reference dependence so central to investor behavior. In particular, investors will only make a gamble if the expected value of the value function increases from its current value. The second ingredient is the *probability weighting function*, which captures subjective probability and maps objective probabilities to subjective probabilities. It captures the empirical fact that rare probabilities are overestimated, whereas the probability of frequent events is underestimated. However, the distortions in probabilities are themselves dynamic and constantly changing and thus provide a lens into the relative cheapness or richness of options on the tails. For instance, immediately prior to the financial crisis, low-probability events were actually underweighted; that is, the probability of a fat-tailed event was underpriced, and tail protection was quite cheap. Once the crisis began, this shifted quickly, and the weighting function rapidly took on a familiar inverse-*S*-shaped structure, where low-probability events were being underweighted (see, e.g., Polkovnichenko and Zhao 2010; Wolff et al. 2009).

As an application of the dynamic nature of the skew, the behavioral component of OTM put options created a relatively large distortion in the pricing of upside versus downside risk. Using risk reversals (sell puts to buy calls), one could have subsequently obtained attractive upside exposure as equity-market substitutes (put strikes, on average, have been two times as far as call strikes for OTM zero-cost risk reversals since the crisis). In addition, this variation in the skew was independent of the movements in volatility, and hence was a separate risk factor.[2]

Let us first focus on the value function in the context of my survey, holding all other variables constant. Applying it to the survey mentioned, in the case of the 20 percent of the respondents who said that there was no difference between investor A's and investor B's perceptions, the value function would be linear and symmetrical, as in Exhibit 7.1.

The 30 percent who selected the "sure thing" or investor B option may have a loss-averse value function, and it looks like the one in Exhibit 7.2. For them, the value of a gain and a loss, added together, was much lower than the value of the sure thing. Their gains are concave, but losses are convex.

Finally, for the majority who preferred investor A (the higher exposure plus tail hedge), the value function may look like the one in Exhibit 7.3 and shows that they value losses as convex, not concave (other value functions are also possible, in particular, ones with more

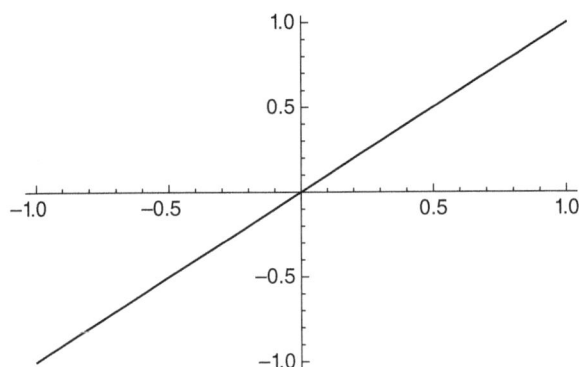

Exhibit 7.1 A risk-neutral value function with losses and gains linear in change of wealth.

A Behavioral Perspective on Tail Risk Hedging

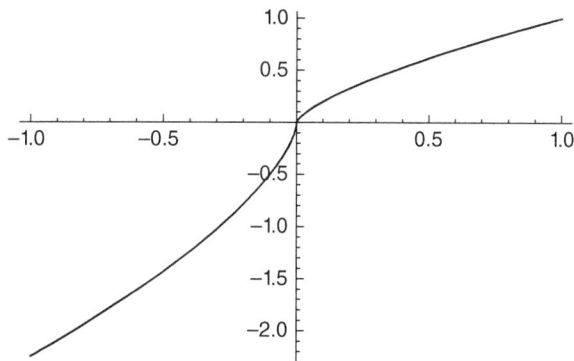

Exhibit 7.2 A loss-averse value function with concave loss function.

risk-loving behavior in the domain of gains). In other words, as losses increase, the investor aversion to further losses increases even more.

Using this value function, we can use the parameters to value the price of options (still assuming that the underlying probability of losses is the same for all investors and has no bias. The mathematics of using behavioral finance for option pricing is detailed in the sidebar to this chapter.)

As an exercise, I priced a one-year 25 percent OTM put on the S&P500 on March 22, 2013 (expiry March 21, 2014), which is a very typical benchmark option for a 60/40 equity/bond portfolio with a

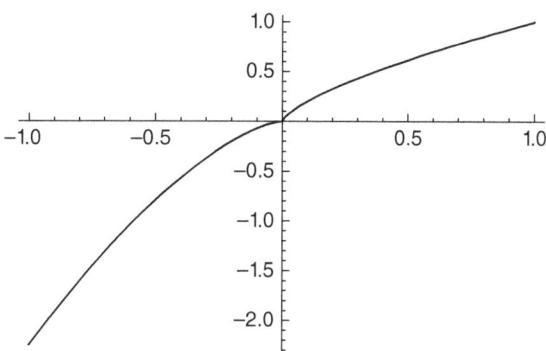

Exhibit 7.3 A loss-averse value function with convex loss function.

15 percent portfolio-level attachment point. The price of the option with the implied volatility of 24.47 percent for the 25 percent OTM strike was approximately 1.46 percent, using Black-Scholes. Note that at the same time, the volatility of the at-the-money (ATM) option was 16 percent, so there was an 8.47 percent additional volatility premium (or volatility skew) from Black-Scholes for the OTM option compared with the ATM option.

Now, instead of assuming a risk-neutral value function, let us assume that the value function is kinked and shows the behavioral form with Kahneman and Tversky's (1992) *cumulative prospect theory* parameters. Holding everything else constant, if we replace $\lambda = 2.25$, $a = 0.88$, and $b = 088$, we find that the price of the 25 percent OTM option almost doubles to 2.77 percent.[3] What if we assume that the value function is risk neutral, but the investor shows probability weighting, that is, overweights low probabilities? We set λ, a, $b = 1$ and $\gamma = 0.65$. Then the price of the option increases more than twofold to 3.10 percent. What if we change both the risk aversion and the probability weighting to the prospect theory parameters? Then the put option price goes up almost fourfold to 6.21 percent. Clearly, behavioral parameters can have a very large influence on the pricing of tail options. And up to this point we have not discussed how we can calibrate these parameters to market observables.

If our interest is in evaluating how the tails are being valued, we can decide to calibrate our model such that the ATM options are equal to the market prices. Denoting the volatility parameter by σ, we basically have five parameters in the behavioral model that we can change, that is, σ, a, b, λ, and γ. Are these enough to fit the whole skew while keeping the ATM option prices matched? Clearly, we should try to keep the volatility (even though it is only a model parameter) σ close to the Black-Scholes volatility because the underlying process for returns is assumed to be geometric Brownian motion, and the volatility should track its realized annualized standard deviation at the money. However, if we assume that put buyers are different from call buyers, we can make the assumption that b is not equal to a to fit the put side of the option market. In other words, we can assume for calibration that the put-option buyer is increasingly risk averse for losses, but in the domain of gains is risk loving. In our example, by doing so, we obtain an ATM put-option price of 7.4 percent with an ATM volatility of 16 percent using Black–Scholes parameters for the behavioral model of λ, γ, a, $b = 1$. Now, if we change the behavioral parameters to the prospect theory parameters $\lambda = 2.25$, $\gamma = 0.65$, and $b = 0.88$ and make the investor risk loving in the domain of gains by using $a = 1.29$, we obtain the same price for the ATM option, showing that the calibration is successful (i.e., 7.4 percent).[4] Next, we can take these parameters (in particular, $\sigma = \sigma$ [ATM]; i.e., the volatility is no longer different for different strikes) and price an OTM option. The 25 percent OTM option with these calibrated behavioral parameters prices to the market price of 1.46 percent, indicating that the behavioral parameters are able to explain the pricing of OTM puts *without* assuming different volatilities for different strikes (*Caveat:* This is only one example and clearly does not guarantee that the whole volatility surface will be priced with such a small number of parameters; in particular, the call options will likely not be priced with the same parameters used to fit the put-option prices). Based on this example, we can see that an alternative explanation of the skew can be constructed by attributing it to a combination of dynamic loss aversion and probability weighting.

Multiple Equilibria and Expected Returns on Tail Hedges

The pricing of OTM options in the context of portfolios adds another important dimension to the analysis. As discussed in the introduction to this chapter, we can explain the market for options by assuming different preferences for sellers and buyers of insurance. If an insurance company is assumed to be risk neutral and a buyer of insurance is assumed to be risk averse, then both can benefit by an insurance transaction at a price that is higher than the actuarially fair price of the insurance. But importantly, we don't have to assume the heterogeneity of market participants to explain the existence of insurance. If we assume that all participants are behavioral (i.e., they invest on the basis of loss aversion, probability weighting, and reference-dependent value functions and with the same aggregate behavioral parameters), then multiple equilibria can exist naturally, and further, there are always some rational investors in this class who will hold tail hedges (and more generally, uncorrelated, highly skewed securities), *even though they know that the expected return on the tail hedges or on the skewed securities is negative*. This conclusion challenges the notion that option buyers are necessarily more risk averse than option sellers, which we simply cannot conclude without reference to the rest of the investor's portfolio.

As shown in work by Barberis and Huang (2008), some investors will prefer the equilibrium in which they are willing to add a positively skewed security such as a put option to their risky portfolio because it improves the skewness of the portfolio. Even though the security has a negative expected return and arbitrageurs will be tempted to sell it to gain arbitrage profits, there are limits to the arbitrage mechanism, and unless the arbitrageur has infinite capital, the overpricing can remain persistent. Note that in their analysis, they did not even have to assume a negative correlation of the skewed security to the underlying portfolio. If this negative correlation is realized, the results that follow are even more powerful and justify a positive premium for the tail hedge (and negative expected return, which is quite rational).

The basic argument is that in an economy in which investors are behaviorally motivated (*prospect-theory investors*), one can obtain multiple market-clearing equilibria; that is, there can be a class of investors that prefers not to hedge, but also a class of investors that is willing to incur a negative expected return on a positively skewed

A Behavioral Perspective on Tail Risk Hedging

security (tail hedge), as long as that security promises a large multiple payoff in a low-probability event.

Here is a mathematical sketch of the argument. Suppose that an investor pays p for a tail hedge on an existing portfolio whose returns are normally distributed with some mean return and volatility. If an adverse event happens, she realizes a payoff of L. Suppose that the probability of this adverse event is q. Now what we want to evaluate is the value to the investor of having this skewed trade/tail hedge in the portfolio. To evaluate this, we have to consider the two states, one in which the hedge pays off and the return is the multiple payoff L/p minus the risk-free return and one in which the hedge does not pay off; that is, the state in which the return is loss of premium paid plus the opportunity loss of not investing the premium in the risk-free investment. With the behavioral-value function and probability-weighting function, the value to the investor can be computed as a function of the allocation to the tail risk hedge by summing over the probability-weighted return distribution as usual. The investor will allocate to the tail hedge if by doing so her value function does not decrease. In Exhibit 7.4 we evaluate this value function as a function of the fraction allocated to the tail

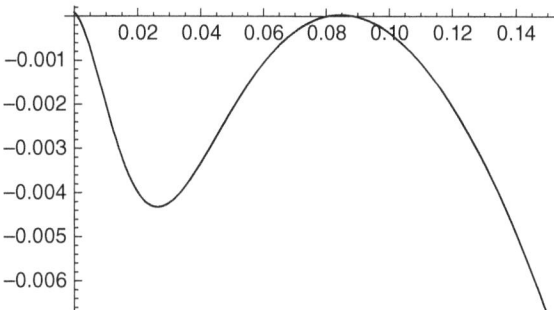

Exhibit 7.4 Value function (vertical axis) versus allocation to positively skewed/tail hedge (horizontal axis) for a 9 percent probability tail event with 10× payoff. *Source:* Author's computations based on Barberis and Huang (2008).

hedge and can see that for a particular choice of parameters, the value function has two equilibria in which it evaluates exactly to zero (which is the neutral point for the investor and hence is the preferred state). The equilibria occur when the allocation to the tail hedge is zero or approximately 8 percent (shown in the exhibit where the behavioral parameters used are the same as the those in Kahneman and Tversky [1992] [$a, b = 0.88, \lambda = 2.25, \gamma = 0.65$] and Barberis and Huang [2008], that is, $\mu = 7.5$ percent, $q = 9$ percent, $p = 0.925$, $L = 10$, $\sigma = 15$ percent).

Using these parameters, it is easy to compute the expected return on the tail hedge ($q \times L/p$ minus the risk-free return), which turns out to be −4.7 percent. What this result demonstrates is that investors are willing to incur a negative return on an investment as long as it improves the skewness of their portfolios. However, the probability of the rare event happening has to be low (so that the probability weighting of rare events can be important), and the potential payoff of the event has to be large.

Another example of this is in Exhibit 7.5. Here we have taken the probability of a tail event to be 5 percent, that is, an even rarer event, and the investor is closer to a risk-neutral investor ($a, b = 0.988, \lambda = 1.25$)

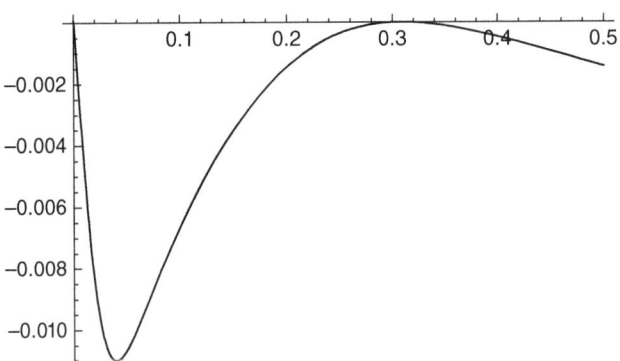

Exhibit 7.5 Value function (vertical axis) versus allocation to positively skewed/tail hedge (horizontal axis) for a 5 percent probability tail event with 9.7× payoff. *Source:* Author's computations based on Barberis and Huang (2008).

but still not completely risk neutral. He overweights tail probabilities ($\gamma = 0.69$). With ($L = 9.72$), we find a solution with two heterogeneous equilibria occuring when investors are either unhedged or allocate 30 percent to the skewed security. Here the expected return on the tail hedge is −52 percent of the premium invested. Clearly, for a very low-probability loss, the investor is rationally willing to incur a substantial premium loss if the payoff in the adverse event is large (while other investors rationally choose not to buy the tail hedges).

Precommitment and Procyclicality

Another behavior we have observed is the time inconsistency of investors in following risk-management rules, which results in procyclical tail risk hedging (buying hedges when they are expensive and running portfolios without hedges when hedges are cheap). I believe that by committing to tail risk hedging as an asset-allocation decision, this procyclicality can be mitigated in ways that are beneficial to the overall portfolio.

The surge in demand for hedging during and after a crisis and the resistance to purchase tail hedges in less volatile periods can be elegantly modeled in terms of a repeated behavioral game. The intuition here is that when faced with a set of unforeseen outcomes, a rational investor will come up with a dynamic hedging (as opposed to static tail hedging) plan that provides positive skewness to her portfolio returns. However, as the situation evolves, the subjective change in probability assessment results in the investor deviating from the plan, unless she is armed with a strategy that precommits her to a particular course of action. As modeled by Barberis (2010), this situation is not dissimilar to a gambler in a casino. Before entering the casino, the gambler with finite capital has a plan to gamble until his cumulative losses hit a particular value, at which point he plans to take his losses and exit the casino. By having this plan, he hopes to truncate his losses while potentially making his gains unlimited. This plan creates a positively skewed distribution of future outcomes and, even in the presence of unfavorable or 50/50 odds, creates the proper conditions for him to enter the casino. However, once he enters the casino, his plans will *rationally* change, and he acts in a manner that actually results in a negatively skewed distribution of outcomes. In other words, his plan allows him to enter the casino, but once he is in, he is more likely to exit when he is winning and keep playing when he is losing. The notable feature of the behavioral model is that it does not require the gambler to be irrational or emotional but only requires him have subjective probability weighting. Intuitively, when he enters the casino, the low probability of a string of wins is overweighted, and this, with his plan to step out if losses reach a threshold, allows him to enter the casino. On the other hand, when he is faced with a history of wins, the 50/50 odds of the next gamble are underweighted, and he chooses to exit. In the same way, when faced with a string of losses, the investor chooses to stay longer than to cut her losses.

To illustrate this in an example, let us assume that a loss-averse investor who overweights tail probabilities is faced with 50/50 objective odds at each round in the casino. Further, in each round, if he wins, he makes 10 units, and if he loses, he loses 10 units. Thus, if he wins five times in a row, he will make 50 units, and if he loses five times in a row, he will lose 50 units (so cumulative −50 payoff). If he wins four times in a row and then loses in the fifth bet, his payoff is 40 minus 10, that is, equal to 30. Now we can compute the average payoff under different assumptions.

If the actual probabilities are one-half at each node, then by following through each node in the tree, we can see that the three positive payoffs (of 50, 30, and 10) cancel with the three negative payoffs (−50, −30, and −10) at the end of five rounds. Thus the expected value is zero. Now suppose that he has had four losses, so the value function is $v(-40)$. At this node, he has a choice to gamble again or exit.

The value function from gambling another round is thus $v(-50)w(1/2) + v(-30)[1 - w(1/2)]$. For $a, \gamma < 1$ (to make the value function loss averse and probability weighted), it is easy to evaluate this value function and see that while both value functions evaluate to negative values, the value of exiting after a loss is more negative than playing another round $[w(1/2) < 1/2]$. In other words, the investor dynamically abandons his plan for attaining a positively skewed outcome when actually losing. Assuming that the investor is aware of his inconsistency when faced with a string of losses, either he can choose to not enter the casino (or take risk) or commit to a precommitment strategy that mitigates any further losses once the loss threshold is breached. Tail risk hedging with explicit options is exactly one such device. By committing premium and contractually outsourcing the risk-management decision, the investor essentially overcomes behavioral uncertainty and makes sure that the rule that is essential to providing him with a positively skewed distribution of returns is actually implemented.

In this chapter I have approached tail risk hedging within a framework where investors evaluate investments with a behavioral framework. We first observed that as a consequence of narrow framing, where tail hedges are evaluated separately from the rest of the portfolio, the overall benefit of tail hedging at the portfolio level can be overlooked if the negative drag from tail hedging is evaluated myopically. We also observed that the option skew, that is, the perceived overpricing of deeply OTM puts, can be explained in the context of a simple behavioral option pricing model and why such a skew can be persistent in the market as long as behavior is persistent. This risk-neutral pricing of the skew and claims of risk-free profit from skew selling should be evaluated more deeply with tools that can quantify variations in investor behavior and sentiment. In particular, both loss aversion and subjective weighting of low probabilities can justify the "overpricing" of OTM put options. We also see that in the context of a portfolio, skewness preference naturally can lead an investor to include tail hedges in her portfolio despite the fact that such tail hedges have negative expected returns. This fact rationally explains why it is important to think of tail hedging in the context of the full portfolio rather than on a stand-alone basis. Further, we see that we can obtain market equilibria where some investors choose to have tail hedges and others choose to run their portfolios naked, and both can be rational. We finally discussed how tail hedging can be justified as a precommitment device against the abandonment of an investment plan that is designed to deliver positively skewed returns. In doing so, tail hedging overcomes "time inconsistency" in investor behavior.

In many ways tail-selling and tail-hedging behavior can be compared with the economics of the natural catastrophe insurance and reinsurance business. The insurance company makes positive expected returns from selling a risk-managed basket of insurance policies. Further, the insurance company diversifies its risks by having, usually, multiple lines of business. Finally, the insurance company reinsures by purchasing direct reinsurance or engaging in the securitization of the catastrophic rare risks that can wipe it out. Management of the portfolio of risks allows it to have a robust business model that it can lean on over multiple insurance market cycles. On the other side of the transaction is the risk-averse buyer of insurance. The fact that the risk-averse buyer of insurance is willing to pay premium and hope for the premium to expire worthless shows that the value of the insurance to the buyer of insurance is higher than the actuarially fair or risk-neutral value to the insurance seller. The fact that the buyer of home insurance does so in order to to stay in the home; that is, he evaluates his portfolio (home plus insurance) rather than the insurance on a standalone basis. The deductible (similar to the attachment level) paid by the insured to the insurance company minimizes moral hazard and speculation on insurance. In this chapter we did not discuss the tendency for insurance purchasers to pay excessively for low-deductible policies that has been documented in the empirical literature. However, it is easy to see that while closer to ATM options can be dynamically hedged and hence their premium might be higher than the actuarial cost of hedging, the relative inability of hedging of tail options using dynamic strategies might make tail options cheaper in the real world. We also know empirically that the value of insurance undergoes a demand surge in the aftermath of a crisis. For example, after the tragic hurricanes in the Atlantic, the pricing of insurance increased multifold, even though the objective probabilities of similar severity items did not increase. In the case of the financial crisis, the pricing of insurance as reflected in the equity-market option skew, pricing of credit-default swap protection, and volatility across all markets structurally rose, and only the explicit and implicit underwriting of downside protection by global central banks has resulted in the slow reversion of the price of protection to precrisis levels. In an environment where central bank reinsurance is likely to be tapered off, investors should take a hard look at the valuation of tail hedges in the context of their overall risk-management objectives at the portfolio level and the pros and cons of tail hedging versus a potentially time-inconsistent dynamic risk-balancing approach.

Put Option Valuation with Cumulative Prospect Theory

The value of a prospective bet (known as a *prospect* in the language of Kahneman and Tversky [1979]) is

$$V = \sum \pi v(x)$$

where x is the monetary value of the outcome, v is a value function that assigns values to the outcome (i.e., whether we like them or not), and π is the probability function that maps objective probabilities into subjective probabilities.

To make this concrete, use a probability-weighting function of Kahneman and Tversky, where γ controls the overweighting and underweighting of small and large probabilities, and p is the cumulative probability. That is,

$$w(p) = p^\gamma / \left[p^\gamma + (1-p)^\gamma \right]^{1/\gamma}$$

Exhibit 7.6 shows the function for different values of the parameter γ as p varies from 0 to 1. The most curved line is for $\gamma = 0.5$, and the straight line is for $\gamma = 1$.

Similarly, the value function determines how outcomes are interpreted relative to the current state, that is, how gains and losses are interpreted. A standard assumption is to use a value function for gains that is, $v^+(x) = x^a$ and for losses that is $v^-(x) = -\lambda(-x)^b$. Exhibit 7.7 plots this value function for $a = 0.7$, $b = 0.65$, and $\lambda = 2.25$.

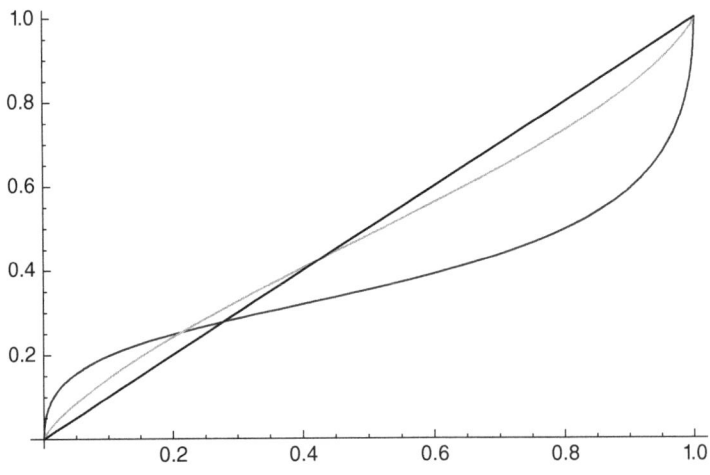

Exhibit 7.6 Probability-weighting function. The horizontal axis shows objective probabilities. The vertical axis shows the subjective probabilities as a consequence of probability weighting for different values of the parameter γ.

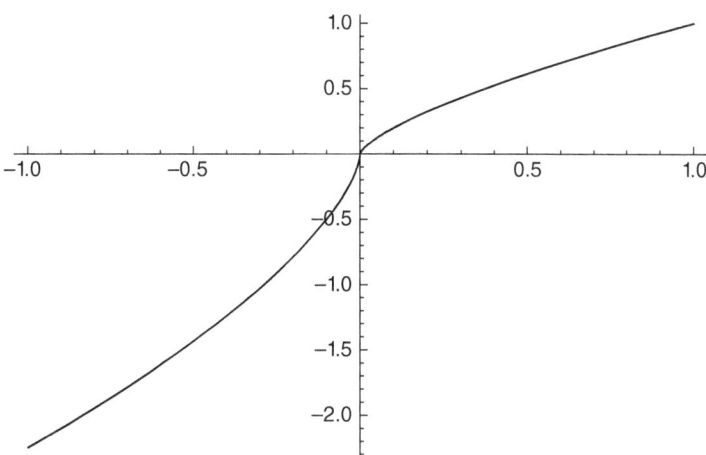

Exhibit 7.7 Value function. The horizontal axis shows gains and losses. The vertical axis shows the value ascribed by an investor to these gains and losses. The gains and losses are relative to a current endowment with a value function of zero as reference.

Finally, we assume here that the underlying market follows a geometric Brownian motion like Black-Scholes (so the dynamics of the market are not changed), with the density for the stock price

$$f(S_T) = \frac{1}{S_T \sigma \sqrt{2\pi T}} e^{-(1/2\sigma^2 T)[\ln(S_T/S_0) - (\mu - \sigma^2/2)T]^2}$$

With its cumulative distribution function

$$F(S_T) = \Phi\left[\frac{\ln(S_T/S_0) - (\mu - \sigma^2/2)T}{\sigma\sqrt{T}}\right]$$

where $\Phi(x)$ is the standard normal cumulative distribution function. To evaluate the option price by integration, we also need to derive the derivative of the weighting function (because they are specified as cumulative probabilities above):

$$\Psi = \frac{dw(p)}{dp}$$

Now, following Wolff (2010), we can derive the continuous time value of a put option in terms of the value function and the density as (here Ψ^- corresponds to the derivative of the weighting function for losses)

$$p_s = e^{-rT} (\lambda \int_0^K \Psi^-\left[F(S_T)\right] f\left[(S_T)(K-S_T)^b dS_T\right]^{1/a}$$

Below I show the *Mathematica* code to evaluate this option price by numerical integration:

```
PutTK[K_,μ_,σ_,T_,γ_,λ_,a_,b_,r_]:=Module[{S,price,S0},
  S0=100;
  f[S_]:=(1/(Sσ Sqrt[2PiT]))*Exp[-(Log[S/S0]-((r-μ)-
  (σ^2/2))T)^2/(2σ^2T)];
  F[S_]:=CDF[NormalDistribution[0,1],(Log[S/S0]-
  ((r-μ)- σ^2/2)T)/(σ Sqrt[T])];
  PsiTK[p_]:=γp^(γ-1) (p^γ+(1-p)^γ)^(-1/γ)-p^γ*
  (p^(γ-1)-(1-p)^(γ-1))*(p^γ+(1-p)^γ)^(-(γ+1)/γ);
  Price=Exp[-r*T]*(λ*NIntegrate[PsiTK[F[S]]*f[S]*
  (K-S)^b,{S,0,K}])^(1/a)
]
```

Note that we can obtain the simple Black-Scholes model by setting $a=1, b=1, \lambda=1$, and $\gamma=1$. For the classic Kahneman-Tversky parameters of $a = b = 0.88$, $\lambda = 2.25$, and $\gamma = 0.65$, we obtain a price of 2.88 percent (we assume that the stock volatility is 20 percent) for a one-year 75 percent strike option. This is more than five times the price of a Black-Scholes option of 0.52 percent.

8

Tail Risk Hedging for Retirement Investments

We really only get one chance to save for retirement. An immediate consequence of this observation is that we cannot simply allocate our retirement dollars to the "market" and hope to have a safe nest egg when we are ready to retire. Averages over all possible outcomes might be interesting for research and analysis, but the reality is that markets take one path, so the law of large numbers is no insurance against market crises.

The impact of a bad market, however short and episodic, can be substantial and permanent. To manage against a knockout punch that can force us to change expectations of our standard of living after retirement, we need to look at the whole path taken by our investment portfolio and keep risks tightly controlled. In this chapter I describe some facts and methods that may be useful for protecting our retirement portfolios.

The first thing to note is that long-term investors generally don't care about volatility if the volatility comes with a promise of ultimately higher gains. What retirees do care about is sharp falls in their portfolio value. These *drawdowns* not only can alter prospects for future savings but also can force us into making irrational decisions at the wrong time—thus crystallizing losses and making them permanent. Protecting against such drawdowns is what a good risk-management paradigm should be designed for. Anecdotally, the financial crisis demonstrated that more risk-averse investors, usually those with a shorter horizon before retirement, indeed illustrated a behavioral bias toward liquidating their portfolio holdings when the equity markets swooned. This resulted in a locking in of losses that the subsequent recovery in the markets was not able to remedy.

First, I make clear the distinction between two types of drawdowns. As typically used, the term *drawdown* is defined as the percentage change in the value of an investment from a newly established high or *peak* to a subsequent low or *trough*. The maximum value of the peak-to-trough drawdown influences how we *feel* about the sudden loss in wealth. Slightly different is the *maximum value* of the loss from its initial value. This measures the economic loss of wealth.

Higher volatility translates both into higher drawdowns and higher potential loss of economic wealth. Because we do not know with certainty when and of what magnitude the drawdowns will be, I will focus attention on the worst case, that is, on the characteristics of expected maximum drawdowns. Fortunately, this area of risk management has been studied recently in much detail (see, e.g., Burghardt et al. 2012).

Some notable features of maximum drawdowns that are relevant to a future retiree include the following:

1. In terms of relative importance of various moments of the return probability distribution, expected maximum drawdown depends primarily on volatility and then on expected returns. Skewness and kurtosis matter less compared with the impact of volatility. Doubling volatility will more than double drawdowns. In the language of risk factors that we use for our asset-allocation approach, a higher equity

Tail Risk Hedging for Retirement Investments

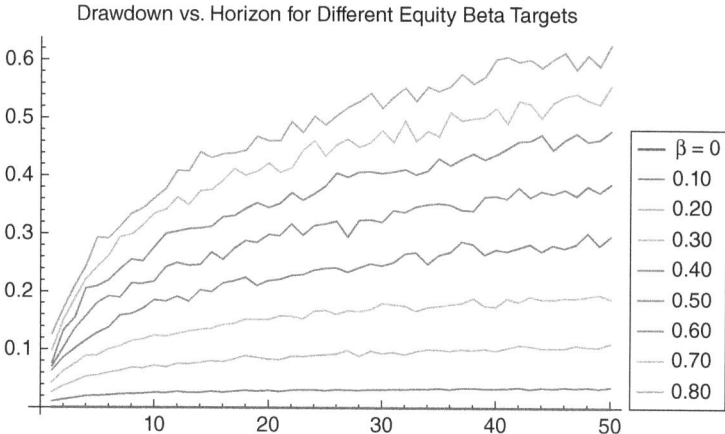

Exhibit 8.1 Maximum drawdown (*vertical axis*) versus horizon (*horizontal axis*) for different equity beta targets. *Source:* Author's computations.

beta translates into higher portfolio volatility and hence to higher expected maximum drawdowns. Exhibit 8.1 shows how increasing the beta increases the potential maximum drawdown[1].

2. Increasing returns or decreasing volatility both decrease maximum drawdowns, but the increase in returns has to be more than twice as much as the increase in volatility to keep the drawdown the same. In particular, increasing volatility and returns at the same time will keep the Sharpe ratio constant but will increase the maximum drawdown. Thus the often-used Sharpe ratio is simply not a good metric for deciding on what investments to pick for retirement—volatility matters via its impact on the potential for large losses. Exhibit 8.2 shows the nonlinear dependence of the volatility-normalized maximum drawdown on the volatility-normalized Sharpe ratio for the same value of returns as the volatility changes (I keep the returns constant at 2 percent per year in this example). For all horizons, this relationship is nonlinear, and the longer the horizon, the higher

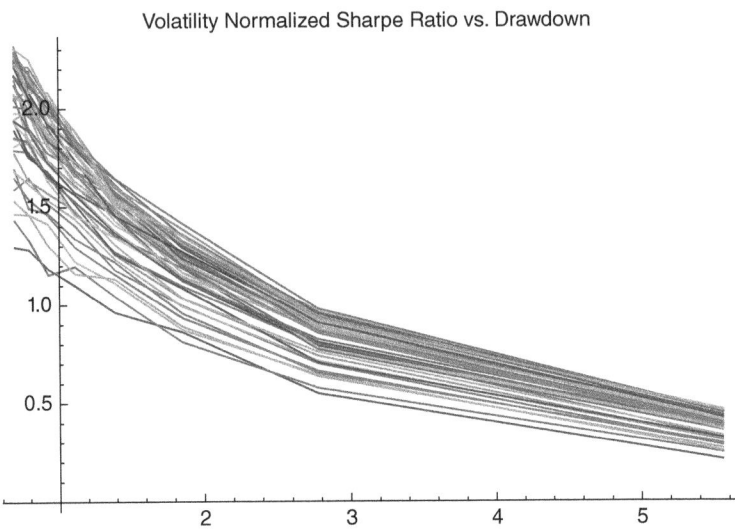

Exhibit 8.2 Volatility-normalized maximum drawdown (*vertical axis*) versus volatility-normalized sharpe ratio (*horizontal axis*) for retirement horizons from 5 to 50 years going from bottom to top line.

is the normalized maximum drawdown for the same normalized Sharpe ratio.

3. Increasing the horizon will increase the expected maximum drawdown and depends very strongly and in a discontinuous manner on whether the expected returns are positive, negative, or zero (see Magdon-Ismail and Atiya 2005). Further, the behavior is qualitatively different for the different signs of the expected return for long horizons that are relevant for retirees.

   a. If the expected return is positive, then the increase in horizon will increase drawdowns logarithmically with time (i.e., very slowly). As volatility doubles, the expected maximum drawdown grows four times as much. As returns double, the expected maximum drawdown halves.

b. If the expected return is zero, then the increase in horizon will increase drawdowns as the square root of time. The famous 1.25 times the volatility rule (see Magdon-Ismail et al.) here suggests that the expected maximum drawdown scales as one and a quarter times the volatility.

c. If the expected return is negative, then the increase in horizon will increase drawdowns linearly (i.e., very rapidly). The scaling of the expected maximum drawdown is largely immune to volatility and increases linearly with falling expected returns.

Note particularly that as expectations of returns fall, the expected maximum drawdown rises quickly and results in catastrophic risk of ruin. In particular, if returns are zero or negative, the possibility of an investor losing over half of his or her investment over the not very far out horizon is a very high-likelihood event. The benefit of high returns in equity markets have been a tailwind resulting in lower drawdowns. However, if returns were to falter, we would need to exercise a high degree of caution to hedge against drawdowns such as the ones experienced in 2008 (see Exhibit 8.3).

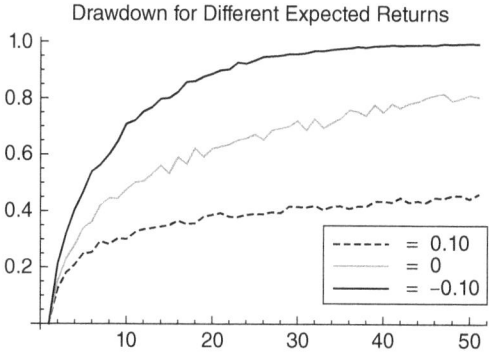

Exhibit 8.3 Maximum drawdown (*vertical axis*) versus horizon (*horizontal axis*) for different expectations of returns.

Having a longer horizon makes the portfolio risk-management problem for a younger retiree more complex than for an older investor close to retirement. The younger investor has to take more risk to save enough and also has a larger length of time in which to recover from losses. However, taking more risk means a higher chance of larger drawdowns. Let's make this concrete. Suppose that we expect returns to be flat over the next few years. Then expected maximum drawdowns for a 20-year-old with 50 years to retirement will be more than twice that for a 60-year-old with 10 years to retirement (square root of 50/10 = square root of 5). But the 20-year-old will have the ability to withstand the drawdown because (1) she has more time to save, and (2) she can expect periods during which she can improve her returns above zero. But her need to manage the downside still exists. So how should she do this in a disciplined manner?

Typical investment portfolios, in my experience, suffer from too much asset-class diversification and not enough risk diversification. In a cosmetically diversified asset mix it is very hard to tell what the potential for drawdowns in the portfolio is because you cannot easily decipher the risks of such a portfolio. However, by using the coarser lens of risk-factor exposures, this exercise becomes somewhat simpler. For instance, we can aggregate the equity beta of all types of assets in a portfolio and change the beta of the portfolio as desired to target a particular risk level. Thus, as a practical tool, I recommend that investors look at the composition of their investments using risk factors. But simply knowing the risks is not enough. We have to control against permanent damage from that risk.

So a relevant question is: How much should we be willing to pay for the option to protect against a particular drawdown for a given horizon? This "budget" for hedging changes with two key variables. First, as the beta rises, the amount of premium spent implicitly (e.g., by keeping excess cash reserves) or explicitly (e.g., by buying put options) rises. Also, as the proximity of the threshold comes closer to the current value of the portfolio, the budget rises. Thus, whereas for a 0.20 beta equity portfolio a 5 percent attachment level would cost 31 basis points (bp) of premium per year (typical of a shorter-dated retirement fund), the same attachment level for a 0.50 beta portfolio would cost almost eight times as much (2.6 percent).[2] On the other hand, if we take the attachment level to 15 percent, the hedge cost of the 0.50 beta portfolio drops back down to 30 bp. Exhibit 8.4 shows the relationship of cost to the horizon of the strategy for different betas. In these examples I have kept the volatility of the equity factor fixed at 18 percent per annum, which is close to the observed volatility over the last 80 or so years. As volatility rise and falls, the price of tail risk protection also rises and falls.

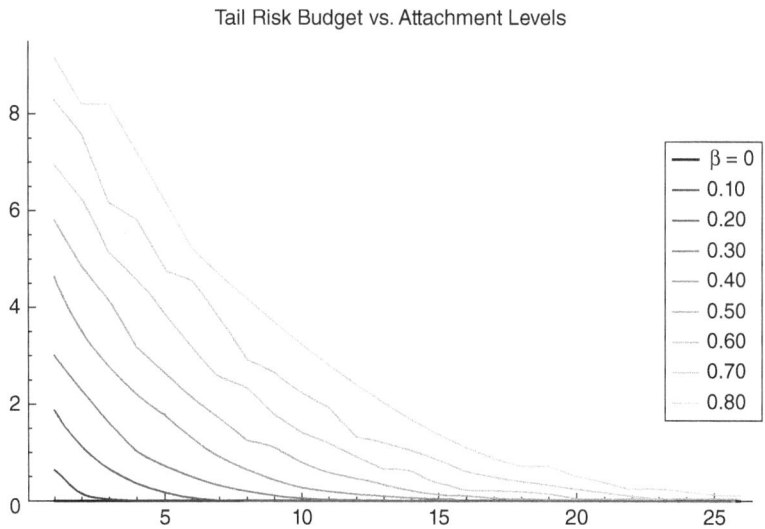

Exhibit 8.4 Tail risk budget vs. attachment level for different amounts of equity beta. The attachment levels are on the horizontal axis in percent.

If we think of this essential tradeoff between hedge cost and beta, we see that for shorter-dated retirement funds, there is very little time to make up for sharp drawdowns. Hence most of the tail hedging has to be done both via defensive positioning and via explicit tail hedges. On the other hand, if the portfolio has a long horizon, we can afford to take more risk via higher equity beta and can simultaneously move the attachment level further out to keep the cost of insuring against tail events relatively low.

As this discussion shows, tail risk hedging of retirement funds has some very interesting and important characteristics because of the interplay among risk aversion, horizon, and the dynamics of markets over long periods of time. All that I have written about in reference to tail hedging for asset allocation in this book still holds true, such as the need for active management, its role as an offensive risk-management tool, and its role in mitigating downside risks. However, the introduction of time to retirement and variables risk tolerance as new variables makes the exercise even more complex and fruitful.

Simulating Drawdowns

Calculating Maximum Drawdown and Expected Maximum Drawdown.

A drawdown is the measure of decline from some peak in the value of an asset. If $X(t)$ is a random process, then the drawdown $D(T)$ at any time is defined as

$$D(T) = \max[0, \max X(t) - X(T)], \ t \, \varepsilon \, (0, T)$$

The maximum drawdown up to time $\text{MDD}(T)$ is defined as

$$\text{MDD}(T) = \max[\max X(t) - X(\tau)], \ \tau \, \varepsilon \, (0, T)$$

When the underlying asset is normally distributed, Magdon-Ismail and Atiya (2004) show that for a positive drift, the maximum drawdown is logarithmic with time; for drift zero, the maximum drawdown grows like the square root of time; and for drift less than zero, it grows linearly with time.

To compute the maximum drawdown of a time series of unit values (asset prices) in Excel, follow this recipe (assuming date is in cells B2 to B500):

1. Compute a column of drawdowns from the maximum return; that is, put in each row =1-B2/MAX($B$2:B2).
2. Copy this formula down (so that in cell C99 you have the formula =1-B99/MAX($B$2:B99)).
3. Take the MAX of the whole column to get the maximum drawdown.

Generating Paths and Visualizing Drawdowns and Option Payoffs

This piece of *Mathematica* code generates sample paths from a normal distribution and computes drawdowns.

```
mu=0.05;sigma=0.20;S0=100;
numsteps=365;
horizon=1; (* in years *)
deltat=horizon/numsteps;
attachment=0.15; (* say a 15 percent attachment
level *)
incr=Table[Exp[(mu-sigma^2/2)*deltat+sigma*Sqrt[de
ltat]*Random[NormalDistribution[0,1]]],{i,1,numst
eps}];
path=FoldList[Times,S0,incr];
ListPlot[path,PlotJoined->True]
```

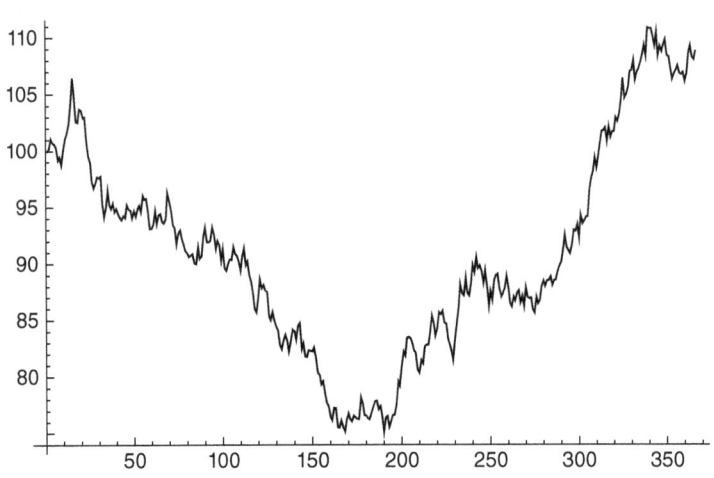

```
runningmax=Drop[FoldList[Max,path[[1]],path],1];
ListPlot[runningmax, PlotJoined->True]
```

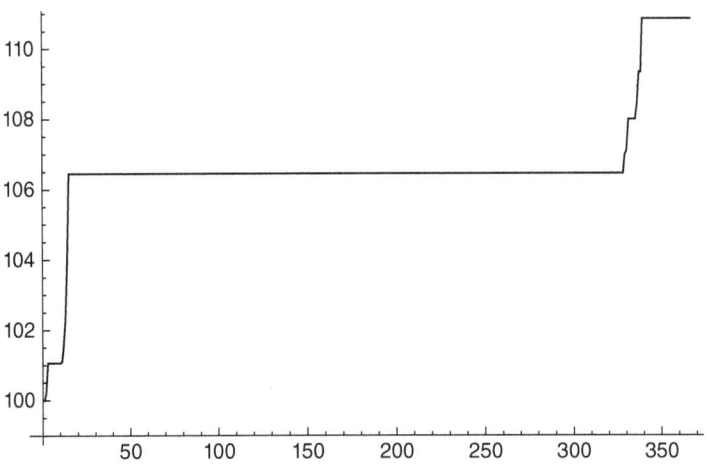

Now show the drawdown:

```
drawdown=runningmax-path;
```

And plot it:

```
ListPlot[drawdown,PlotJoined->True]
```

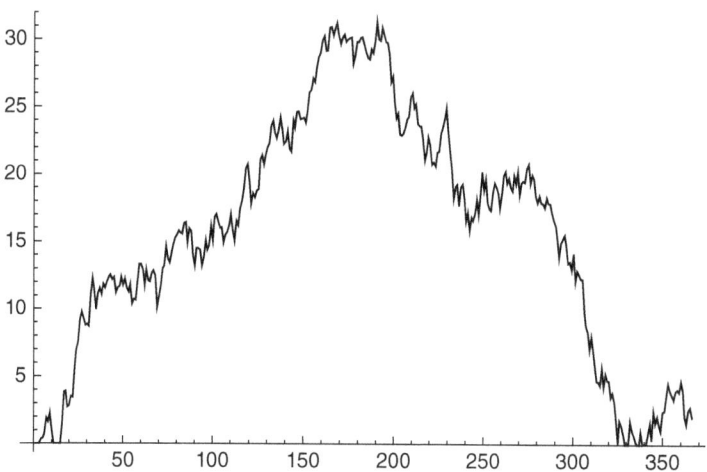

Plot drawdown in percentage terms:

```
relativedrawdown=Table[(runningmax[[i]]-path[[i]])/
runningmax[[i]],{i,1,Length[drawdown]}];
ListPlot[relativedrawdown,PlotJoined->True]
```

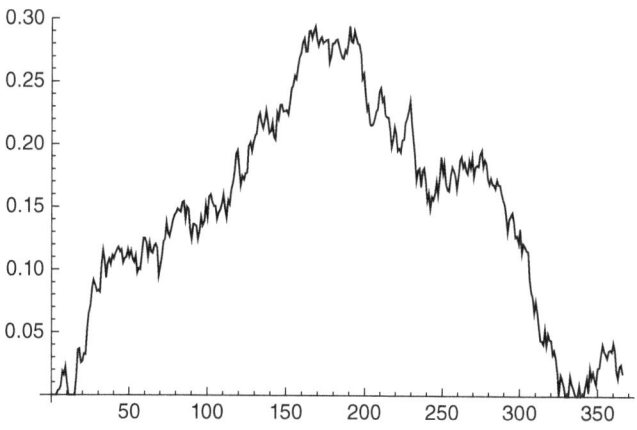

Now compute the payoff to a put on the drawdown:

```
ddpayoff=relativedrawdown-attachment;
ListPlot[ddpayoff,PlotJoined->True]
```

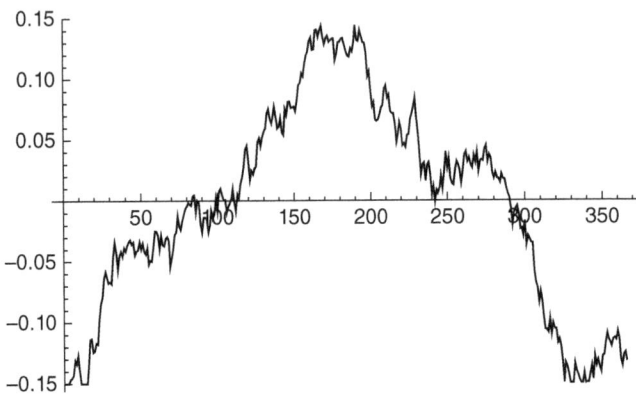

```
ddpayoffseq=Map[f,ddpayoff];
ListPlot[ddpayoffseq,PlotJoined->True]
```

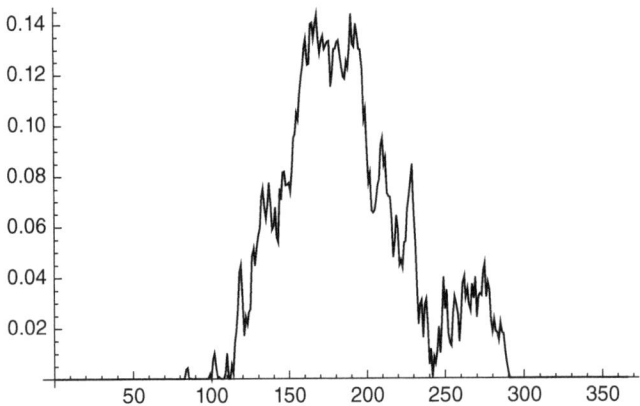

```
ListPlot[{path,runningmax,relativedrawdown,ddpayoff
seq},PlotJoined->True]
```

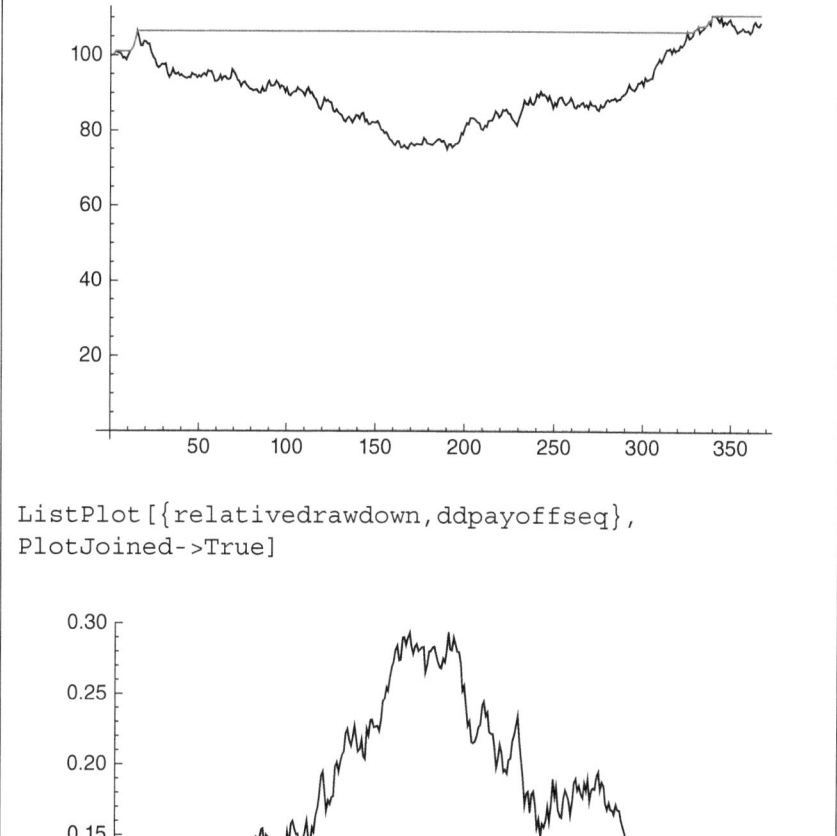

```
ListPlot[{relativedrawdown, ddpayoffseq},
 PlotJoined->True]
```

9

Inflation and Duration Tail Risk Hedging

In the aftermath of the 2008 crisis, the term *tail risk hedging* has entered the vernacular of financial market participants with a speed and intensity unmatched by any other market concept in recent memory. However, this concept so far has largely been limited to the hedging of risks related to rapid declines in equity-related markets. Policy makers are well aware of these equity-market-related risks, which from a macro perspective are associated with a deflationary fat tail and have flooded the markets with unprecedented amounts of liquidity via low interest rates, an increasing quantity of money, and outright asset purchases. These extreme measures, by most metrics, have resulted in a historically unprecedented set of market conditions and raises the question of whether there are other risk factors "under our noses" whose tail risks now need to be anticipated and managed proactively.

Indeed, both theoretically and empirically, there are reasons to believe that in addition to the equity risk factor, the duration risk factor, or sensitivity to interest rates, is the second key variable that drives investment risks over long horizons. This is economically sensible because growth largely drives the returns of equity markets, and inflation largely determines the returns to credit-risk-free fixed-income instruments. Clearly, equity-market risk is more volatile and has a higher frequency than inflation risk, and hedging techniques have to be adapted appropriately to the inherent difference in the nature of the risk factors. Even though I believe that whereas the last five years may have made it possible for us to ignore the tail risks arising from the rise in interest rates (given the tail wind of central bank liquidity injections of various sorts and low realized and expected inflation and low interest rates), continuing with this assumption may no longer be very safe.

First, because global central banks around the world are injecting unprecedented amounts of liquidity into the financial markets to boost asset prices and raise inflation expectations, expecting inflation to remain subdued for a very long period of time seems to be a biased bet. Other than the direct influence of a ballooning money supply, the demand for food and energy globally, not the least from newly emerging nations, could result in consequential inflation spikes not unlike those witnessed in the early 1970s. The direct purchase of mortgages by the Federal Reserve has resulted in a lowering of mortgage interest costs that plays an important role in the computation of the inflation index such as the U.S. Consumer Price Index (CPI). A rise in these mortgage rates can result in a substantial percentage rise in the CPI because the cost of servicing the loans flows directly into the inflation indices. Indeed, in today's low-inflation environment, these events seem much too remote and unlikely in terms of both probabilities and potential severities, but so did the possibility of a rapid credit-market widening prior to the 2008 crisis.

Second, rising inflation can affect not only fixed-income assets, which occurs directly as yields and prices move inversely to each other, but also the prospective returns of all risky assets. This occurs conceptually because most risky assets derive a significant part of their value from the discounting of future cash flows, and the discount factor used for the present-value computation is driven mostly by the path of policy rates, inflation expectations, and inflation risk premium. There are hidden options in many markets that also can get activated by a rise in interest rates. For instance, the municipal bond market has seen a large amount of issuance in recent years at low yields. Given how taxation of municipals is treated (see Ang, Bhansali, and Xing 2008), many of these bonds are adversely affected if yields were to rise suddenly.

Finally, even without actual inflation rising, the rise of inflation uncertainty can result in rising inflation risk premiums (there is plenty of empirical evidence and theoretical basis to justify that high levels of inflation will be correlated with high inflation volatility, which is the primary driver of inflation risk premia), and thus result in adverse performance of inflation-sensitive assets. This variability, while currently low, can have an amplification effect on the impact of rising inflation and inflation expectations as and when they occur.

Whereas the impact of rising inflation on liabilities is well understood and managed, the impact on the pricing of asset portfolios is equally relevant for inflation tail risk management. For the purpose of this chapter, I do not fixate on predicting which part of portfolios inflation is going to have a larger impact on. I believe that the tail risks on the total value of portfolio assets and liabilities and the techniques described here can be practically useful for both aspects.

Hedging at the Money Inflation versus Inflation Tails

Before diving into the details of inflation tail hedging, I would like to clarify some important issues that have an impact on implementation. First, when one thinks of inflation hedging, it is important to distinguish between hedging of inflation risks that are closer to current levels and expected and large, unanticipated inflation spikes. Because asset markets discount expected inflation fairly efficiently, an approach that uses asset-allocation techniques efficiently is best suited for small and expected deviations from current inflation. Below I discuss how to find and scale allocations to such assets.

Second, for hedging purposes, it is not sufficient to find assets that have exhibited anecdotal contemporaneous positive correlations with inflation in particular episodes because many of these correlation relationships are horizon and period-sensitive. For the hedge to be robust, it is critically important that the cumulative returns over a period of time on the hedging instruments are positively correlated with the factors that drive the cumulative increase in inflation. Because most assets exhibit a much higher volatility than the inflation rate over short periods of time, the efficacy of short-term correlations (or betas) for hedging becomes questionable if one relies too heavily on simplistic anecdotal and episodic correlation analysis.

Third, we should be prepared for the same assets to exhibit different hedging behavior as a function of the time horizon. For instance, there is a large amount of academic and practitioner literature that discusses the weak hedging nature of equities against inflation over short horizons but a more reliable hedging relationship over a longer horizon. Rather than have this change of inflation hedging potency become a detractor, we should think of this horizon-dependent variability as an essential ingredient in the construction of actively managed portfolios that are robust over a variety of hedging horizons.

To illustrate these issues specifically, assume that the current inflation rate (e.g., as measured by the CPI) is 2.5 percent. I believe that dynamic asset allocation should be the first line of defense in controlling against the initial and persistent rise in inflation, say, for instance, for a range of 2.5 to 4 percent. This can be implemented by shifting the allocation to inflation-sensitive assets. For example, it is well established that outright long positions in traditional asset classes such as stocks and nominal bonds, in aggregate, deliver lackluster nominal returns under inflationary scenarios over short horizons (particular combinations, such as yield-curve steepeners, implemented by going short longer-dated bonds while hedging the duration risk with shorter-dated bonds, allow one to benefit from rising inflation expectations). To be clear, outright long positions in equities show a mixed sensitivity to inflation as the horizon changes. Whereas in the short term rising inflation risk premia (which accompany rising inflation) lead to an inverse relationship of equity returns and inflation, over longer horizons, high earnings yield (accompanied by high interest rates) may lead to positive correlations between inflation and equity expected returns. Alternative asset classes, such as treasury inflation protected securities (TIPS), gold, commodities, real estate investment trusts (REITs), certain foreign currencies, timber, intellectual property, farmland, and long-short baskets of inflation-sensitive equities are other examples that can be used to create more robust portfolio mixes against moderate persistent rises in inflation. Of course, for practical implementation, we would need to estimate the potential transaction costs of switching from traditional assets to these alternatives, and liquidity concerns might prohibit the use of many of the less liquid categories.

In contrast, and importantly so, when we talk about inflation spikes or tails, the dynamic asset-allocation approach to managing inflation needs to be complemented with more convex inflation-hedging strategies. There are three main reasons for this. First, as mentioned earlier, large inflation shocks can result in larger unanticipated movements in asset prices. The linear instruments mentioned earlier cannot capture the convexity inherent in market responses to inflation spikes. This issue is especially important when initial inflation and inflation expectations are at very low levels. Second, hedging against inflation spikes by rebalancing alone would require a much higher than normal allocation to inflation-sensitive assets in the steady state. Because this portfolio rebalance has an implicit cost (in terms of lower nominal yields from underweighting nominal bonds, for example), the cost of a static inflation-sensitive portfolio using asset allocation alone would be a permanent drag if inflation spikes are not realized or inflation is not persistent. Inflation spikes are, by definition, low-probability events; thus the expected implicit cost of insurance from asset allocation should be compared with the potential benefits. Finally, and this follows from both the inherent instability of correlations of assets to inflation and the trouble with forecasting inflation with accuracy, if instead of inflation rising we actually realize deflation, a static asset-allocation approach would prove to create large portfolio underperformance or at least additional tracking error.

For these reasons, if the object of hedging is to control against inflation tail risks, I believe that a powerful approach is to directly use an extension of the framework I have developed for equity/risky-asset/deflationary-scenario tail risk hedging that commits a finite amount of hedge "premium" to potentially inflation-sensitive derivatives. This approach relies heavily on applying an option theoretic framework to hedging inflation risk. To achieve these objectives in practice, the framework relies on both linear and nonlinear option-like instruments across multiple asset classes. Surprisingly, volatility across macroeconomic markets has been driven to historic lows on the back of the supply of central bank liquidity and creates the opportunity, albeit short-lived, to hold assets and hedge them too. Thus, in my view, today's macroeconomic environment creates an attractive set of conditions for implementing inflation tail hedging relatively inexpensively.

Tail-Hedging Realized Inflation versus Inflation Expectations

The simplest metric for inflation risk is the percentage gain or loss on a price index. In the United States, the CPI (Exhibit 9.1) is such a metric (the Fed's preferred metric is the personal consumption expenditure

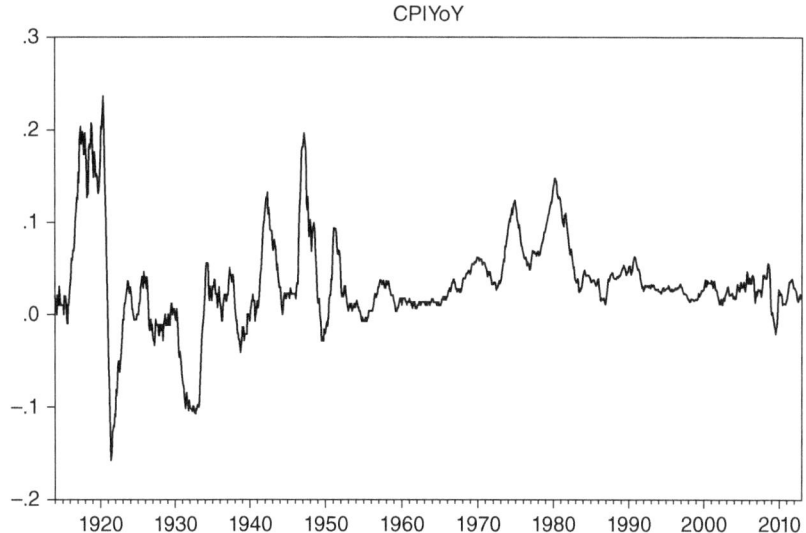

Exhibit 9.1 CPI inflation in the United States. *Source:* PIMCO.

index). Inflation-linked securities such at TIPS derive their value from the change in CPI. Thus, to target inflation risk management, the simplest dynamic approach would be to create a portfolio of securities that are sensitive to the CPI.

For instance, a direct linear hedge against inflation would consist of inflation swaps, where one receives the inflation rate measured by such an index in exchange for a contractually fixed payment (these trade with a fair amount of liquidity). Another alternative is to purchase an inflation option, which typically trades in the form of inflation caps (for rising inflation protection) and offers more convexity if inflation starts to rise quickly. These caps come in the form of both year-over-year caps and zero-coupon caps. Quite simply, year-over-year caps pay off if the inflation measured over a yearly period exceeds a predefined strike. Zero-coupon caps pay off if the actual value of the inflation index (e.g., the CPI) exceeds a predefined strike level of the index.

However, limiting to observed CPI for inflation risk management could be a rather restrictive way to manage inflation tail risks, especially in today's market environment. There are two main reasons for this. First, a cursory look at the components that make up the CPI shows that a dominant part (over 40 percent) of the CPI is related to housing and another major portion to food and energy. Because the housing market is recovering from the excesses of the crisis and there is ample supply of housing to keep inflation in this sector moderated, focusing on CPI inflation could miss the impact of inflation in other sectors of the economy. From a forward-looking and broader perspective, macroeconomic considerations such as low rates of capacity utilization can keep the short-term inflation rate low, whereas longer-term inflation and inflation expectations can rise as a result of policy, expectations, and uncertainty. Second, for longer-term investment decisions, including sensitivity to inflation expectations is likely to be a key input. There are, of course, many metrics for inflation expectations. One could use directly observable market metrics such as the pricing of inflation swaps (although they also carry exposure to counterparty risk and illiquidity). As another alternative we could look at surveys (e.g., the Philadelphia Fed Survey of Professional Forecasters or the Thomson Reuters/ University of Michigan Survey). As a third alternative we could use implicit market metrics such as the steepness of the Treasury yield curve or inflation breakeven rates. This last metric, that is, inflation breakeven, is simply the difference between a nominal government bond yield and the corresponding maturity real yield.[1]

As can be observed in Exhibit 9.2, the 10-year breakeven is currently hovering around 2.5 percent.

If instead of using the spot-yield differentials we use the differential of forward yields, the result is the forward breakeven rate. For example, the five-year forward five-year breakeven is the difference between the nominal five-year forward five-year yield and the real five-year forward

Inflation and Duration Tail Risk Hedging 201

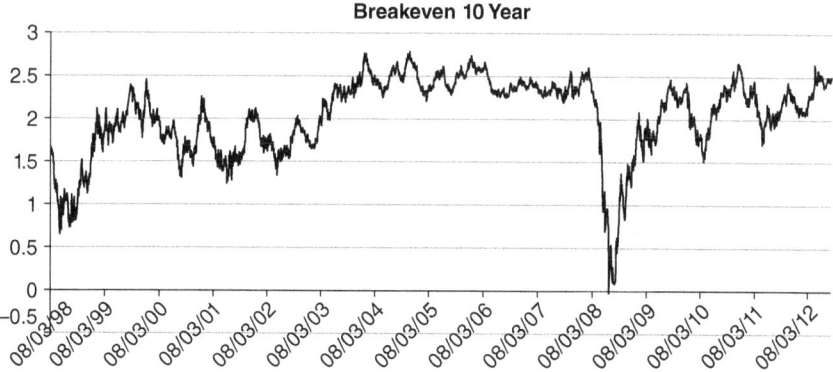

Exhibit 9.2 Breakeven 10-year inflation. *Source:* PIMCO and Bloomberg.

five-year yield (shown in Exhibit 9.3). Each five-year forward yield can be computed by observing the 10-year spot yield and the five-year spot yield and using traditional compounding formulas for the yield curve. This has also gained some notoriety as the gauge that reflects in real time the inflation-fighting credibility of the Fed (see Gurkaynak et al. 2008). Thus, as an added benefit, this metric and tail hedges on it are directly related to the liquidity risk/inflation-risk tradeoff to which central bankers are also paying attention.

Exhibit 9.3 Five-year forward five-year breakeven inflation. *Source:* PIMCO and Bloomberg.

To recap: using a linear instrument to protect against realized inflation, we can use CPI swaps on the observed inflation rate, or to protect against expected inflation, we can use "four-legged" breakevens (sell a 10-year nominal and 5-year real bonds and buy the 5-year nominal and 10-year real bonds) or their nonlinear option counterparts.

These linear instruments such as swaps and breakevens are always *delta-one*; that is, they will respond one for one to changing inflation rates or inflation expectations. As mentioned earlier, because both the swaps and the breakeven trade can result in unlimited mark-to-market losses if inflation falls, the risk budget allocated to the hedge is hard to quantify exante compared with their option counterparts. To enter into such swaps, counterparties would require both maintenance and variation margins against the mark-to-market volatility of the positions.

The linear strategies are also always at the money, (ATM) compared with more flexibility in picking the "strike" for options-based strategies. Also note that we can combine options-based strategies to reconstruct the linear strategies, but not vice versa. In this sense, the options-based strategies allow for more customization of inflation-protection portfolios.

Inflation Dynamics and Inflation Spikes

Before we can dive deep into the quantitative aspects of options-based inflation tail hedging, it makes sense to explore briefly the theory and empirical properties of rising inflation. I should note that both the economics and empirics of inflation have been well studied over multiple decades[2], but the ability to forecast bouts of high or hyperinflation remains difficult as ever. In the interest of focusing on practical methods for inflation tail hedging, I will not discuss the fundamental economics of inflation but rather summarize the data on its time-series and cross-sectional properties.

Inflation and Duration Tail Risk Hedging

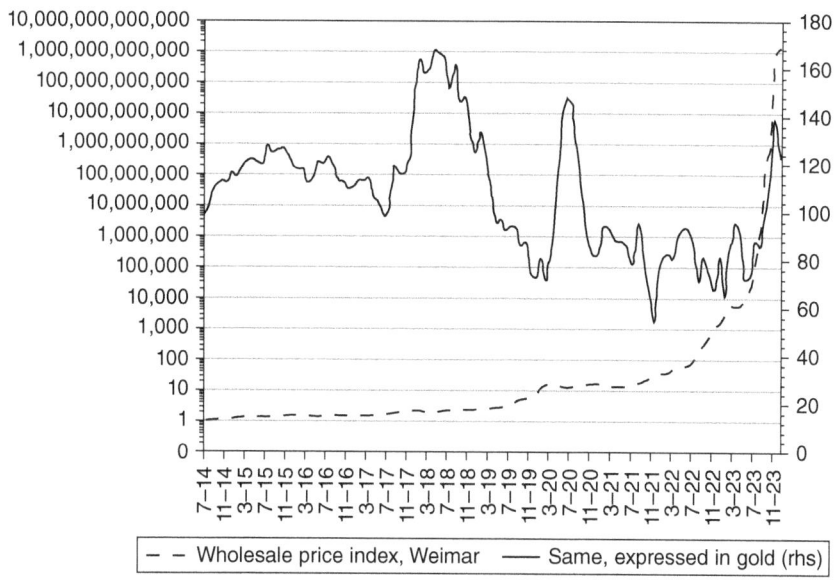

Exhibit 9.4 Wholesale price index in Weimar Germany during hyperinflation. *Source:* Shadow Government Stats website.

The two canonical examples of inflation superspikes (with episodes of high inflation present essentially in all developed and developing economies over the last 300 years) are from the experiences of the Weimar Republic (early 1900s Germany) and Zimbabwe (late 1900s early 2000s) (see Exhibit 9.4).[3]

While prices shot up 1 trillion times higher in terms of marks, prices remained stable in terms of gold, widely considered to be an inflation hedge. In Zimbabwe, the inflation rate in August 2008 went up to 6.5 sextillion (1021). In effect, this meant that the currency had no residual exchange value.

Whereas these anecdotes are interesting in their own right, any currently popular inflation-modeling paradigm does not allow for the possibility for rapidly rising inflation, let alone hyperinflation In Exhibit 9.5, we display recent high and persistent inflation periods.

	Initial CPI	End CPI	Initial 1y ΔCPI	End 1y ΔCPI	Number of Months in the Period	Number of Months with 1y ΔCPI YOY > 2%	Number of Months with 1y ΔCPI YOY > 3%	Number of Months with 1y ΔCPI YOY > 4%
5/1973 – 1/1975	5.5	11.8	2.3	2.4	21	21	18	14
10/1978 – 6/1980	8.9	14.4	2.5	3.5	21	21	17	5
4/1987 – 1/1988	3.8	4	2.2	2.5	10	9	3	0
10/2007 – 9/2008	3.5	4.9	2.2	2.1	12	7	2	0
12/2009 – 9/2010	2.7	1.1	2.6	2.4	10	9	2	0

Exhibit 9.5 Recent periods of high and persistent inflation in the United States as measured by CPI.

CPI YOY Range	Probability of Exceeding
2.50%	54%
3.50%	38.60%
4.50%	27.70%
5.50%	21.60%
6.50%	17.32%
7.50%	14.50%
8.50%	12.80%
9.50%	10.90%
10.50%	9.00%
11.50%	7.40%
12.50%	5.90%
13.50%	4.60%
14.50%	3.90%
15.50%	3.20%
16.50%	3.00%
17.50%	2.50%
18.50%	1.70%
19.50%	1%

Exhibit 9.6 Probability of exceeding inflation based on empirical inflation distribution in the United States for the last 100 years. *Source:* PIMCO.

Exhibits 9.6 shows inflation episodes in the United States over the last 100 years. As is obvious, although there are sustained periods of higher than normal inflation, the actual experience in the developed markets recently has not supported fears of very high inflation. Thus, any empirically calibrated model for inflation to recent experience would find the probability of hyperinflation to be negligible.

The distribution of inflation over this supersecular period has also shown no signs of being normally distributed (see Exhibit 9.7). As a matter of fact, if we compute the raw probability of CPI inflation

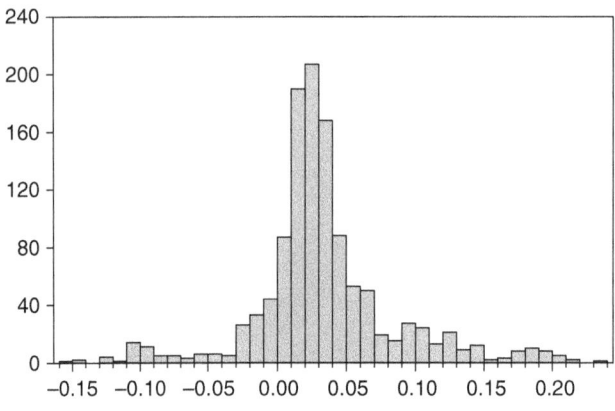

Tabulation of CPI_YOY

Date: 01/17/13   Time: 11:20

Sample: 1914M01 2012M12

Included observations: 1,188

Number of categories: 9

Value	Count	Percent	Cumulative Count	Cumulative Percent
[−0.2, −0.15)	1	0.08	1	0.08
[−0.15, −0.1)	22	1.85	23	1.94
[−0.1, −0.05)	29	2.44	52	4.38
[−0.05, 0)	114	9.60	166	13.97
[0, 0.05)	742	62.46	908	76.43
[0.05, 0.1)	163	13.72	1071	90.15
[0.1, 0.15)	78	6.57	1149	96.72
[0.15, 0.2)	31	2.61	1180	99.33
[0.2, 0.25)	8	0.67	1188	100.00
Total	1188	100.00	1188	100.00

Exhibit 9.7   CPI inflation distribution in the United States. *Source:* PIMCO.

exceeding 5 percent per annum, the long history suggests that year-over-year (YOY) inflation measured monthly exceeded 5 percent more than 20 percent of the time. Note, however, that the low levels of realized inflation and low inflation volatility as embedded in the pricing of inflation options (CPI options) suggest that the cumulative probability of exceeding 5 percent inflation in one year is only 2.2 percent, in five years, 6.4 percent; and in 10 years, 9.5 percent.[4] So, clearly, the "risk-neutral" pricing of inflation risk is not compatible with the very long history of realized inflation unless we make the heroic assumption that credible monetary policy has the power to quash inflation and inflation expectations unconditionally to keep them within a short range of current levels. Indeed, in recent research based on inflation caps and floors, Fleckenstein et. al. have demonstrated that the inflation options market is implying very low probability that inflation will exceed 2.5 percent over a very long horizon, and subsequently, the compensation required by seller of inflation protection is relatively low compared to the protection for deflation protection (Fleckenstein 2013).

One of the reasons why rapidly rising inflation is out of the zone of common expectations of current theoretical models is that inflation modeling has relied generally on the same technology of continuous-time finance that is used in the pricing of options on equities (where adjustments have to be made to explain tail behavior). In one such popular model, inflation rises to a certain level, but the further it deviates from a long-term average, the more likely it is to revert back to the longer-term mean (the *mean-reverting Ornstein-Uhlenbeck model*). This dynamic is ultimately based on the credibility of the central bank not being challenged. If long-term inflation expectations are anchored in this way and remain fixed, these class of models predict that the mean and variance of inflation are always well behaved and converge to a finite value; thus they cannot reach values that are out of the ordinary with any large probability. Note that whereas this approach is reasonable for modeling inflation under well-behaved economic conditions, it might not be appropriate under the presently observed economic conditions, low realized and expected inflation, and policy-maker activism, not to mention the increasing challenges to the notion of central bank independence and credibility.

Another similar approach that is more econometrically motivated but still backward-looking and rooted in empirical data analysis is to model year-over-year inflation as an autoregressive process. The economic rationale behind this assumption of "inertia" is that rising inflation results in a recalibration of expectations, and hence inflation-rate changes show momentum; that is, rising or falling inflation is likely to be followed by rising or falling inflation.[5] Thus, discontinuous changes, especially reversals, cannot be accounted for within this approach either.

Abandoning the assumptions of continuity, at the other extreme we can model the inflation process as a compound jump process. A compound jump process marries randomly occurring jumps with randomly distributed magnitudes of jumps. The easiest approach assumes that inflationary jumps occur randomly, following, for instance, a Poisson process, and that the size of the jumps is also random (e.g., the size of the shocks can be normally distributed about a mean jump size).[6]

The modeling of hyperinflation from a purely macroeconomic viewpoint is based on the classical quantity theory of money, which relates money times the velocity (circulation) of money to price times economic output (i.e., $M \times V = P \times Y$). Under this theory, holding all else constant, if the supply of money increases, then the price level has to increase. The expected increase in the money supply (i.e., under the promise of continued central bank quantitative easing, so-called $QE \infty$) would result in such an outcome for inflation expectations.[7]

I do not believe that any of these simplified dynamics are the complete and unique answer to modeling inflation, let alone forecasting its future evolution. Indeed, not one of these theoretical approaches does very well in fitting the actual distribution, especially the tails of the inflation distribution. Given the inability of these models to fit actual experience both in the United States and elsewhere, pinning too much faith in inflation-hedging strategies on such foundations is likely to prove erroneous for practical portfolio construction.

As Exhibit 9.8 shows, the empirical distribution of realized inflation is much fatter tailed than either an autoregressive model, normal distribution, or even a calibrated jump process. What this suggests is that while modeling inflation dynamics with an eye toward tail hedging, we might have to make a larger leap than any of the traditional models would allow.

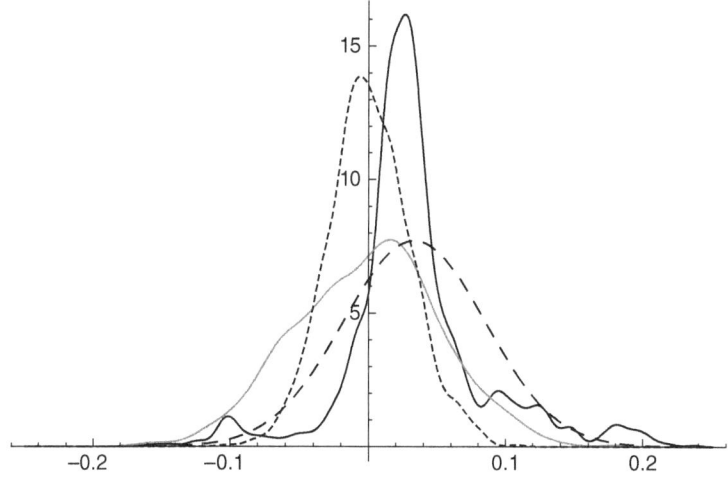

Exhibit 9.8 Empirical and theoretical inflation rate distributions. Distribution of realized CPI inflation. The heavy solid line is a kernel fit to the actual year-over-year CPI inflation. The long dashed line is the normal distribution with long-term mean and standard deviation from realized inflation. The short dashed line is from a compound jump process, and the light solid line is from an autoregressive *AR*(1) model. None of the theoretical models can explain the fat tails in realized inflation.

Framework for Inflation Tail Hedging

Given that there are severe limitations to forecasting the dynamics of inflation, I take the view that investors ought to be less concerned about forecasting the probability of inflation spikes and more concerned about the severity of such events and their impact on portfolios. This "Pascal's wager" approach to tail risk hedging necessarily forces us to reflect on the exposures within the portfolio to construct the hedging program.[8]

I also believe that any tail-hedging program is best implemented with reference to the underlying asset and liability portfolio being hedged. This holistic picture allows for active management, proper accounting of hedging costs, and the ability to rebalance opportunistically. This asset-allocation perspective also makes it possible for the tail-hedged portfolio to perform better over long-term horizons because inflation tails, by definition, are low-frequency, high-severity events, and excessive reliance on our ability to forecast the timing of such events is fraught with danger.

Three essential ingredients are critical to the understanding of any tail-hedging program, whether for equity-type risk or, more relevant to the current discussion, for interest-rate or inflation sensitivity. First, we need to understand portfolio risk exposures. As is well known, for fixed-income portfolios, we can condense and encapsulate the exposures in terms of a handful of key risk factors. The most important ones are duration, curve duration (sensitivity to yield-curve steepening and flattening), spread duration (sensitivity to option adjusted spread [OAS] changes), and convexity. Of these, the primary risk factor is duration. For equity-heavy portfolios, this means various equity factors, such as betas (overall market betas, growth, value, etc.). For a blended portfolio, a look-through into both these factor exposures is important. Just as high-yield bonds carry a substantial amount of equity beta, many risky assets thought of as pure equities carry a large amount of inflation or duration exposure. For example, think of utility-sector equities, which are exposed to economic cycles and interest-rate levels, or even the financial-sector equities, which are exposed to the level of interest rates as well as the shape of the yield curve (because financial-sector companies derive profits primary from borrowing short and lending long—the "carry" trade).

Second, we need to specify tail risk *attachment levels*. For hedging purposes, the attachment levels are simply the level of inflation or interest rate beyond which we want the portfolio to be protected. If we estimate the duration of a portfolio to be five years (e.g., for a portfolio similar to the Barclays Aggregate Bond Index), then a 100-bp rise in yields (say, from inflation) would result in roughly a 5 percent fall in the value of such a portfolio. Thus we can translate easily from the portfolio loss tolerance to the attachment level in terms of inflation if we assume a pass-through from inflation to interest rates.

Third, we need to specify the horizon of the tail hedge. Is the hedge for a *cyclical* six-month horizon or for a *secular*, say, five year or even longer, horizon? Because inflation is a much lower frequency and longer lasting than equity-market shocks, I believe that inflation tail-hedging horizons necessarily have to be longer than equity-market tail hedging.

Finally, we need to have some estimate of the cost of the hedge and whether the budget will be used upfront or on an ongoing basis.

Obviously, these inputs have to be iterated to find appropriately priced hedges in the market, or the parameters have to be varied until a suitable exposure, attachment, and cost can be found. For instance, if the attachment level is too close to the current level of rates and the cost budget is not large enough, then either the duration exposure has to be reduced by portfolio repositioning or cheaper, indirect hedges have to be used.

Benchmarking Inflation Tail Hedges

When we discuss tail hedging for typical equity-like risks, it is important to define a benchmark hedge that we can call the *direct* hedge. For instance, let us look to hedge the equity component of a 60 percent equity, 40 percent bond portfolio at an attachment level of 15 percent of the portfolio value (i.e., when the portfolio falls 15 percent or more, it is hedged) for one year. The reference hedge is a 25 percent out-of-the-money (OTM) equity put on 60 percent of the notional for the same one-year maturity. We can price this option directly using the price of an index option that replicates the equity component. Of course, if volatilities are high, then the hedge might be too expensive, and one might make the decision to reduce the total size of the hedge, look at correlated "indirect" hedges, or actively manage the quality (e.g., strikes, maturities, or mixes) of the hedges.

For inflation hedges, we can take the same approach. We can either benchmark the hedge in terms of the total expected payoff if the CPI (or the five-year forward five-year breakeven as an alternative) rises beyond a particular level, or we can price the theoretical CPI cap or breakeven option and then try to make the actual hedge more attractive relative to the direct inflation hedge. This exercise in benchmarking leads us to a discussion of the pricing of inflation options.

Pricing of Inflation Options[9]

While options on both realized and expected inflation currently do not have liquid markets, we will find it instructive to use this pricing for setting a theoretical benchmark. To this end, we go through the steps of pricing a CPI option and a breakeven option.[10]

Options on CPI[11]

To set the stage, we first compute the pricing of options on the CPI (CPURNSA on Bloomberg). These options come in two forms. The first form is the zero-coupon (ZC) option on the cumulative CPI. The second form is options on year-over-year CPI inflation (YOY).

Party A (buyer):	
Party B (writer):	
Option type:	CAP
Notional Amount:	USD $100,000,000.00
Inflation index:	CPURNSA
Inflation Base Index:	CPURNSA for November 2012
Strike inflation rate:	5 %
Premium:	X bps
Trade Date:	1/30/2013
Premium Payment Date:	2/1/2013
Effective Date:	2/1/2013
Maturity Date:	2/1/2023
Date Convention:	Modified following business day, as determined by New York and London holidays

Schedule of Payment:

Party A pays and Party B receives:

USD $ [X bps * Notional] on the Premium Payment Date

Party A receives and Party B pays:

Notional * Max [0, Inflation Adjustment − (1 + Strike Rate)^10] on Maturity Date

Inflation adjustment will be defined as USCPI (N) / Inflation Base Index, where USCPI (N) is the CPURNSA published 3 months prior to the maturity date.

Exhibit 9.9 Example of indicative terms for a zero-coupon CPI cap.
Source: Deutschebank.

To price these options, the market convention is to assume that the CPI itself is a lognormal variable. Term sheets for these options are provided in Exhibits 9.9 and 9.10.

As of December 2012, the index had a value of 230.221. The forward CPI for one year (using data from the survey of professional forecasters was 238.28 (using a CPI YOY forecast of 3.5 percent). If we assume that the last 12 months of volatility of the CPI are a good estimate of volatility for option pricing, we can compute an input

Party A (buyer):	
Party B (writer):	
Option type:	CAP
Notional Amount:	USD $100,000,000.00
Inflation index:	CPURNSA
Inflation Base Index:	CPURNSA Index level 3 Months prior to the Effective Date
Strike inflation rate:	4%
Premium:	Y bp
Trade Date:	1/30/2013
Premium Payment Date:	2/1/2013
Effective Date:	2/1/2013
Maturity Date:	2/1/2018 (5 YEARS)
Roll Date:	Feb 1st, annually
Date Convention:	Modified following business day, as determined by New York And London holidays

Schedule of Payment:

Party A pays and Party B receives:

Notional Amount * Y bps on the Premium Payment Date

Party A receives and Party B pays (on roll dates):

USD 100,000,000.00 * Max [0, Inflation adjustment-4%]

Inflation adjustment will be defined as: USCPI(N) / USCPI(N-1)-1 Where: USCPI(N) is the inflation index published 3 months prior to the payment of the Nth period and USCPI(N-1) the one published 15 months prior to the payment of the Nth period.

Exhibit 9.10 Example of indicative terms for a YOY CPI cap.
Source: Deutschebank.

annualized volatility of approximately 1.5 percent (although please note that this volatility has been quite variable, and some practitioners use the volatility implied from the implicit floor in TIPS prices to price such options).

Using these inputs, an at-the-money (ATM) forward CPI option for one year would cost 1.24 percent (of notional). Similarly, a 1 percent out-of-the-money (OTM) option would cost 62 bp, and a 2 percent OTM option would cost 24 bp. From 1968 onward, the average annualized volatility of the CPI has been approximately 1.15 percent, so the average price of an ATM option at the theoretical volatility would be approximately 0.5 percent. Similarly, the average theoretical price of a 1 percent OTM CPI option would be 19 bp, and that of a 2 percent OTM CPI option would be approximately 8 bp.

Just to be clear, market participants also quote the volatility in terms of basic points per day for inflation option pricing. If ATM volatility is 1.5 percent for the CPI, this translates roughly to 10 bp/day basis-point volatility. This increases to 2 bp/day more (or 180 bp/year) for a 5 percent strike cap, reflecting the skew in the pricing of inflation options.[12] Of course, we do not doubt that the pricing will be variable based on models and demand and supply considerations, but having these estimates allows us to do basic analysis in terms of the relative richness or cheapness of these "straight" hedging alternatives.

Options on the Breakeven Inflation Rate[13]

In a similar vein, as discussed earlier, if we are concerned that the rise in inflation expectations needs to be hedged, we need to price options not on the current CPI or inflation rate but rather on longer-term inflation expectations. The best metric (of many such metrics, none of which is really perfect), as displayed earlier (and watched by the Fed), is the forward inflation rate as embedded in the pricing of nominal and inflation-linked bonds. The theoretical benchmark pricing of options on these breakevens is slightly more involved, and to be clear, these options do not trade currently.

Suppose that we take the current five-year forward five-year breakeven to be 3 percent, and want to price an option on the breakeven struck at 4 percent. To price this option, we will require the volatility of the breakeven rate itself. The difficulty is that options on the breakeven do not trade, so there is no direct way of inferring the breakeven volatility. One alternative is to use historically realized breakeven volatility. The historical estimate (since 2007) of the volatility of the five-year forward five-year breakeven is approximately 100 bp/year.

The other alternative is to use the fact that the breakeven rate is basically the difference between the nominal and real yields. The variance of the breakeven can be estimated if we can use the volatility of the nominal rates, real rates, and the correlation between them. The nominal-rate volatility can be read from the actively traded swaption market (it's on the order of 80 to 100 bp/year). The volatility of the real rate also can be implied from options on TIPs (called *TIPtions*), but these options again don't trade with much volume or liquidity. To make things simple, we assume that we can forecast real-rate volatility (which ultimately should be related to real-growth-rate variability).

As an illustrative example, if we assume that the volatility of the real yield is 75 bp/year and the correlation between the real yield and the nominal yield is 70 percent, then we obtain an estimate of the volatility of the forward breakeven of approximately 65 bp/year using the formula relating the variances. We can now use this volatility as an input in the pricing of a breakeven call option. An option struck 100 bp OTM (say, at a forward breakeven rate of 4 percent) would cost approximately 96 bp upfront. If we annualize this number, the cost is approximately one-fifth or 20 bp/year. In practice, there is likely to be a substantial skew to the volatility surface; that is, because the volatility of inflation is expected to be higher for higher inflation, the input volatility for a deeply OTM call option on the breakeven is likely to be closer to 100 bp.[14]

As mentioned earlier, these computations for both the CPI and breakeven options are largely theoretical as of this writing because breakeven options really do not trade in any real volume. But the real value of benchmarking the price of these options is to set a reference for indirect hedging of inflation tail risk. To replicate the payoff of such direct options, we have to create proxy or "indirect" hedges whose relative attractiveness may be graded with reference to the theoretical "direct" options. I will discuss this approach now.

Indirect Inflation Tail Risk Hedging and Basis Risk

Given that many direct inflation tail options are practically not implementable, we now turn our focus to approximations. I will do this systematically, but starting with underlying assets that are fundamentally most correlated with inflation and then with assets that have less predictable comovements with inflation under normal situations, but high comovements especially under inflation shocks.

Whereas it may seem that our task would be done if we could find assets that show a high positive beta to inflation by doing a simple correlation analysis, it is important, as mentioned earlier, to note that the potency of an inflation hedge also depends on the persistence of inflation. Because inflation itself is a low-frequency time process, incorporating inflation persistence in to estimation of the hedge betas is critical before we select hedges.

Following the framework of Schotman and Schweitzer (2000), if inflation evolves as an autoregressive process (with the caveats discussed previously on making this assumption),

$$\pi_{i+1} = \mu + \alpha(\pi_i - \mu) + \eta_{i+1}$$

and asset returns are a function of expected and unexpected inflation

$$r_{i+1} = v + \beta E_t(\pi_{t+1}) + \phi \eta_{t+1} + \epsilon_{t+1}$$

(where α, β, ϕ, σ_ϵ, and σ_η are inflation persistence, inflation beta of asset, beta of returns to unexpected inflation, return volatility, and inflation volatility), then the estimate of the long-term beta (the *hedge ratio*) of the hedge is

$$\Delta = \frac{[(1-\alpha)\phi + \alpha\beta]\sigma_n^2}{(1-\alpha)^2 \sigma_\epsilon^2 + [(1-\alpha)\phi + \alpha\beta]^2 \sigma_n^2}$$

which requires $[(1 - \alpha)\phi + \alpha\beta] > 0$ for the hedge to be a bonafide hedge (i.e., for the beta to be positive to inflation).

Equally important is the case where inflation becomes a "random walk," that is,

$$\pi_{t+1} = \pi_t + \eta_t$$

Then for any time horizon k, the estimate of the hedge beta is

$$\Delta = \frac{\left[\phi + \frac{1}{2}(k-1)(\beta + \phi) + \frac{1}{6}(k-1)2k-1\right]\beta)\sigma_n^2}{\sigma_\epsilon^2 + \left[\phi^2 + (k-1)\beta\phi + \frac{1}{6}(k-1)(2k-1)\beta^2\right]\sigma_n^2}$$

If we were to plot this hedge ratio as a function of time horizon k, we would find that the hedge potency increases monotonically, but at a decreasing rate as a function of the horizon. What this tells us is that even though the short-term behavior of indirect inflation tail hedges may be open to much debate, the potential longer-term benefits of a diversified basket of inflation tail hedges, purchased attractively, is quite predictable.

Intuitively, the reason why one might not see short term benefits of hedging inflation from assets such as equities but still see long term benefits is the following. Over short horizons, the volatility of equities (of the order of 18%) can swamp the volatility of inflation (of the order of 1.5% per annum). But if inflation is persistent, then the cumulative volatility of inflation can become the same order of magnitude as the equity volatility.

Pricing of Tail Interest-Rate Swaptions

Our first step toward deriving an indirect hedge is to assume that the effect of rising inflation is reflected in rising nominal interest rates while real rates remain relatively static. If this assumption is borne out, then options on the nominal yield curve (i.e., swaptions) would be the simplest replication of the option on the breakeven inflation. Indeed, as a matter of practice, I have recently observed that most inflation tail hedgers have been using OTM swaption hedges (which explains the payer skew for swaption volatilities).

Here is an example of the pricing of a payer swaption (the right to pay fixed swap rates at a predefined strike). Assume that the current five-year forward five-year swap rate is 2.97 percent. Suppose that we fix the premium budget at 50 bp/year, which equals 2.50 percent for the next five years. Using a Black model for swaptions and an implied volatility of 95 bp, we can price the option and solve for the strike that this cumulative premium gets us (strike turns out to be 3.64 percent). The distance of this strike from the current value of the forward is 0.67 percent. Based on a Black model, the delta of the swaption turns out to be 0.38. To evaluate the potency of this hedge in a portfolio and perform risk analysis, we can shock the interest-rate curves and reevaluate the new value for the portfolio with and without the hedges. This exercise is quite standard, and most of the computations can be done with ease.

Note that swaptions allow the customization of both the option expiry and the rate (underlying) of the hedge. If we are worried about inflation rising in the short term and the short end of the nominal curve reacting to it, shorter-dated swaptions (say, one year expiry into the five-year swap curve) can be used. On the other hand, if we think that the rise in inflation will be a gradual process and it really happens through expectations changing, then longer options (say, 10-year options on the 10-year swap) might be warranted. In doing do, swaptions allow for an implicit view on the impact of rising inflation or inflation expectations on the shape of the yield curve to be simultaneously expressed with the most attractive point to buy volatility. In the current environment, the swaption volatility curve illustrates a *hump*; that is, it peaks around the two-to five-year point and declines both for shorter- and longer-dated swaptions. This allows for efficient volatility positioning as well. For instance, the purchase of a long-dated swaption results in volatility *roll-up*; that is, as time passes, the longer-dated swaption becomes a shorter-dated swaption with a higher implied volatility. In doing so, the natural time decay incurred as part of buying an option is reduced. Any active inflation tail risk management paradigm should pay attention to such opportunities in the volatility term structure.

As we move further afield from interest-rate options such as swaptions, we are faced with the problem of forecasting the correlations between these instruments and the rise in inflation and especially the robustness of the correlations. Theoretically, we can try to anticipate which assets are likely to have positive inflation sensitivity by noting that the value of any asset is the expected net present value (NPV) of its future cash flows. If the NPV is calculated using the discount factor given by $d = e^{-(r+i+\lambda)t}$, where r is the real rate, i is the inflation rate, and λ is the risk premium or credit risk, then we can see that the lower the sum of the three, the higher is the discount factor. We can empirically partition the returns of any asset into their loadings onto these factors and keep the inflation-sensitive component as a hedge. If we linearize the preceding equation by expanding the exponential, essentially what we are looking for are asset classes and combinations of securities that will show positive relationship with inflation. To evaluate this, we looked at various inflationary periods and some core inflation-sensitive asset classes. Over most periods it is clear that among other proxy instruments, gold and oil have tracked both realized and expected inflation fairly well and, given our preceding discussion, are also robust hedges when inflation is persistent.

While some assets such as gold clearly show persistent positive relationships to rising inflation, especially if we condition our analysis on large rises in inflation, the paucity of data for periods similar to the current era makes dependence on backward-looking data analysis dangerous. To address this issue, we take a three-step approach. First, we forecast which assets qualitatively are expected to respond to inflation in a dependable manner. Second, we estimate the relative cost of inflation-protection options on these assets against the cost of the more direct hedges. Finally, we iterate different mixes of such options in the portfolio to arrive at a probability distribution of possible outcomes that captures the basis risk versus the relative cheapening of the hedges compared with the most direct hedge. The spectrum of combinations measured through the lens of the cost versus basis risk allows a practical hedge program to select what point of the spectrum is appropriate.

Indirect Hedges

As an example of indirect hedges that we can build theoretical and empirical support for, we can look at gold, crude oil, and some foreign currencies as proxy hedges. Even a cursory look at the historical returns on the CPI (YOY) and YOY returns on gold shows that the two series are highly correlated, especially in the extremes. Other than the empirical correlations (which happen to be close to 0.5 for inflationary episodes), there are good fundamental reasons to believe that gold and oil are robust inflation tail hedges, especially if inflation is persistent. Simplistically put, if central banks are printing money to devalue their currencies, then gold, which is in limited supply and the currency of no one central bank, is clearly the beneficiary. In addition, there is anecdotal evidence that central banks are generally underweight gold as an asset, and a rebalancing toward reducing this underweight could easily be correlated with an inflation shock. Whereas the empirical beta and the correlation are highly variable, we can easily see for fundamental reasons why options on gold at proper valuation levels can prove to be a potent indirect hedge for both realized and expected inflation. For crude oil, the relationship might indeed be even more fundamental. First, rise in oil prices have a direct flow through into the pricing of finished products because of both the energy cost of production and the fact that many oil derivatives are actually components of consumer products. Shocks to energy supply are naturally positively correlated with rising inflation and inflation expectations.

Example of Gold Options as a Proxy Tail Hedge

In this section I will illustrate an indirect tail-hedging exercise with gold. The analysis can be easily extended to options on oil in a parallel fashion.

Let us return to the example discussed earlier, where we priced a CPI call option for one year at a theoretical price of 24 bp for a 2 percent OTM attachment point. We also priced an option on the five-year forward five-year breakeven for approximately 20 bp/year. I will focus on comparing the breakeven option with the gold option as an indirect hedge.

To show how the computation of gold as a proxy hedge works, we first estimate the comparable attachment point in gold terms. If, for instance, we believe the conditional tail correlation between gold and the CPI to be 0.8 and assume that the volatility of gold for one year is 15 percent (we could read this from option implied volatilities on gold, for instance), then we can approximate the beta of gold to the CPI to be approximately the volatility ratio of gold to the CPI times the correlation. With this predicted beta of 8, we can see that a theoretical call option on gold will require a strike price that is scaled to be proportionately further away. In other words, in percentage terms, we want the strike of the gold call option to be eight times away from the equivalent strike for the direct inflation option. The price of this indirect option is easy to obtain from the market. However, we still need to figure out how much of the indirect option to buy.

Thus the second step is to compute the future value of both the inflation option and the gold option conditional on the inflation variable crossing the targeted inflation attachment point and scaling the size of the gold option such that when such an event happens, their future dollar values are equal. This step is necessary to make sure that the indirect option can be exchanged with a high degree of certainty against the theoretical inflation option at that unknown (random) future date. This step also allows us to measure the potential basis risk from selecting an indirect hedge. The final step in the analysis is to compare the present price of this appropriately scaled indirect gold option against the price of the direct inflation option.

Continuing with our example, suppose that the breakeven option crosses the threshold of 4 percent inflation rate in six months. Assuming that the volatility of the 4.5-year forward now increases to 100 bp/year (see the discussion of skew earlier), the new price of the theoretical breakeven option is 384 bp, that is, the initial 96 bp has realized a mark-to-market gain of three times and is now worth four times its original value. Thus the proper way to scale the gold call option is such that its dollar value increases to the same amount. Of course, ultimately, we need to apply judgment on how much of the ultimate hedging portfolio should consist of indirect hedges. To achieve this, we include the mix of direct and indirect options in the portfolio at different weights and compute the distribution of scenario payoffs versus costs. This tradeoff of basis risk versus cost savings is standard for any tail-hedging practice and ultimately is one that the end user has to make based on considerations of the desire for certainty in hedge performance against the budget available.

The longer the time for crossing the threshold, the more certain we can be that the indirect hedges will actually realize the tail correlation that we theoretically expect them to. In other words, the basis risk of indirect hedges is effectively reduced as the horizon of hedging increases.

The unprecedented creation of liquidity in the aftermath of the credit crisis, the massive debt burden emanating from this liquidity, and the well-advertised and potent threat of inflation-loving central banks raise the risk of an unanticipated inflationary tail event. Whereas a spike in actual inflation is not impossible, the magnitude of the adverse impact to investment portfolios is likely to occur via an unanticipated increase in inflationary expectations and real yield shocks. In this chapter I discussed how to address systematically inflation tail hedging via the framework that so far I have had the opportunity to apply to equity-market risks. To do so, I first introduced direct, non-linear options on both realized and expected inflation. Unfortunately, becuase these options do not have a liquid market at the time of this writing, I am lead to working with approximations to the direct hedges. To do so, I first laid out the key elements for building an inflation tail-hedging program using benchmarks, exposures, attachment points, and cost and basis risks as parameters. Finally, I illustrated by simple examples how to incorporate indirect hedges from other asset classes.

In summary, there is need today for crude yet potent inflation-hedging solutions against persistent, unanticipated rises in both realized and forward inflation. Whereas the actions of central banks have possibly mitigated short-term deflation risk and the risk to equity markets, in their wake, inflation and duration tail risk are not far behind. I believe that the framework in this chapter can be used to create a portfolio of potent hedges against such an adverse tail event.

Notes

Chapter 1

1. R. Cont and L. Wagalath, "Running for the Exit: Distressed Selling and Endogenous Correlation in Financial Markets," *SSRN*, 2011.

Chapter 2

1. For example, if we assume that the underlying assets are jointly distributed in the form of a bivariate normal distribution, then, in *Mathematica*, the payoff is

    ```
    payoff[w1 _ , w2 _ , a _ , mu1 _ , d1 _ , mu2 _ , d2 _ , sigma1 _ ,
    sigma2 _ , t _ ] := Max[a - w1*(Exp[(mu1 - d1 - 0.5*sigma1^2)*t +
    alpha1*Sqrt[t]*sigma1] - 1) - w2*(Exp[(mu2 - d2 -
    0.5*sigma2^2)*t + alpha2*Sqrt[t]*sigma2] - 1), 0];
    ```

    and this can be numerically integrated over the bivariate normal density, which has a built-in *Mathematica* symbol.
2. This Section was originally published in the May–June 2012 edition of the *Journal of Indexes*, www.indexuniverse.com.

Chapter 3

1. This and the following two chapters are based on joint work with my colleague Josh Davis.
2. In this chapter, *expected return* means mathematical expectation or the first moment of a random variable calculated as the integral of the variable with respect to its probability measure.
3. The actual shape of the second distribution is derived from an iterative optimization procedure that specifies different allocations to equities and different strikes to the option hedge.

Chapter 4

1. Portions of this chapter are based on V. Bhansali and J. M. Davis, "Offensive tail risk management. II: The case for active tail risk hedging," *Journal of Portfolio Management*, Vol. 37, No. 1, 2010, pp 78–91.

Chapter 5

1. This chapter relies heavily on joint work done with Josh Davis and described in our paper, "Active Tail Risk Hedging. III: Managing Basis Risk." PIMCO, 2009, unpublished.
2. We can simulate the time for crossing using a variety of dynamics for the underlying assets. For a normal distribution, the probability density for crossing a barrier is explicitly known: $P(a,\sigma,\mu,t) = a/\sqrt{2\pi\sigma}\, t^{-3/2} e^{-(\mu t - a)^2/(2\sigma^2 t)}$, where a, σ, μ, and t are, respectively, the barrier, volatility, drift, and time horizon. The expected time to crossing can be computed by integrating time over this density.
3. For small v, a Taylor expansion yields

$$N(v) \approx \frac{1}{2} + \frac{1}{\sqrt{2\pi}} v$$

Thus

$$\left[\frac{N(\gamma \times v) - \frac{1}{2}}{N(v) - \frac{1}{2}}\right] \approx \gamma$$

Chapter 6

1. Here is a piece of *Mathematica* to generate a mixed density from two normal distributions to explore fat tails and bimodality. Here mu1, sigma1, mu2, and sigma2 are the mean and volatility of the two processes, and t is the mixing between the two distributions.

   ```
   Manipulate[Plot[t*PDF[NormalDistribution[mu1,sigma1],x]+(1-t)
       *PDF[NormalDistribution[mu2,sigma2],x],{x,-10,10},PlotRange
       →All],{mu1,0,1},{sigma1,0.5,10},{mu2,0,1},{sigma2,0.5,10},{t,0,1}]
   ```

2. Optimal allocations: For those who are mathematically inclined, computation of the optimal allocation to risky assets begins by specifying a very standard power utility function $U(W) = W^{1-a}/1-a$, which represents the preferences

of a typical investor with constant relative risk aversion where W is the initial wealth of the investor. We used a typical parameter of $a = 5$. The investor has a choice to allocate between the risky asset (stocks) and keep money in cash at a return rate of 25 basis points (bp) annually.

3. Barra is a brand of MSCI. Barra factors are represented by MSCI indexes and are meant to reflect target exposure to factors such as momentum, earnings, or leverage.

4. The CBOE also publishes a skew index, which empirically shows little correlation to the VIX—demonstrating that the skew and the VIX are independently important variables and measures of risk.

5. This section was coauthored with Josh Davis.

6. Option values assume the Black-Scholes model used to generate prices and delta-hedge ratios. The interest-rate assumption corresponds to 3M USD LIBOR, the dividend yield is the most recent yield reported at the time in Bloomberg for the S&P500, and implied volatility is assumed to correspond to 90-day historical realized S&P500 daily volatility. The dynamic trading is done once per day at the close of the market assuming execution at closing prices.

7. Option values obtained from using actual data on option prices. Dynamic hedging uses the Black-Scholes delta-hedge ratios.

Chapter 7

1. In the jump-diffusion model, the stock price S_t follows the random process $dS_t/S_t = \mu dt + \sigma dW_t + (J-1)dN(t)$, which is made up of, in order, drift, diffusive, and jump components. The jumps occur according to a Poisson distribution, and their size follows a lognormal distribution. The diffusive volatility is σ, the average jump size is J (expressed as a fraction of S_t), the frequency of jumps is λ, and the volatility of jump size is v.

2. For instance, the VIX was at 12.9 on May 15, 2013, which was almost 1 percent higher than the VIX when the SPX was 100 points lower on March 15, 2013. The April 2009 skew, right at the height of the crisis, was lower, but this was largely due to all volatilities being higher. In May 2010, the skew was high because the market had just rallied from 700 to 1,200 on the SPX, and hedgers were buying OTM puts. The market had priced SPX skew relatively flat in 2009 due to "bimodal" outcomes (high volatility, low put-call skew), elevated skew in 2010 due to "fear" (high volatility, high put volatility), and flat skew due to "optimism" on the upside (low volatility,

low skew). Thus, clearly, a behavioral calibration of the skew is of interest to participants because it explains how volatility and the skew premium can be dynamically variable.
3. The parameters λ, a, b, and γ correspond, respectively, to the loss aversion, convexity in the value function for gains and for losses, and degree of overweighting of tails.
4. Note that we can see the impact of changing the parameters by taking derivatives with respect to each of the parameters. Increasing γ from 0.65 to 0.66, the price of a 25 percent OTM option falls by 2 percent. Increasing λ from 2.25 to 2.26 increases the put option price by 0.5 percent. Increasing a from 0.88 to 0.89 decreases the put option price by 2 percent, and increasing b from 0.88 to 0.89 increases the put option price by 3 percent.

Chapter 8

1. For the purpose of this discussion, I used a simple Monte-Carlo simulation assuming that the retirement portfolio net asset value (NAV) follows a lognormal process and the volatility of the underlying equity risk factor is 18 percent per annum. Eighteen percent is consistent with the long-term volatility of the U.S. equity markets.
2. Computations based on Monte-Carlo with 18 percent volatility for the equity risk factor.

Chapter 9

1. However, two qualifiers are important before one takes this metric seriously. First, the TIPS market is less liquid than the nominal Treasury market; hence some of the breakeven spread is really a liquidity differential. Second, given the purchase of both TIPS and nominal bonds by the Fed, care needs to be exercised in relying on the breakeven rate as a pure metric of inflation expectations.
2. For instance, the time-tested Cagan model for hyperinflation is an elegant framework that dates back to the 1960s. One consequence of the model under a wide variety of assumptions is that expectations of an uncontrolled and rapid increase in the supply of money in the future will inevitably lead to an increase in inflationary expectations.
3. There are numerous books and websites that discuss these historic episodes. The website Shadow Government Stats (www.shadowstats.com) has a compendium of such anecdotes and further references.
4. Please see *Barclays Inflation Volatility Digest*, January 2013.

5. If one naively fits the CPI year-over-year inflation series to an $AR(1)$ process (i.e., with one lag), the dependence on the first lag is almost 0.98 percent, so there is indeed a lot of momentum in inflation as measured over short periods.
6. This is exactly the same as a Merton jump process that has been used for the modeling of fat tails and the volatility skew for equity markets.
7. Critics of the quantity theory of money would argue that hyperinflation only results if there is an accompanying supply shock, for example, shocks that arise from wars or famines, but these nuances are really irrelevant for the task at hand of creating portfolios robust to rapidly rising inflation or inflation expectations.
8. Pascal's wager in this context simply means that because expected losses are the probability of loss times the severity of loss, we should behave as if we cannot forecast the probability becuase the severity of the event can easily overwhelm any minor differences in the probability forecast error. Pascal used this logic in the context of whether one should believe in the existence of God.
9. I am grateful to colleagues at Wall Street dealer desks for updating me on the recent state of the art and volume trading in the market related to this section.
10. For a robust hedge construction, we also need to manage the counterparty risk of the over-the-counter (OTC) options and carefully select the currency in which the hedge payment will be made. In the extreme case, if the settlement for a dollar inflation option is in less valuable dollars, the price of the inflation hedge has to be adjusted appropriately. This quanto adjustment is standard.
11. I would like to thank my colleague Qinqxi Wang for her assistance in the computations in this section.
12. C. Mirani et. al., "Inflation Volatility Digest," Barclays Interest Rate Research, January 29, 2013.
13. I am grateful to my colleague Mitch Handa for the computations in this section.
14. The simplest way to use this in the pricing of breakeven options is to use a class of models know as SABR (stochastic alpha beta rho), where both the inflation variable, either the CPI or the breakeven rate, and the respective volatility are stochastic, and the inflation variable and the volatility have a positive correlation.

Bibliography

Ang, A., V. Bhansali, and Y. Xing, (2008). "Taxes on Tax-Exempt Bonds," *Journal of Finance* 65(2):565–601.

Asness, C. S., T. J. Moskowitz, and L. H. Pedersen (2008). *Value and Momentum Everywhere*. Cambridge, MA: National Buvean of Economics Research (NBER), 2008.

Barberis, N. (2012). *The Psychology of Tail Events: Progress and Challenges*, New Haven, CT: Yale University Press.

Barberis, N. "A Model of Casino Gambling." *Management Science* 58(1):35–51.

Barberis, N., and M. Huang (2008). "Stocks as Lotteries: The Implications of Probability Weighting for Security Prices." *American Economic Review* 98(5):2066.

Barberis, N., and M. Huang (2009). "Preferences with Frames: A New Utility Specification that Allows for the Framing of Risks." *Journal of Economic Dynamics and Control* 33:1555.

Bhansali, V. (2007a). "Markowitz Bites Back: The Failure of CAPM, Compression of Risky Asset Spreads and the Path Back to Normalcy." *PIMCO Viewpoints*.

Bhansali, V. (2007b). "Putting Economics (Back) into Quantitative Models." *Journal of Portfolio Management* 33(3):63–76.

Bhansali, V. (2007c). "Volatility and the Carry Trade." *Journal of Fixed Income* 17(3):72–84.

Bhansali, V. (2008a). "Tail Risk Management." *Journal of Portfolio Management* 34(8):68–75.

Bhansali, V. (2008b). "Correlation Risk: What the Market Is Telling Us and Does It Make Sense?" In N. Wagner (ed.), *Credit Risk: Models, Development and Management*. Boca Raton, FL: Chapman and Hall.

Bhansali, V., and J. Davis (2010a). "Offensive Risk Management: Can Tail Risk Hedging be Profitable? SSRN February 2010.

Bhansali, V., and J. M. Davis (2010b). "Offensive Tail Risk Management. II: The Case for Active Tail Risk Hedging." *Journal of Portfolio Management* 37(1):78–91.

Bhansali, V. (2010). "The Ps of Pricing and Risk Management, Revisited." *Journal of Portfolio Management* 36(2):106–112.

Bhansali, V., and M. B. Wise, "Forecasting Portfolio Risk in Normal and Stressed Markets." *Journal of Risk* 4(1):91–106.

Bhansali, V., and M.B. Wise, (2002). "Diversification and Generalized Tracking Errors for Correlated Nonnormal Returns." *Quantitative Finance* 2(6):482–486.

Bhansali, V., and M.B. Wise, (2005). "Implications of Correlated Default for Portfolio Allocation to Corporate Bonds." *Journal of Investment Management* 3(1).

Bhansali, V., Y. Schwarzkopf, and M. B. Wise, (2011). "Fat-Tails and Stop-Losses in Portable Alpha." *Journal of Investment Management* 9(3):19–32

Bhansali, V., R. Gingrich, and F. A. Longstaff, (2008). "Systemic Risk: What Is the Market Telling Us ?" *Financial Analysts' Journal* 64(2):16–24.

Bhansali, V., M.P. Dorsten, and M. B. Wise, (2009). "Asymmetric Monetary Policy and the Yield Curve." *Journal of International Money and Finance* 28:1408–1425

Bhansali, V. (2009). "Market Crises: Can the Physics of Phase Transitions and Symmetry Breaking Tell Us Anything Useful?" *Journal of Investment Management*.

Bhansali, V. (1998). *Pricing and Managing Exotic and Hybrid Options.* New York, McGraw-Hill.

Bhansali, V., and M. B. Wise, (2009). *Fixed Income Finance: A Quantitative Approach.* New York: McGraw-Hill.

Bhansali, V. (2010). *Bond Portfolio Investing and Risk Management.* New York: McGraw-Hill.

Deng, Geng, C. McCann, and O. Wang. (2012). "Are VIX Futures ETPs Effective Hedges?" *Journal of Indexing* Winter 2012, 3(3):35–48.

Bhansali, V., J. Davis, G. Rennison, J.C. Hsu, and F. Li (2012). "The Risk in Risk Parity." *Journal of Investing* 21(3):102–110.

Bhansali, V., Y. Schwarzkopf, and M. B. Wise, (2009). "Modeling Swap Spreads in Normal and Stressed Environments." *Journal of Fixed Income* 18(4):5–23

Burghardt, G., R. Duncan, and L. Liu (2003). "Understanding Drawdowns." Working paper, Carr Futures.

El-Erian, M. (2008). *When Markets Collide: Investment Strategies for the Age of Global Economic Change.* New York: McGraw-Hill.

Fleckenstein, Matthias and Longstaff, Francis A. and Lustig, Hanno N., Deflation Risk (July 2013). Available at SSRN: http://ssrn.com/abstract=2293210 or http://dx.doi.org/10.2139/ssrn.2293210.

Fung, W., and D. A. Hsieh (2001). "The Risk of Hedge Fund Strategies: Theory and Evidence from Trend Followers." *Review of Financial Studies* 14(2):313–341.

Graham, John R., and Campbell R. Harvey, (2005). "The Long-Run Equity Risk Premium." Working Paper 79, Fuqua School of Business, Duke University, Durham, NC.

Gurkaynak, Refet S., Brian Sack, and Jonathan H. Wright (2008). *The TIPS Yield Curve and Inflation Compensation.*

Heston, S. (1993). "A Closed-Form Solution for Options with Stochastic Volatility with Applications to Bond and Currency Options." *Review of Financial Studies* 6: 327–343.

Kahneman, D., and A. Tversky (1979). "Prospect Theory: An Analysis of Decision under Risk." *Econometrica* 47(2): 263–291.

Leibowitz, M., and A. Bova, (2010). "Illiquidity Surges, Capital Calls and Bargain Scenarios." Portfolio Strategy, Morgan Stanley, New York.

Magdon-Ismail, M., and A. Atiya (2004). "Maximum Drawdown." *Risk Magazine* (October) 17(10):99–102.

Merton, R. (1998). *Continuous-Time Finance.* Oxford, UK: Blackwell.

Nardon, Martina, and Paolo Pianca (2012). "Prospect Theory: An Application to European Option Pricing." Economics Paper No. 34, Ca' Foscari University.

Polkovnichenko, V., and F. Zhao (2010). "Probability Weighting Functions Implied by Option Prices." *Journal of Financial Economics* 107(3):580–609.

Schotman, P., and Schweitzer M. "Horizon sensitivity of the inflation hedge of stocks." *Journal of Empirical Finance* 7(2000):301–315.

Sornette, D. (2003). *Why Stock Markets Crash: Critical Events in Complex Financial Systems.* Princeton, NS: Princeton University Press.

Taleb, N. (2012). *Antifragile: Things that Gain from Disorder.* New York: Random House.

Thaler, R. H. (1999). "Mental Accounting Matters." *Journal of Behavioral Decision Making* 12(3):183–206.

Tversky, Amos, and Daniel Kahneman (1992) "Advances in Prospect Theory: Cumulative Representation of Uncertainty." *Journal of Risk and Uncertainty* 5(4):297–323.

Wolff, Christian, C. Versluis, and T. Lehnert (2009). "A Cumulative Prospect Theory Approach to Option Pricing." LSF Research Working Paper Series, University of Luxembourg.

Index

Numbers
3M USD LIBOR, 227
10-delta options, 83
60/40 portfolios
  behavioral perspectives on, 163
  benchmarking in, 40, 211–212
  inflation tail hedges in, 211–212
  offensive tail risk hedging in, 51–55
  put option values in, 63
  risk vs. return in, 59–62
  rolling tail hedges in, 33–37
  tail risk management in, 28–31
70/30 portfolios, 52
1928, 86, 89–91
1950, 88–89
1987
  buy-and-hold strategies in, 87
  narrow framing in, 157
  static vs. dynamic hedging in, 148–150
1988, 87
2005, 78–79, 81–83
2006, 78–79, 81–83
2007
  backfilling volatilities in, 78–79, 81–83
  credit crisis in, 43
  credit-market hedges in, 4
  S&P500 in, 88
2008
  backfilling volatilities in, 78–79, 81–83
  credit crisis in, 43, 194
  delta of tranches in, 5
  fixed-income markets in, 12
  hidden tail risk in, 18
  S&P500 in, 88
  static vs. dynamic hedging in, 150–151
  tail risk hedging after, 193
2009
  backfilling volatilities in, 78–79, 81–83
  credit crisis in, 43
  S&P500 in, 88
  skew indexes in, 227–228
2010
  backfilling volatilities in, 78–79, 81–83
  skew indexes in, 227–228
  stock market flash crash in, 43
2011, 44
2012, 213
2013
  inflation in, 227
  mini tail event in, 126
  Nikkei Index in, 20

235

A

accounting
  constraints, 19, 23
  cost-benefit, 16
  mental, 160
active monetization rules, 71–76, 84–91
active tail risk management. *See also* tail risk management
  backfilling volatilities in, 78–84
  basis risk and, 116
  introduction to, 71–78
  monetization rules in, 84–91
adjusting tail hedges. *See also* tail risk management, 15
algorithms
  for dynamic hedging, 146
  efficacy of, 33
  for targeting volatility, 7
alternative betas mode, 7–9
annual return distributions, 58–59
Anti-fragile, 10
anticyclical asset-allocation, 16
arbitrage strategies, 157
asset-allocation
  in active tail risk management, 73–74
  anticyclical asset-allocation, 16
  derisking, 133
  inflation and, 196–198
  optimal, 226–227
  rolling tail hedges and, 37
  in tail risk management, 17, 129–134
asset classes. *See also* assets
  cash-and-options-based tail hedges from, 46
  correlation of, 107–117
  diversification of, 184
  inflation and, 196–198, 220
  monetization multiples in, 86
  risk factors and, 11–13, 28, 72
asset returns, defined, 12–14

assets
  allocation of. *See* asset-allocation
  cheap, 71–73
  classes of. *See* asset classes
  correlated classes of, 107–117
  decay of, 45
  diversification of classes of, 184
  factor exposure and, 27–29
  fixed-income, 194
  inflation and, 194–198, 217–221
  net value of, 228
  risky. *See* risky assets
  tail risk and, 3–4, 12–14, 38
at-the-money (ATM) options. *See also* out-of-the-money (OTM) options
  in 1987, 148
  behavioral perspectives on, 164–165, 173
  benchmarking inflation tail hedges and, 214–215
  correlated asset classes and, 107–112
  in indirect hedges, 99, 103–104, 117
  introduction to, 83
  linear strategies and, 202
  in "soft" indirect hedges, 104–107
  strikes for. *See* at-the-money (ATM) strikes
at-the-money (ATM) strikes. *See also* at-the-money (ATM) options
  hitting times and, 104
  indirect hedges and, 111–112
  puts vs. put spreads and, 104–107
Atlantic, 173
ATM (at-the-money) options. *See* at-the-money (ATM) options
ATM (at-the-money) strikes. *See* at-the-money (ATM) strikes
attachment points
  benchmarking and, 38–39
  direct vs. indirect hedges and, 94–95
  for inflation tail hedges, 211
  introduction to, 11

attachment points (*Cont.*):
  matching hedges at, 98–104
  put options and, 65
  in retirement investing, 185
  in tail risk management, generally, 27–32
AUD/JPY (Australian dollars/Japanese yen), 107
AUD/USD (Australian dollars/US dollars), 107–110
autoregressive models, 208–209

B

β-scales, 30–31
backfilling volatilities, 78–84
banks. *See* central banks
Barberis, N., 155, 166, 169
Barclays Aggregate Bond Index, 40, 211
barra factors, 227
barrier crossings, 226
basis points (BP), 4–5
basis risk
  attachment points and, 98–104
  from correlated asset classes, 107–117
  inflation and, 217–218
  introduction to, 93–95
  matching hedges and, 98–104
  quantification of, 95–98
Bear Stearns, 11–12
behavioral perspectives
  cumulative prospect theory in, 173–177
  expected returns in, 165–169
  introduction to, 153–154
  multiple equilibria in, 165–169
  narrow framing in, 154–160
  precommitment in, 169–173
  procyclicality in, 169–173
  put option valuation in, 173–177
  in retirement investing, 179–180
  standalone put option pricing in, 161–165

benchmarking
  for inflation tail hedges, 211–215, 221–222
  for rolling tail hedges, 33–35
  in tail risk management, generally, 35, 37–43
benefit frameworks, 5–9
bespoke tail hedge portfolios, 43
betas
  alternative betas mode, 7–9
  of direct hedges, 107–108
  diversifying, 7–9
  equity, 38–40
  inflation and, 196
  in retirement investing, 181, 184–186
  of stock market, 13–14
  in tail risk management, generally, 27–31
bimodality, 130–134, 226
Black model. *See also* Black-Scholes model, 219
Black Monday, 149
Black-Scholes model
  delta-hedge ratios in, 227
  dynamic hedging in, 147
  evaluation of option prices with, 156–159, 176–177
  implied volatilities in, 74, 82, 156, 158–159
  introduction to, 10–11
  option values and, 227
  OTM vs. ATM options in, 164–165
  quantifying basis risk and, 95–97
  risk-free rates in, 84–85
  rolling tail hedges in, 33
  simulating generic paths in, 125
  in tail risk management, generally, 26
  volatility in, 56, 59–60
The Black Swan, 10
bond market, 12–14

238   Index

Bond Portfolio Investing and Risk Management, 31
bonds
   correlations between stocks and, 31–32
   factor exposure and, 27–28
   interest rates and, 138
   municipal, 195
   in offensive tail risk hedging, 55
   in tail risk management, generally, 41
   Treasury, 12
bootstrapping, 14, 126
BP (basis points), 4–5
breakeven premiums, 60
breakeven rates
   forward, 200–202, 215
   "four-legged," 202
   inflation options and, 215–217
Brownian motion, 164, 175
bubbles, 21–22
bullet one-year hedges, 33
buy-and-hold strategies, 73–76, 86–91
buying on dips, 88

C
Cagan model, 228
calibrating models, 57–66
carry-currency pairs, 107
cash-and-options-based tail hedges, 46–47
cash mode, 7–9
cash vs. explicit tail hedges, 43–47
CBOE (Chicago Board Options Exchange), 227
CDX Index, 5–6
central banks
   activism of, 20
   inflation and, 207–208, 221–224
   liquidity injections by, 194, 198
   underwriting downside protection by, 173
charm, 121, 125

Chicago Board Options Exchange (CBOE), 227
Chicago Board Options Exchange Volatility Index (VIX). *See* VIX (Volatility Index)
cliff effects, 32
commodities, 197
commodity trading advisors (CTAs), 8
complexity vs. transparency, 41–42
conditional value-at-risk (cVaR), 63
constant-proportion debt obligations (CPDOs), 6
constant volatility, 56–57, 59–60
Consumer Price Index (CPI)
   benchmarking tail hedges and, 212–215
   gold options and, 222–223
   inflation and, 194, 198–207, 209
   year-over-year returns in, 221
Cont, R., 18
conversion, 72–73
convex loss functions, 163
correlations
   between asset classes, 107–117
   between companies and sectors, 93–94
   inflation and, 196
   instability of, 2
   "risk-on, risk-off," 13
   sensitivity to, 11
   between stocks and bonds, 31–32
   stress, 126–127
cost-benefit accounting, 16
cost of hedges
   benchmarking and, 38–43
   cash vs. explicit tail hedging and, 43–47
   conversion and, 72–73
   in dynamic vs. static hedging, 146–151, 173
   historically, 95
   market costs and, 66

Index 239

cost of hedges (*Cont.*):
    option cost vs. benefits and, 5–9
    in rolling tail hedges, 32–37
    S&P500 and, 117
costless collars, 138–141
countercyclical approaches, 16–17
covariance, 18–19
CPDOs (constant-proportion debt obligations), 6
CPI (Consumer Price Index). *See* Consumer Price Index (CPI)
credit derivatives, 12
credit-market crises. *See also* financial crises
    of 2007-2009, 43, 194
    carry currency put options in, 19
    unifying frameworks for hedging in, 5–9
credit-market hedges, 3–4
credit-market indices
    equity markets and, 93
    mortgage rates and, 194
    systemic risks and, 11
CTAs (commodity trading advisors), 8
cumulative prospect theory
    behavioral perspectives in, 173–177
    introduction to, 161
    OTM vs. ATM options in, 164
cVaR (conditional value-at-risk), 63
cyclical horizons, 211

D
decay, 45
defense strategies
    benchmarking in, 37–43
    buy-and-hold, 88
    cash vs. explicit tail hedging in, 43–47
    factor hedges in, 30–32
    overview of, 25–29
    probability estimation in, 47–49
    quantifying performance in, 42–43
    rolling tail hedges in, 32–37

deleveraging, 5, 15
delta-hedge ratios, 227
delta-ones, 202
deltas
    decay of, 121
    option, 4–5, 83
    in puts vs. put spreads, 119–122
    replication of, 137
    of swaptions, 219
    in tail risk management, generally, 35–37
demand surges, 17
denominator effect, 13
density, 225–226
derisking of portfolios, 133–138
direct hedges. *See also* indirect hedges
    attachment points and, 98–104
    benchmark hedges as, 211
    correlated asset classes in, 107–116
    introduction to, 94–95
    matching hedges and, 98–104
    puts vs. put spreads and, 105–107
    quantifying basis risk and, 95–98
    volatility-based, 141–145
disaster insurance, 1–2
distressed liquidation, 18–20
diversification
    of asset classes, 184
    of betas, 7–9
    failure of, 18–20
    of portfolios, 28–32
    of risk, 184
    in tail risk management, 2
dollar gamma, 146
downside volatility, 63
drawdowns
    introduction to, 179–186
    simulation of, 186–191
    visualization of, 187–191
duration tail risk hedges
    basis risk and, 217–218
    benchmarks for, 211–215, 221–222

duration tail risk hedges (*Cont.*):
   dynamics in, 202–209
   framework for, 210–211
   gold options and, 222–224
   indirect, 217–218
   introduction to, 193–195
   money inflation vs. inflation tails and, 195–198
   options on breakeven rate in, 215–217
   pricing of options in, 212
   pricing of options on CPI in, 212–215
   pricing of swaptions and, 219–221
   proxy, 222–224
   realized inflation vs. inflation expectations in, 198–202
   spikes in, 202–209
dynamic hedges, 146–152
dynamic replication, 9–10
dynamic risk rebalancing, 7–9
dynamic variation in pricing, 154
dynamics of inflation. *See also* inflation, 202–209

E
earthquakes, 20–21
economic bubbles, 21–22
economic loss of wealth, 180
empirical kernel distributions, 47–48
endowment style portfolios, 28–29
equilibria, 129–130, 154
equity beta, 38–40
equity markets
   since 2009, 55
   active monetization rules and, 84–88
   behavioral perspectives and, 180, 183, 193
   credit-market indices and, 93
   direct volatility-based hedging in, 141–145
   driving risk, 25–27
   introduction to, 2, 9, 12–14

equity markets (*Cont.*):
   long-term volatility in, 52
   narrow framing and, 154–156
   in offensive tail risk hedging, 55
   probability density of returns in, 47–49
   risk aversion and, 74–77
   in stochastic volatility models, 159
   tail correlations and, 19
   variance swaps and, 141–145
   VIX and, 134–135
   volatility in, 26–27, 35, 80–83
estimating probabilities, 47–49
ETFs (exchange-traded funds), 37
European options, 26, 147–148
ex post analysis, 71–72
exchange-traded funds (ETFs), 37
exchanging indirect hedges, 96
expected inflation, 198–202
expected maximum drawdowns, 186–187
expected returns, 165–169, 225
explicit tail risk hedges
   in defense strategies, 43–47
   dynamic risk rebalancing in, 7–9
   introduction to, 2
explosive liquidity, 43
exposures, 38
extension, 72

F
factor–augmented vector autoregression model (FAVAR), 80–81
factor exposure, 27–29
factor hedges, 30–32
failure of diversification, 18–20
fair value of put options, 63
farmland, 197
fat-tailed distributions, 53–54
fat tails, 226
FAVAR (factor–augmented vector autoregression model), 80–81

Federal Reserve Bank, 194, 198–199, 201
financial crises
    of 2008, 150–151
    credit-market crises as. *See* credit-market crises
    loss-aversion and, 160–161
    pricing of insurance and, 173
    retirees and, 180
    static vs. dynamic hedging and, 150–151
    systemic risk in, 11
financing
    basis risk and, 96
    continuous-time, 207
    of put option protection, 140
    as risk, 3
    by self, 39
    by selling an OTM call options, 139
Fleckenstein, B., 207
Fooled by Randomness, 10
forecasting risk, 3
foreign currencies, 197
foreign exchange, 9–10
forward breakeven rates, 200–202, 215
"four-legged" breakevens, 202
fragile systems, 10
frameworks
    for inflation tail hedges, 210–211
    option cost vs. benefit, 5–9
    for quantifying basis risk, 95–98
    unifying, 9
framing. *See also* narrow framing, 160
frequency of rebalancing, 32–37

G
gamma
    in dynamic vs. static hedging, 146
    introduction to, 41
    in puts vs. put spreads, 119, 122–123
generation of paths, 125–126, 187–191
generic path generation, 125–126

Germany, 203
gold, 197, 203, 220–224
government's role, 11–12
Great Depression, 77–78, 89–90
Greeks, 41

H
happiness, 154–158
hedge funds, 37
hedge ratios, 147, 218
hedge value, 134–138
hedges
    adjusting, 15
    benchmark, 211
    cost of. *See* cost of hedges
    credit-market, 3–4
    direct. *See* direct hedges
    duration tail risk. *See* duration tail risk hedges
    explicit tail risk. *See* explicit tail risk hedges
    factor, 30–32
    implementation of, 5–9
    indirect. *See* indirect hedges
    monitoring, 15
    offensive tail risk. *See* offensive tail risk hedges
    rolling tail hedges, 25
    valuing, 10–12
Heston model
    cost of hedging and, 67
    introduction to, 57
    narrow framing and, 159
high-frequency estimations, 126–127
high-frequency signatures, 19
history
    of cost of hedges, 95
    of monetization, 71–72
    of stock performance, 77–78
holding cash, 43–46
home insurance, 1–2

horizons
  cyclical vs. secular, 211
  in indirect tail hedging, 218
  inflation and, 196, 218
  long, 51
  in offensive tail risk hedging, 56
  in retirement investing, 181–186
Huang, M., 155, 166
humps, 220
hurricanes, 173
hyperinflation, 208, 228–229

I

implementation of hedges, 5–9
implied volatility
  active monetization rules and, 84–86
  backfilling of, 78–84
  in Black-Scholes model, 156, 158–159
  in costless collars, 140–141
  introduction to, 74–78
  market-, 57, 60
indirect hedges. *See also* direct hedges
  basis risk in, 95–98, 107–117
  charm in, 121
  correlated asset classes in, 107–117
  delta decay in, 121
  delta in, 119, 122
  gamma in, 119, 122–123
  generic path generation in, 125–126
  inflation and, 217–218
  introduction to, 93–95
  matching at attachment points, 98–104
  put theta in, 120
  puts vs. put spreads in, generally, 104–107, 118–125
  sensitivities of puts vs. put spreads in, 118–125
  simulations of, 125–126
  soft form of, 104
  spot prices in, 118–122
  stress correlations in, 126–127

indirect hedges (*Cont.*):
  theta in, 123
  underlying (spot) prices in, 118–122
  value of, 118–119, 122
  vanna in, 120, 124
  vega in, 120–121, 123–124
  volatility in, 121–122
  volga in, 121, 124
inflation
  basis risk and, 217–218
  benchmarking and, 211–215, 221–222
  breakeven rates and, 215–217
  CPI year-over-year, 229
  in current economy, generally, 194–195
  dynamics in, 202–209
  gold options and, 222–224
  hyperinflation, 228–229
  indirect tail risk hedges and, 217–218
  interest-rate swaption pricing and, 219–221
  introduction to, 193–195
  money inflation vs. inflation tails, 195–198
  pricing of options based pm, 212–215
  proxy tail hedges and, 222–224
  realized vs. expected, 198–202
  spikes in, 202–209
  tail hedging and, 210–211
inflation swaps, 200
instability of correlations, 2
insurance
  behavioral perspectives on, 165, 172–173
  holding cash vs., 46
  narrow framing and, 154–155, 157–158
  tail risk management as, 1–2
  in tail risk management, generally, 4–5

intellectual property, 197
investor behavior. *See* behavioral perspectives
ITRAXX index, 5–6

J
Japan, 20
Journal of Portfolio Management, 91
jump-diffusion model, 227
jumps, 159, 208

K
Kahneman, D., 161, 168
Kahneman-Tversky model, 176–177
kurtosis, 132, 180

L
left tails, 47
Lehman Brothers, 12
leverage, 3
liquidation, 18–20
liquidity
  active monetization of hedges and, 71
  bid/ask spreads and, 149
  credit-market crises and, 5
  explosive, 15–16, 43
  inflation and, 193–201, 216, 224
  injections of, 194, 198
  as macroeconomic risk, 3
  mark-to-market values and, 87–88
  market shocks and, 28
  nonlinear, explosive, 15–16
  return enhancement and, 51
  taking advantage of reduced, 2
log-periodic oscillation, 21–22
long-horizon investing, 51
loss aversion, 160, 162–164, 170
lottery-ticket risk, 13–14

M
macroeconomic risks, 3

mark-to-market value
  inflation and, 202
  losses in, 5
  peaking of, 86
market costs, 66
market implied volatility, 57, 60
matching hedges, 98–104
Mathematica code
  evaluating option prices with, 176
  generating paths with, 187–191
  payoffs in, 225
  in risk management, 47
  simulating generic paths with, 125–126
  stochastic volatility in, 67
maximum drawdowns, 186–187
mean-reverting Ornstein-Uhlenbeck model, 207
mean-variance optimization, 6, 58–59
mental accounting, 160
Merton model
  introduction to, 13
  jump processes in, 229
  narrow framing and, 159
  in risk management, 147
model-derived implied volatility, 82
models
  autoregressive, 208–209
  Black, 219
  Black-Scholes. *See* Black-Scholes model
  Cagan, 228
  calibration in, 57–66
  FAVAR, 80–81
  Heston. *See* Heston model
  jump-diffusion, 227
  Kahneman-Tversky, 176–177
  Merton. *See* Merton model
  for offensive hedging, generally, 56–57
  option, 10–11
  Ornstein-Uhlenbeck, 207

models (*Cont.*):
  risk-neutral, 10–12
  SABR, 229
  stochastic volatility approach to, 67–69
  vector autoregression, 81–84
momentum
  in 2007-2009, 129
  dynamic risk rebalancing and, 7–9
  in tail risk management, 134–138
monetization
  active, 71–76, 84–91
  example of, 74–76
  history of, 71–72
  introduction to, 15
  multiples, 85
  rules for, 71–76, 84–91
  setting stage for, 73–74
money inflation, 195–198
moneyness. *See also* strikes
  deltas vs., 140
  of put options, 54, 59–60, 63–66
monitoring hedges, 15
Monte-Carlo simulations, 228
mortgages, 194
MSCI factors, 227
MSCI World, 40
multimodal worlds, 129–134
multiple equilibria, 130–132, 165–169
multiple-market equilibria, 154
municipal bonds, 195
mutual funds, 37

N
narrow framing, 153, 171
NAV (net asset value), 228
net asset value (NAV), 228
net benefits, 66
net present value (NPV), 5, 220
Nikkei Index, 20–23
nonlinear, explosive liquidity, 15–16
nontraditional portfolios, 28–29

notionals, 27
NPV (net present value), 5, 220

O
OAS (option adjusted spread), 210
offensive tail risk hedges
  definition of, 16
  introduction to, 16, 51–55
  model calibration in, 57–66
  models for, generally, 56–57
  stochastic volatility model of, 67–69
oil, 222
optimal allocations, 226–227
optimal frontiers, 6
optimization procedures, 225
option adjusted spread (OAS), 210
option costs. *See also* cost of hedges, 8–9
option deltas, 4–5
option payoffs, 187–191
option straddles, 137
options
  ATM. *See* at-the-money (ATM) options
  behavioral perspectives on, 160
  on breakeven rates, 215–217
  costs vs. benefits, 5–9
  European, 26
  models of, 10–11
  OTM. *See* out-of-the-money (OTM) options
  pricing of, 160
  put. *See* put options
  tail hedges based on, 41–43
  on TIPs, 216
  zero-coupon, 212–213
Options Exchange Volatility Index (VIX). *See* VIX (Volatility Index)
Ornstein-Uhlenbeck model, 207
oscillation, 21–22
OTC (over-the-counter) markets, 41, 229

OTM (out-of-the-money) options. *See* out-of-the-money (OTM) options
OTM (out-of-the-money) strikes. *See* out-of-the-money (OTM) strikes
out-of-the-money (OTM) options. *See also* at-the-money (ATM) options
  in 1987, 149
  in 2008, 150–151
  behavioral perspectives on, 161–165, 171
  benchmarking and, 212–215
  in costless collars, 139–141
  in indirect hedges, 103–104, 107–113, 116–117
  inflation and, 228
  multiple equilibria and, 165
  narrow framing and, 157
  in "soft" indirect hedges, 104–107
  strikes for. *See* out-of-the-money (OTM) strikes
  in tail risk management, generally, 27
out-of-the-money (OTM) strikes. *See also* out-of-the-money (OTM) options
  AUD/USD exchange rate and, 108
  indirect hedges and, 108–109, 112–113
  puts vs. put spreads and, 104–107
  volatility and, 164
outsourcing of risk management, 147
over-the-counter (OTC) markets, 41, 229

P

Pascal's wager, 210, 229
peaks, defined, 180
performance quantification, 42–43
Poisson processes, 208, 227
policy activism, 10–12
portfolios
  60/40. *See* 60/40 portfolios
  70/30, 52

portfolios (*Cont.*):
  bespoke tail hedge, 43
  context of, generally, 16
  derisking of, 133–138
  diversification of, 28–32
  endowment style portfolios, 28–29
  level of, 3
  managing risk in, generally, 3, 7–9
  nontraditional, 28–29
  retirement. *See* retirement investments
positively skewness, 166–172
precommitment, 169–173
prediction, 20–23
prices
  behavioral perspectives on, 160
  Black-Scholes model for, 156–159
  in CPI. *See* Consumer Price Index (CPI)
  dynamic variation in, 154
  evaluation of, 156–159, 176
  of inflation options, 212
  Mathematica code for, 176
  of options on CPI, 212–215
  of put options, 160–165
  in puts vs. put spreads, 118–122
  spot, 118–122
  for standalone put options, 161–165
  of tail interest-rate swaptions, 219–221
  underlying, 118–122
probability
  estimation of, 47–49
  severity of tail events vs., 14–15
  of stock market decline, 77
  weighting, 156, 161–165, 170–174
procyclicality, 169–173
prospect-theory investors, 166
prospects, 173
proxy tail hedges, 222–224
put-option spreads. *See also* put options
  charm in, 121, 125
  delta decay in, 121

put-option spreads (*Cont.*):
  delta in, 119, 122
  gamma in, 119, 122–123
  in indirect hedging, 104–107, 118–125
  put theta in, 120
  sensitivities of, 118–125
  spot prices in, 118–122
  theta in, 120, 123
  underlying (spot) prices in, 118–122
  value of, 118–119, 122
  vanna in, 120, 124
  vega in, 120–121, 123–124
  volatilities in, 122
  volatility in, 121
  volga in, 121, 124
put options. *See also* put-option spreads
  in 1929-1930, 78
  in active tail risk management, 74–76
  basis risk and, 95–98
  behavioral perspectives on, 161–165, 173–177
  cash vs. explicit tail hedging and, 43–44
  fair value of, 63
  in offensive tail risk hedging, 53–54
  pricing of, 161–165
  on standalone basis, 161–165
  theta in, 120
  valuation of, 173–177
pyramiding, 136

Q
quantifying performance, 42–43
quantity theory of money, 229
quarterly rebalancing, 32

R
random walks, 218
rational change. *See also* behavioral perspectives, 170
rational multiple-market equilibria, 154

real estate investment trusts (REITs), 197
realized inflation, 198–202
realized volatility, 79–83
reference market instruments, 40–41
regression, 142
REITs (real estate investment trusts), 197
renting processes, 46
retirement investments
  introduction to, 179–186
  net asset value in, 228
  simulating drawdowns in, 186–191
return distributions, 52–56
return enhancement. *See* offensive tail risk hedges
risk-free rates, 84–85
risk management. *See also* tail risk management
  active approach to. *See* active tail risk management
  basis risk in. *See* basis risk
  benchmarking and, 38–40
  compensation for risk in, 14
  correlations in, 13
  derisking of portfolios in, 133–138
  diversification of risk in, 184
  dynamic risk rebalancing in, 7–9
  offensive approach to. *See* offensive tail risk hedges
  outsourcing of, 147
  in retirement investing. *See* retirement investments
  risk-factor based approaches to, 45–46
  risk-neutral approaches to. *See* risk-neutral approaches
  risky assets in. *See* risky assets
  thresholds in, 64
risk-neutral approaches
  behavioral perspectives on, 162–164, 169, 171
  inflation and, 207
  introduction to, 10–12

risk-neutral approaches (*Cont.*):
  narrow framing in, 159
  offensive tail risk hedging and, 57
"risk-on, risk-off" correlations, 13
risk-premium compensation, 14
"riskless" premium-gathering, 157
risky assets. *See also* risk management
  inflation and, 194, 210
  in offensive tail risk hedging, 53–55, 63–65
  optimal allocation to, 133–134
  puts vs. call options on, 158
robust systems, 10
roll-ups, 220
rolling tail hedges, 25, 32–37
rotation, 72–74
rule-of-thumb monetization strategies, 84–85

S
S&P500 (Standard & Poor's 500 Index). *See* Standard & Poor's 500 Index (S&P500)
SABR (stochastic alpha beta rho) models, 229
Scholes. *See* Black-Scholes model
Schotman, P.C., 217
Schweitzer, M., 217
secular horizons, 211
securities. *See* U.S. Treasury securities
sensitivities, 11, 118–125
severity of tail events, 14–15, 47
Shadow Government Stats, 228
shadow values. *See also* offensive tail risk hedges, 61, 64–66
Sharpe ratio, 181–182
short-term interest rates, 56
simulations
  of drawdowns, 186–191
  of indirect hedges, 125–126
  of tail events, 14

skewness. *See also* volatility skews
  in 1009-2010, 227–228
  positive, 166–172
  preferences, 171–172
  in retirement investing, 180–185
  skew roll-ups in, 140–141
  variance swaps and, 145
slice distributions, 69
soft indirect hedges, 104
Sornette, D., 21–22
spikes in inflation, 202–209
spot prices, 118–122
SPX (S&P500 Index). *See* Standard & Poor's 500 Index (S&P500)
standalone put option pricing, 161–165
Standard & Poor's 500 Index (S&P500)
  in 1928, 86–87
  from 1928- 1949, 90
  since 1950, 88–89
  since 1988, 87
  in 2009-2010, 55, 227
  in active tail risk management, 74, 85
  basis risk and, 94, 114–115
  benchmarking and, 40
  bimodal vs. unimodal distributions in, 131
  costless collars and, 140
  decline in 2007-2008, 77
  direct vs. indirect hedges in, 107–113
  dynamic hedging and, 147
  empirical kernel distributions in, 48
  equity risk premiums in, 66
  hedging costs in, 117
  historical cost of hedging with, 95
  history of monetization and, 71
  long-term equity volatility in, 52
  narrow framing and, 159
  put options in, 43–44
  rolling tail hedges and, 33–34

Standard & Poor's 500 Index (S&P500) (*Cont.*):
  in tail risk management, generally, 25–26
  variance swaps and, 144–145
  VIX and, 58, 134, 144
  volatility in, 52, 227
static hedges, 146–148
stochastic alpha beta rho (SABR) models, 229
stochastic volatility
  constant volatility and, 59–60
  narrow framing and, 159
  in offensive tail risk hedging, 67–69
  offensive tail risk hedging and, 56
stock market. *See also* Standard & Poor's 500 Index (S&P500)
  beta of, 13–14
  bond market vs., 2
  credit crises and. *See* credit-market crises
  equity markets and. *See* equity markets
  financial crises and. *See* financial crises
  implied volatilities and. *See* implied volatility
  probability of decline in, 77
  realized volatilities and, 79–83
  risk vs. return in, 61
stress correlations, 126–127
strikes
  active monetization rules and, 84–86
  ATM, 104–107, 111–112
  attachment levels and, 40
  attachment points and, 98–104
  basis risk and, 95–98, 107–117
  buy-and-hold strategies and, 76
  changing volatilities and, 122–125
  cumulative prospect theory and, 164–165

strikes (*Cont.*):
  expiry and, 44
  in factor hedges, 30–31
  indirect hedges and, 223
  inflation and, 199–202, 215, 219
  introduction to, 11
  moneyness as. *See* moneyness
  OTM, 104–109, 112–113, 164
  put delta and, 119
  of put options, 54, 64–66
  put theta and, 120
  in risk management, 40
  in rolling tail hedges, 33
  skew effects and, 82–83
  spot prices and, 74
  in tail risk management, generally, 26–27
  variance swaps and, 144–145
  volatility and, 158
surveys of inflation, 200
systemic risk, 3

T
T-bills (Treasury bills). *See* Treasury bills (T-bills)
tail risk management. *See also* risk management
  active. *See* active tail risk management
  adjusting hedges in, 15
  asset-allocation and, 17, 129–134
  asset returns in, 12–14
  benchmarking in, 37–43
  cost-benefit accounting in, 16
  costless collars in, 138–141
  countercyclical approaches in, 16–17
  direct volatility-based hedging in, 141–145
  distressed liquidation in, 18–20
  diversification in, 2, 18–20

tail risk management (*Cont.*):
  duration tail risk in. *See* duration tail risk hedges
  dynamic hedging in, 146–152
  dynamic replication in, 9–10
  explicit hedging in, 2
  failure of diversification and, 18–20
  hedging value in, 134–138
  implementing hedges in, 5–9
  insuring against risk in, 4–5
  introduction to, 1
  liquidity in, 15–16
  modes of, 6–7
  momentum in, 134–138
  monitoring hedges in, 15
  in multimodal world, 129–134
  narrow framing in, 154–160
  need for, 1–2
  nonlinear, explosive liquidity in, 15–16
  option cost vs. benefit frameworks in, 5–9
  policy activism in, 10–12
  portfolio context in, 3, 16
  prediction in, 20–23
  probability vs. severity of tail events in, 14–15
  quantifying performance in, 42–43
  for retirement. *See* retirement investments
  risk-neutral models in, 10–12
  strategies for, generally, 129
  systemic risk in, 3
  trends in, 134–138
  unifying frameworks in, 9
  valuing tail hedges in, 10–12
  variance swaps in, 141–145
  volatility-based hedging in, 141–145
Taleb, Nicholas, 10
Taylor expansions, 226
theta, 41, 123

threshold FAVAR (threshold factor–augmented vector autoregression model), 80–81
timber, 197
time consistency, 154, 169–173
time decay, 41, 149
time horizons. *See* horizons
time-series momentum, 138
TIPS (treasury inflation protected securities). *See* Treasury Inflation Protected Securities (TIPS)
TIPtions (options on TIPs), 216
tranches, 4–5, 11
transparency vs. complexity, 41–42
Treasury bills (T-bills)
  active monetization rules and, 84–85
  breakeven rates and, 228
  debt ceiling and, 44
  futures, 40
  inflation and, 200
  risk vs. return and, 53, 59–61
Treasury bonds, 12
Treasury Inflation Protected Securities (TIPS)
  benchmarking and, 215
  inflation and, 197, 199, 228
  options on, 216
trends
  in 2007-2009, 129
  strategies for following, 137
  in tail risk management, 134–138
troughs, defined, 180
Tversky, A., 161, 168

U
underlying prices, 118–122
unifying frameworks, 9
unimodal distributions, 130–131, 133–134
U.S. Consumer Price Index (CPI). *See* Consumer Price Index (CPI)

U.S. Treasury securities
  TIPS. *See* Treasury Inflation
    Protected Securities (TIPS)
  Treasury bills. *See* Treasury bills
    (T-bills)
  Treasury bonds, 12
utility theory, 155

V

value
  behavioral perspectives on, 167–172
  cumulative prospect theory on,
    161–164, 173–175
  mark-to-market. *See* mark-to-market
    value
  net asset, 228
  net present, 5
  of puts vs. put spreads, 118–119, 122
  at-risk, 63
  shadow, 61, 64–66
  of tail hedges, generally, 10–12
value-at-risk (VaR), 63
vanna, 120, 124
VaR (value-at-risk), 63
variance swaps, 141–145
vector autoregression model (VAR),
  81–84
vega, 41, 120–121, 123–124
visualization of drawdowns, 187–191
VIX (Volatility Index)
  equity index in, 14, 23, 227
  futures in, 141–145
  hedge fund strategies on, 134–135
  narrow framing and, 159
  S&P500 and, 58, 134, 144
VNKY volatility index, 23
volatility
  in active tail risk management,
    74–76
  backfilling, 78–84
  constant, 59–60

volatility (*Cont.*):
  curves of, 33–37
  direct vs. indirect hedges and,
    94–98
  downside, 63
  hedges based on, 141–145
  implied. *See* implied volatility
  index of. *See* VIX (Volatility Index)
  market implied, 57, 60
  model-derived implied, 82
  offensive tail risk hedging and,
    52–58
  parametric models of, 77
  in puts vs. put spreads, 121, 122
  ratios, 2
  realized, 79–83
  rolling tail hedges and, 33–37
  in S&P500, 227
  skews. *See* volatility skews
  stochastic. *See* stochastic volatility
Volatility Index (VIX). *See* VIX
  (Volatility Index)
volatility skews. *See also* skewness
  in active tail risk management, 116
  behavioral perspectives on, 154
  in Black-Scholes option-pricing
    model, 59–60
  breakeven rates and, 103
  indirect vs. direct hedges and, 109
  long-term vs. short-term, 83–84
  market crashes and, 83–84
  narrow framing and, 157–159
  in retirement investing, 180–185
  in zero-cost structures, 140–141
volga, 121, 124

W

Wagalath, L., 18
weekly return frequency, 57–58
Weimar Republic, 203
whipsaw effect, 8, 137–138

Index

wholesale price indexes, 203
Wolff, C., 176

Y

year-over-year (YOY)
   caps, 199
   CPI inflation, 212–214
   CPI returns, 221
   inflation, 207

YOY (year-over-year). *See* year-over-year (YOY)

Z

zero-coupon (ZC) caps, 199
zero-coupon (ZC) options, 212–213
zero-premium options strategies, 129, 139–141
Zimbabwe, 203

CPSIA information can be obtained
at www.ICGtesting.com
Printed in the USA
BVHW04*1657081018
528978BV00005BA/7/P